KILLER ANIMALS

BY EDWARD R. RICCIUTI

Killers of the Sea
Do Toads Give You Warts?
To the Brink of Extinction
The American Alligator, Its Life in the Wild
Shelf Pets
Dancers on the Beach

KILLER ANIMALS

BY EDWARD R. RICCIUTI

WALKER AND COMPANY
NEW YORK

First published in the United States of America in 1976 by the
Walker Publishing Company, Inc.

Published simultaneously in Canada by Fitzhenry & Whiteside,
Limited, Toronto.

ISBN: 0–8027–0509–X

Library of Congress Catalog Card Number: 75–12193

Printed in the United States of America.

10 9 8 7 6 5 4 3 2 1

FOR HOWIE BARON
AND HIS FRIEND PAT HOGAN

ACKNOWLEDGMENTS

DURING THE MORE than two years required for the preparation of this book, scores of people and institutions provided valuable assistance and guidance. I have tried to keep a record of individuals and organizations responsible for special help. As is often the case, I am certain that I have been neglectful of some, but at least I can express my appreciation to those listed below. (The fact that they helped in no way implies endorsement of any material in this book.)

—New York Zoological Society Library

—Dr. F. Wayne King, New York Zoological Society

—John Behler, New York Zoological Society

—Robert Brandner, New York Zoological Society

—Joan Van Haasteren, New York Zoological Society

—American Museum of Natural History Library

—*Audubon* magazine, for material on monk parakeets and nature television which appeared in its pages

—Thomas Livers, East Bay Botanical and Zoological Society

—The Honorable Anthony D. Marshall, United States Ambassador to Kenya

—Robinson McIlvaine, African Wildlife Leadership Foundation

—Nairobi Snake Park

—Kenya National Parks

—Iain Douglas-Hamilton

—Killingworth (Conn.) Library

—Connecticut Audubon Society Library

—Richard Sweeney, Beardsley Zoological Gardens

—Lederle Laboratories

—Gray Williams, Center for the Humanities

—William Partington, Environmental Information Center of the Florida Conservation Foundation

—Romano Boncore

—Fred Muerrle

—Dr. Findlay Russell, Los Angeles County-U.S.C. Medical Center

—David Hendin, Newspaper Enterprise Association

—Dr. Alan Beck, New York City Bureau of Animal Affairs

—Albert Einstein Medical Center

—Charly Baumann, Ringling Bros. and Barnum & Bailey Circus

—Dr. James Layne, Archbold Biological Laboratory

—Mr. and Mrs. Duard V. Lawson

—George Speidel, Milwaukee County Zoological Park

—Dr. George Raab, Chicago Zoological Park

—Clayton Freiheit, Denver Zoological Society

—Carol Towne, San Diego Zoological Society

—Prof. Aharon S. Shulov, Hebrew University

—Fred Blair, Jungle Habitat

—Larry French, *New Haven Register*

—Bayard Webster, *New York Times*

—Warren J. Iliff, National Zoological Park

—Wesleyan University, for library facilities

—Richard Winslow, for his patience as an editor

CONTENTS

INTRODUCTION

Ever Since Man first emerged from his animal origins, violent encounters have occurred between man and beast, frequently with damaging results for one or the other. Ancient man was a rather rare and sparsely distributed breed; so on a global basis such encounters were statistically few. At the same time, however, early man lived among wild animals, often engaging in basic fang-and-claw competition with them.

Today, the situation is more complex. Vast numbers of people live packed into great population centers and have little exposure to wild animals except vicariously, through zoos, circuses, and television. Yet the ingredients of conflict between man and animal have intensified, as has the potential for disaster for both man and beast. The reason for this state of affairs, the paradoxes that stem from it, and its meaning for the future, will be explored in the pages to come.

The paradoxical nature of the situation is typified by the fact that man has exterminated large predators from much of the land, yet has filled his cities with them in the form of the domestic dog. People who have never seen wolves nevertheless fear them immensely, but fail to recognize the danger posed by the wolf's canine cousins, roaming in packs on city streets and through suburban neighborhoods. Other people, believing themselves lovers of animal life, are blind to the threat of disease and injury that accompanies the wild pets they invite into their

I

homes, and oblivious to the fact that every wild animal taken for the pet trade is one less in the wild.

All about man are the Frankenstein monsters he has created within the animal kingdom: dogs bred and trained to kill people, black bears taught by handouts from national park visitors that people mean food, and deadly snakes kept as pets in people's homes.

By carrying animals with him, knowingly and accidentally, man has changed zoogeography for the worse. Starlings from Europe bespatter American cities with their droppings and displace native birds, less adaptable than the sharp-beaked European immigrants. Snails capable of carrying horrendous tropical diseases thrive in the southeastern United States. And, it now seems possible, a deadly species of cobra may live among the palms of southern Florida.

Paradox again emerges. For the first time on a worldwide scale, man is trying to preserve animals that can make a meal of him, trample him into the landscape, consume his crops, and otherwise cause him travail. While people in India starve, a fortune is being amassed to save the last of India's tigers, some of which ease their own hunger pangs by consuming a sizable number of India's citizens.

Conservationists want to save the grizzly bear and set aside the wilderness, isolating it from humans, that this great beast requires. But into the wilderness pours a horde of people starved for contact with nature and stuffed with fallacies about the animals they may encounter.

The most damaging of such fallacies for both man and beast are those arising from the tendency many people have to view the behavior of animals in human terms. The sight of a buck deer in the peak of breeding season, for example, evokes in such people the image of Bambi —noble, courageous, and kind lord of the forest. In reality, however, the buck in rut is the essence of bestiality. The buck stalks the forest, his neck swollen by gorged blood vessels, tongue lolling, and body stiff with desire for any female that he can batter into submission. A man who comes upon such a beast unawares stands a good chance of being charged, gored, and slashed to ribbons by razor-sharp hooves.

When people humanize animals they ascribe rational motives to acts triggered by instinct. If such acts are deemed unfriendly or nasty, the animals commiting them quickly assume the role of villians and thus become objects of persecution.

Man is a great classifier. He categorizes other creatures egocentrically, by their proximity to him on the evolutionary tree, and according to whether they benefit him. Within the latter frame of reference, an animal that is "good" is one which pleasures man, provides him with sustenance or shelter, or at the very least does not interfere with human affairs. An animal is "bad," on the other hand, if it competes with man for food, shelter, or territory, or poses a threat—even imagined—to human life or limb. It follows from these definitions that, depending on circumstances, an animal can be "good" one moment and "bad" the next, like a dog which fends off a burglar and then bites the postman.

While understandable in human terms, this attitude reflects a distorted view of the natural world, where adjectives such as "good" and "bad" have no meaning. Only from a human point of view is the insect that pollinates flowers more valuable than the one which chews on them.

So dominant is the human species, however, that man's view of nature ultimately will determine the fate of the animal kingdom. Although the often-hidden but nevertheless powerful forces of adaptation may have fitted an animal perfectly into its evolutionary niche, if that creature is considered inimical to human interests, it has little or no place in the world as re-created by man.

Evidence occurs with dreary regularity. Cases in point: the government of the central African country of Rwanda ordered most of that state's elephants destroyed in 1975 because the great beasts continued to forage on their ancestral feeding grounds, which unfortunately for the elephants had been converted to farmland. Grizzly bears, once kings of the North American wilderness, are captured and carted off to the back country if they habitually visit campgrounds in the national parks that are their last havens south of Canada. If a grizzly persists in its visits after a few relocations, it is shot. "Three times and you're out," says a National Park Service publicist in explaining its bear policy.

With the ascendancy of man, the rules for animal survival have changed. Fang, claw, horn, and sting, the urge to defend territory, to feed on flesh or fruit, are in a biological sense natural adaptations for survival, not instruments for good or evil; but when any instinctive action or physical characteristic of an animal is seen by man as threatening, it marks the creature as man's enemy. Adaptations that are the key to survival in nature thus may be maladaptive in the world of man. No matter how justified an animal's actions are in terms of its evolution, if they imperil human interests, the creature can become a killer in human eyes, and is so treated.

Considered objectively, no species is harmful; each contributes to the totality and diversity of life. A killer is not an enemy of nature, only of man. Moreover, man's own attitudes and actions, particularly those related to his exploitation of the animal kingdom, generate the conditions that trigger conflict between man and beast. The nature of this conflict, which all of us live with throughout our lives, and the conditions that spawn it, are the subject of this book.

The human act that turns a killer into an enemy may be as innocent as treading on a venomous snake in a rice field, or blundering into a grizzly sow with cubs on a narrow trail. It can be deliberate—taken with clear knowledge of risk—such as stepping into a ring with a fighting bull, or hunting a jaguar with a spear. Or it can be purposeful but based on ignorance, such as poking one's hand into a cage at a zoo.

The way people behave toward animals derives from ancient attitudes that have accumulated in man since he himself was half beast, together with images that are the products of our modern world. Emotions rooted in prehistoric nightmares, childhood experiences, and the contents of books, films, and television programs combine to create a confused picture of the animal kingdom and its relationship to man. It is with an examination of some of the forces that shape our attitudes toward animals, and how they contribute to the conflict between man and beast, that this book begins.

1. THE BEAST WITHIN

FIGURES CROUCH in the dripping gloom of a cave on a day now lost in time. Squatting in the dimness, they are unquestionably human, although on occasion a narrowing of the eyes or tensing of the muscles ever so faintly suggests the brute, like the echo of a whisper far along an empty corridor. Even so, an immense evolutionary gulf, forever unbridgeable, separates these primal men of 50,000 years ago from the beast which shambles towards them in the subterranean darkness, unaware of their ambush.

Concealed on a ledge the men wait for the beast with their hands clutching wooden spears and large jagged stones. Perhaps some of them gasp as they sense the approach of the creature. They know the power and savagery embodied in the shadowed form, with its massive head swaying from side to side under huge humped shoulders as it moves heavily through the passageway below.

At a wordless signal the men rise fluidly, one waving a firebrand snatched from a hidden receptacle, the others raining their weapons upon the now-raging animal, the great cave bear of prehistory.

Rearing on its hind legs the gigantic bear tears at the air a dozen feet above the cave floor with its clawed sledgehammer paws, but to no avail. It cannot reach the men that torment it from above. Pounded with rocks, pierced by wooden points hardened in fire, its coarse coat smoldering from a hurled brand, the bear snarls and foams at its attackers, who now sense the kill.

One of the men hoists a large boulder with his two hands, and heaves it down to thud against the high-domed skull of the bear. As the hunters' guttural cries echo through the underground vault, the beast shudders, then collapses to the cave floor, where it lies in a bleeding, battered heap. After some moments, certain that the great bear has died, the men file down from their parapet. Muttering sounds permitted by their primitive vocal tracts, they stare down at the beast they have killed in the bowels of the earth.

CULT OF THE CAVE BEAR

Archaeological evidence hints tantalizingly of encounters like the one described above occurring repeatedly during prehistory. Starting about 100,000 years ago, and for thousands of years after that, Neanderthal man hunted and killed the great cave bear *(Ursus spelaeus).*

While killing a one-ton relative of the modern grizzly bear with weapons of wood and stone is no mean feat, it was not a remarkable accomplishment for the Neanderthals. These ancient men routinely killed animals as large as the woolly rhinoceros and mammoths of the ice ages. What makes the killing of the cave bear so intriguing is not that it was done, but why ancient men sought encounters with it in caverns beneath the earth.

Man did not kill the bear because the bear preyed on him; the blunt cusps on the teeth of the bear indicate it was a vegetarian. It is reasonable to assume, however, that bear and man came into conflict over possession of caves in which both sought shelter, particularly during glacial periods. But that is not the whole story. Combat to the death between man and bear was prompted by something much less material and far more mysterious than competition for shelter. The cave bear was killed as part of a cult ritual whose exact meaning has vanished with the mind of prehistoric man.

Evidence for the existence of the cave bear cult has been gleaned from the heaps of bones discovered in European caves, and the manner in which some of these relics were arranged, obviously by the hands of ancient man.

Thousands of bones have been found in some caves. In the Austrian cave of Drachenhöhle (Dragon's Cave) alone, the bones of 30,000 cave bears, young and adult, had accumulated before the end of the last ice age 11,000 years ago.

Generations of cave bears made their dens in Drachenhöhle and similar caves as the vast glaciers of the ice ages grew and melted. During the course of such long-term occupation, countless bears died in their caves from disease, accident, wounds resulting from combat with other bears and, on rare occasion, old age.

Scientists who have explored the caves and examined their contents say that many of the bears also died violently under the weapons of prehistoric men, who fell upon the big animals as they slept, or ambushed them in the dark. Drachenhöhle contains a narrow passageway near the bottom of a waterfall that is a likely site for such an ambush.

Once a bear was killed, its head and bones were used as objects in some sort of ritual, which we can only guess. Ancient men arranged the skulls and bones of the bears in purposeful patterns, sometimes with considerable effort. Long before the appearance of modern man, Nean-

A French artist's depiction shows primitive men battling the great cave bear of the ice ages. The illustration is somewhat fanciful, but there is proof such battles really took place, perhaps as rituals.

derthal man ventured into one Alpine cave and placed the heads of seven bears within a stone box, then covered it with a stone lid of considerable weight. Each of the heads in the box was stationed with sightless eyes gazing in the direction of the cave entrance which served as a Neanderthal dwelling.

The skulls of five bears were arranged on a natural shelf in the wall of a German cave, while a grotto in France contained several skulls, arranged concentrically. Within another French cave, a site called Regourdou, Neanderthal man took the trouble to place the bones of more than twenty cave bears in a pit, then covered it with a chunk of stone that must have strained the muscles of several men to budge.

The ritual placement of bear bones might have been an afterthought, a ceremony to propitiate the spirits of bears killed for food, but that is unlikely because almost no cave bear remains have been discovered in the refuse of Neanderthal kitchens.

STEALING THE BEAST'S POWER

Perhaps the Neanderthals worshiped the bear, or offered it to dimly imagined supernatural beings. Either of these possibilities could be true, but there is another that seems even more likely. Mountainous in form, awesome in strength, apparently without fear, the cave bear possessed superb survival qualities. By killing the bear, Neanderthal man could have sought to transfer to his own self these qualities so much at a premium in his primitive world.

Animals that display superior strength, speed, sexual vitality and other physical attributes esteemed by humans have long been envied by man. How many people have wished for the strength of the lion, or the grace of an eagle? It is as true today as it was in the time of Neanderthal man, although its impact on us is somewhat less obvious.

Contemporary advertising and marketing techniques play upon man's innate desire for the physical attributes of certain animals. Not by accident are many high-performance, sporty automobiles named after big cats and other large, powerful beasts. Skim through any popular magazine and the chances are good that you will find advertisements

The common brown bat, despite its fierce appearance, is harmless
—except if it has rabies. Then its bite is fatal unless treated.

appealing to the animal we wish we had in us. Typical is an advertise-
ment extolling the pleasures of wearing diamond jewelry. It pictures an
attractive woman cheek to cheek with a sleek black cat which wears a
diamond bell on its neck. The copy reads:

> Embellish your ego.
> Or your alter ego.
> Wear diamonds on anything you love.

Wherever you roam.
Morning, noon or night alleys.

Somewhat more exotic is the attitude of many Orientals towards certain animals believed able to restore flagging virility. The chief among these is the rhinoceros. Preparations made from the rhino horn are supposed to do the trick. It is a very unfortunate notion as far as the rhinos of the world are concerned, because it has led to their relentless slaughter by poachers, who seek the price of $300 an ounce that rhino horn brings in Far Eastern markets. Birds of prey and hornbills also carry the same significance, and are hunted in the Far East for this reason. Bear paws and deer antlers are sold over the counter in scores of shops in Hong Kong to Chinese who deem these products restorative of strength and vitality.

The human longing to invest oneself with the powers of the beast is not restricted to old Oriental men and American consumers, but manifests itself even on the part of entire nations. Keep in mind that the United States and the Soviet Union, so advanced technologically that their astronauts rendezvous in space and their industries make weapons capable of ending life, still represent themselves in the respective guises of a bird of prey and a shaggy brown bear.

THE BEAST RELEASED

Historically, people who have aspired to incorporate animal attributes into their being sometimes cloak themselves in the guises of beasts. Perhaps after killing the cave bear, Neanderthal man skinned the beast and dressed its bloody hide in order to acquire its power. I have always suspected that at least part of the appeal of fur coats to women arises from this tendency.

Donning the garb of animals often has had the effect of releasing the beast within man. Disguised as animals, like children cloaked in the anonymity of Halloween costumes, people have felt free from the restraints of reason and society and have committed all sorts of wild and horrendous acts. Until early in this century, and perhaps as some people think, even today, members of a secret African society masked themselves in the pelts of leopards for ritual murders. Throughout much of west and central Africa, the leopard cultists pounced upon their victims by night, ripping them to death with razor-sharp metal claws. Women, children, and elderly people were frequently the victims of the leopard men, who commonly would remove the breasts of women victims and cannibalize the bodies of the slain.

More than two thousand years ago, the maenads of ancient Greece, female devotees of the wine god Dionysus, clad themselves in the skins of wild beasts for orgiastic worship of their deity. Their drunken, uninhibited orgies, actually fertility rites, sent the maenads staggering and raging about the countryside, draped in the skins of wolves, leopards, and similar animals. Disheveled and wild-eyed, these women in effect became the beasts whose pelts they wore.

As they roamed, the maenads coupled with men they happened to meet and slaughtered small animals they found in their path, rending the creatures with their teeth and nails. In very ancient times the orgy ended with human sacrifice. Biting and clawing, the frenzied women tore to bits a young man who represented the god. Some parts of his body were eaten in bloody communion, and the others were scattered in the fields to fructify the land. In the more gentle atmosphere of later times, a bull or goat was substituted for the human victim.

Myths rooted in the earliest days of ancient Greece, more than 3,500 years ago, hint of another group of worshipers in animal garb performing human sacrifice, in this case atop a mountain in Arcadia. The echoes of what took place on that peak in central Peloponnesus still haunt the dark corners of our dreams today, for the sacrifices that occured there might well have spawned the legend of the werewolf.

THE MYTH OF THE WOLF MAN

The story of the werewolf has strong links with early worship of no less a deity than Zeus, the chief of the Olympian gods of Greece. According to one ancient tradition, Zeus was born on Mount Lycaeus, or Mount Lykaion, in Arcadia, a region which was inhabited by large numbers of wolves.

Mount Lycaeus was, according to classical writers, the scene of human sacrifices in quite ancient times. Among other stories told of the mountain were those about people who ate the flesh of children and then became wolves. One such tale is the myth of King Lycaon, whose daughter had a son sired by Zeus. The king killed the child, had his flesh prepared as a meal, and served it to Zeus, who on discovering what had transpired, turned Lycaon into a wolf for his impiety. Today the supposed ability to transform oneself into a wolf is known as lycanthropy.

Scholars have speculated about the reality behind such tales; they suggest that before the Greeks of later times elevated Zeus to the status of chief of the gods, he was worshiped as a rain god atop Mount Lycaeus. In this role he was consort of the great mother goddess of the ancient Mediterranean. Among her symbols was the moon, and among the animals associated with her was the wolf. Very long ago, a sacred king representing the rain god may have been sacrificed atop the mountain. Eventually, rather than kill the king to bring the rain, worshipers substituted children as victims. The priests who performed the ritual might have carried on their grim duties while wearing the pelts of wolves. Dimly remembered, the sacrifices on Mount Lycaeus gave rise to the legend of a tormented human being transformed into a killer wolf under a gleaming, full moon.

The snarling, slavering beast-man preying on human victims is a staple tale of the occult. Stories of wolf-men whispered in the smoky interiors of medieval huts chilled those who heard them and caused many a man to glance towards the doorway and cross himself. Today the werewolf snarls at us from the motion picture and television screen, and still prompts an occasional nervous glance over the shoulder.

Now as in the past, too, the legend of the werewolf has another consequence. Like the story of Little Red Riding Hood it promotes the image of the wolf as an evil monster, intent on killing human victims, rather than as a highly intelligent predator with a key role in the natural scheme. This is unfortunate, for people need little enough excuse to persecute the wolf. Exterminated throughout much of its range, the wolf needs all the friends it can get.

This is not to say that the story of the werewolf is responsible for all of man's ill-will towards wolves, but it certainly has not helped the wolf's cause. Over the centuries, it has helped create the erroneous impression that the wolf is a cruel deliberate killer of men. In this sense the real victim of the werewolf myth has been the wolf itself.

THE WINGS OF SATAN

Superstition of one type or another has adversely affected the attitudes of people towards many animals, particularly creatures of the night, among these, the bat. Although the bat symbolizes good luck in the Orient, it had the opposite connotation in Europe. Westerners regard the bat as darkly as the night through which it flies. Artists of medieval times and the Renaissance endowed Satan with bat wings, but to many, if not most people, the bat signifies one thing—that frightening horror of the supernatural, the vampire.

Before the Spanish conquistadors trekked into the jungles of the American tropics, however, the association between the bat and the vampires of European legend did not exist because the vampire bat, which feeds on the blood of mammals and birds, lives only in the New World, from northern Mexico to the middle of South America. Nowhere else in the world do bats that feed on the blood of other creatures exist.

Cortez is credited with conferring the appellation "vampire" on the bats—there are three species in the family Desmondontidae—that now bear the name. Word of blood-drinking creatures that preyed on their victims by night spread rapidly in a Europe that was haunted by vampire legends. Soon, regardless of their dietary preferences, all bats became linked with the vampire, a situation which the Dracula stories have fostered down to this day. Ask almost any child and many an adult, and he will tell you, "Bats suck blood."

THE NATURAL HISTORY OF THE VAMPIRE

Contrary to popular belief, not even the vampire bat *sucks* blood, nor does it take enough of the fluid to pose harm to its human victims. There are reports about sleeping horses covered with vampires, and about repeated attacks by these creatures weakening fowl and puppies to the point of death, but the slightest movement by a human will send the bat flitting to safety. Vampire bats are small, with bodies no longer than a man's hand.

The manner in which the vampire feeds is fascinating. Its razor-

Bats issuing forth from caves, like these ones at the Carlsbad Caverns, New Mexico, evoke images of demons in the minds of many people.

sharp teeth scoop out a tiny slice of its host's skin, deep enough to allow blood to trickle forth. An anticoagulant in the bat's saliva keeps the blood flowing steadily, although not heavily. As the blood flows, the bat laps it up with incredible speed, inverting its tongue to form a trough through which the fluid spurts into the mouth, perhaps creating a slight vacuum in the process.

The bite of the vampire apparently has some sort of anesthetic quality for it seldom awakens a sleeping animal or man. William Beebe, the famed explorer and naturalist of the New York Zoological Society, once experimented on a colleague to assess the sensitivity of sleepers to the bat's bite. His subject had been bitten twice by bats the night before without awakening. Beebe tried several times to draw blood from the man's finger by pricking it with a pin while the subject slept but each time woke the fellow, who must have been a good-natured sort.

Beebe also allowed a vampire to alight on his arm, and observed the bat crawl up his limb. He reported hardly feeling it as it moved, wings neatly folded, over his flesh.

Another illustration of the ability of the vampire to bite without awakening sleeping victims occurred around 1920 when several members of a University of Michigan expedition to Colombia were bitten by bats during the night. In the morning the victims awoke to find themselves dabbed with smears of blood, but not one of them had been disturbed as the bats had fed in the dark of night.

REAL AND IMAGINED DANGERS OF THE VAMPIRE

Furnishing a meal for a vampire bat cannot be described as a pleasant experience, but in itself does not endanger human well-being. The wound made by the bite of the bat is minuscule and the amount of blood it takes slight. On occasion, however, the bite of the vampire, and, as we shall see, of other bats as well, can visit man with a horror far more terrible than the imagined menace of its blood meal: rabies, which bats, like other mammals, can carry and transmit to man. Several million cattle die yearly in Latin America because rabid vampire bats have fed on them. The cost of the loss totals $350,000,000 annually.

In their superstitious fear of bats, people often forget the real hazard that these winged mammals can pose. Like so many other animals, bats are feared for the wrong reasons. When man looks at the animal kingdom he often sees chimeras, created not only by superstition but by cultural attitudes, religion, and sometimes just plain foolishness. The results of man's distorted view make it difficult for him to relate to animals objectively, and seldom are positive for our fellow creatures.

No better example of this exists than the way people feel about snakes. All too many of us react in one of two ways at the sight of a serpent; we either bash it or run. There is no doubt, of course, that this deep fear of snakes stems in part from the fact that some species of serpents can kill a man with the touch of their fangs. And, although venomous snakes constitute but a small number of the total species, many people who do not know that treat all snakes like poison.

THE ETERNAL ENEMY

Stacked as they are against the snake, the odds are made even worse by Judeo-Christian scripture which presents the serpent as the symbol of evil incarnate. Exactly why the biblical author picked the snake to symbolize Satan probably never will be known, but it may have to do with the role of the snake in the ancient Summerian epic of Gilgamesh.

In the Mesopotamian epic of one of the world's first national heroes, considered by some scholars to preview the account in Genesis, the serpent is pictured as the thief of human immortality. The hero, Gilgamesh, left the plant that held the key to eternal life by the shore of a pool while he bathed. The serpent spied the plant and stole it.

If this story did not inspire the biblical depiction of Satan as a snake, then the reason may simply have been a matter of politics. The Caananites, enemies of the Hebrews, worshiped snake gods. What better way to defame one's foes than to picture their gods as the source of evil in the world?

The Hebrews were not the only people to cast the snake in the role of the Evil One. The serpent is the figure of the evil spirit Ahriman in the Zoroastrian religious system founded in the sixth century B.C.

Occasionally the snake was depicted in a favorable light. The periodic shedding of the snake's skin as the animal grows symbolized renewal and rebirth to the ancient Egyptians, who nevertheless feared snakes and offered prayers against their bite. As a phallic symbol the snake was associated with fertility worship in ancient Crete 5,000 years ago, and the Greeks who came later linked the serpent to healing powers —an association still with us in the twin serpents on the staff of Asklepius, badge of the physician. Snakes, including cobras and kraits, are eaten in the fall by Chinese who believe the flesh of the serpents will keep them warm in the winter.

Despite occasional regard for the snake, people generally have seen it as a symbol of evil, something to be summarily dispatched, without regard to whether or not it is dangerous to man. As predicted in Genesis, eternal enmity has existed between the serpent and the children of Eve.

ANIMALS, GODS, AND MEN

Even when religion or superstition confers a favorable image upon animals, they often suffer for it, as the cave bears killed by Neanderthal man testify. It has been suggested, in fact, that Neanderthal man killed so many cave bears he helped hasten the extinction of that species, which was vanishing by the time modern man had established himself in the caves of Eurasia about 40,000 years ago.

Not even holding the status of a god guarantees an animal's safety and, in fact, the sacred animals of many ancient religions were offered as sacrifices because they represented gods. The bull and the goat that substituted for the wine-god Dionysus met a bloody end, as did the Egyptian ram-god Ammon, which was sacrificed once a year and buried in a holy tomb.

THE AINU BEAR RITUAL

Until quite recently, the Ainu, an aboriginal people of northern Japan, killed a sacred bear in a ritual that scholars have compared to the Neanderthal bear cult. The Ainu, a Caucasian people of mysterious origin, have been nearly assimilated into Japanese society, so the bear ritual is all but lost, although it may persist in a few back-country villages. Even so, several vivid accounts record it in detail.

Ainu hunters killed the Asiatic black bear *(Selenarctos thibetanus)* for its hide and flesh and also posted skulls of the creature in their villages.

The ritual significance of the bear to the Ainus is uncertain, however, perhaps even to most people of Ainu extraction living today. Some Ainu have told scholars who inquired about it that their people believed they were descended from a bear. Others insisted that the bear was a sacred messenger dispatched by sacrifice to a forest god, or else the Ainu ritual may be a means of restoring good relations with the spirits of bears killed by the hunters.

Whatever its meaning, the ritual is quite bloody. A cub, caught at the end of the winter, is given to a woman of the village to suckle. After

weaning, it is stuffed with food and caged, but still treated as an honored guest.

One day, however, a village orator informs the bear that, sorrowfully, the people must kill it although they dearly love it. Praising the bear as the "divine one," the people drag it from its cage with ropes, tie it to a stake, and pummel the frightened beast with blunt arrows. The men of the village then scissor the bear's neck between two large poles, strangle it, and sometimes shoot it in the heart with an arrow.

After skinning the bear, the celebrants decapitate it and offer the severed head a piece of the flesh. The celebrants then may drink some of the bear's blood, or smear it over them to invest themselves with the courage they attribute to the animal. Next they post the hide atop a wooden pole and, consuming the flesh, dance around the raised bearskin.

MAN AGAINST NATURE

Rituals such as bear sacrifices in recent times and in the dim past may play upon a chord hidden deep in man and linked to his longing for the physical prowess of animals. Possessing natural powers beyond those of man, animals symbolize the awesome forces of nature which rule human existence. Taking the life of the bear might well be a way of demonstrating that man indeed has some control over nature.

It has been suggested that the appeal of Tarzan of the Apes to millions of people rests upon this same ancient human desire to overcome elemental forces, personified by animals. How many of us have killed their cave bears vicariously, identifying with the figure of Tarzan standing over the lifeless body of a bestial foe, man triumphant over beast?

MAN VERSUS BEAST

The need to be reassured about man's ascendancy over nature may be the reason people always have been fascinated by confrontation between man and beast. Manifested in many ways, some hidden beneath

The Minoans of ancient Crete worshipped a mother goddess often shown holding snakes, symbols of fertility. This statue dates back to 1500 B.C.

the conventions of modern society, human fascination with the contest between the powers of man and animal are at the heart of the drama of the bull ring, and behind the tremendous popularity of the performance of the animal trainer at the circus. In this connection it is worth mentioning that one of the most long-lived and popular programs in the history of television, "Mutual of Omaha's Wild Kingdom," is a show that has frequently featured its zoologist personalities in the act of wrestling, roping, netting and otherwise pitting their brains and brawn against wild animals.

The compulsion to demonstrate our dominance over nature probably is the unconscious motivation for many of the ways people use animals, if indeed, it does not bias the entire gamut of relations between man and beast. Does the need to show our mastery over animals drive many of us to hunt wild animals when we do not need them for subsistence? Has man's fear and envy of the physical abilities of animals inspired the craze for keeping wild animal pets? Is it the reason why increasing numbers of people parade about the streets with large aggressive dogs in tow? Are the countless zoo visitors who flock to see the big cats being fed by their human keepers seeking reassurance that man, after all, is ruler of his world?

IN THE IMAGE OF MAN

Hand in hand with man's need to prove superiority over animals is his inherent inclination to recast animals in his own image by ascribing human motives to their behavior. All of us give in to this tendency, and in fact people delight in bestowing human characteristics upon animals. Perhaps it lessens the threat that the physical prowess of animals poses to man, or perhaps it is merely a symptom of human ego that we find it easiest to discuss animals in our own terms.

This humanized view of the animal kingdom encourages the mistaken idea that some creatures are evil, some good. It ignores the fact that animals are not driven by the reasoning, emotions, and impulses that motivate people, but largely by instinct, and less so by lessons learned through personal experience. Strictly speaking, an animal cannot love, or even lust, although it can be loyal, but only to a thing, never a concept.

An animal can react fearfully to something it sees or hears, but it cannot fear an idea. For an animal, out of sight really is out of mind.

An animal behaves one way or another not for motives that are good or bad but for its survival. Man has been able to yoke some of these instincts for survival to his service, as in the case of dogs trained to save people, or to kill them.

The tendency to make animals into people in furry suits emerges not only in stories of Peter Rabbit and the Big Bad Wolf, but in contemporary depictions of animals that are intended to represent realism. No where is this more apparent than in some of the television programs about wildlife whose enormous popularity with American audiences has made them a dominant factor in the television industry.

A major special on the beaver contained these gems, intoned by Henry Fonda:

> "Castor [the beaver] has been thinking about settling down and finding himself a wife, but he's surprised when he finds out that his parents want him to leave the pond."
> ". . . it doesn't take very long before Castor discovers a friend in need. It's his good luck that she's just about the most beautiful thing he's ever seen. Look at those sensitive eyes; and, of course, any girl wearing a fur coat is hard to resist: . . . It's love at first sight."

This anthropomorphic mush was from Survival Anglia Limited, a firm which has also produced some of the finest, most intelligent documentaries about wildlife ever shown on American television.

FANG AND CLAW IN PERSPECTIVE

The whole idea of beavers falling in love may seem harmless—even fun—but when presented as reality, the humanization of animal behavior can be damaging to man and beast, in that it thwarts man's understanding of animals and how they live. Animals mate, fight, kill, and play out of motives that have nothing to do with reason. They have little choice in the matter and, allowing for some individual differences, must respond to a particular situation in a way dictated by their evolution.

If the proper response to a particular set of conditions is to pounce

Japanese hunters of today confront a bear with spears in the way
men have fought bears for countless thousands of years.

on something and tear it to ribbons, that is what the animal will do. If
the repertoire of an animal's feeding behavior includes a predatory response to creatures the size of man, you may become its dinner. Instinct
may tell an animal to flee or fight; the animal's response is a matter of
following a command, not a reasoned course of action.

The mother robin defending her young acts not out of courage, but
because her instincts demand she fight for the survival of her offspring.

Beavers mate only under very specific conditions—the right combination of time, place, and the peaking of complex chemical processes within their bodies, interacting with such external triggers as the length of day. Love has nothing to do with it.

In stressing the differences between man and beast, it would be an oversight to disregard that some similiarties exist, too. Certainly the shadow of the beast still lurks in a hidden corner of man's being, and some animals hint faintly of the evolutionary giant step that led to the human race, but differences are what count and must be recognized if we are to understand the nature of animals.

When the mass media humanize animal behavior such as courtship and killing of prey, they can warp the perspective of millions of people on the animals that share the world with man, and more importantly, on what must be done to insure their survival. Typically, motion pictures and television often miscast hawks, snakes, big cats, and other predators as the miscreants of the animal world. The killing these creatures do is presented as something that is malicious, not in its true light as part of the predator's role in maintaining the balance of nature.

An example can be drawn from an exchange of letters between a leading zoologist, recognized as an authority on the world's crocodiles, and an executive associated with the television program "Last of the Wild." The zoologist, Dr. F. Wayne King of the New York Zoological Society, wrote the executive, complaining that one episode of the program depicted the crocodile as a villain, rather than a simple predator. King's comments in part were motivated by the fact that crocodiles are threatened with extinction throughout virtually all of their range.

The executive dismissed King's complaint, stating, "It would seem that a simple predator ready to strike at anything that moves might well be portrayed as a villain."

At the other end of the spectrum from this view of predators is that expressed in the *Born Free* trilogy of books by Joy Adamson, and the films and television programs based on these works. Millions of people have been influenced by Adamson's story of Elsa, the lioness reared by Adamson and her husband George, a game warden in Africa.

Essentially, the *Born Free* approach tells people that they can establish a loving relationship with a big, savage predator that is capable of killing a man with a love tap. The outlook fostered by Adamson's works

is reflected particularly well in the following extract from promotional material for a brief-lived television series based on the book:

> Elsa, who came to the Adamsons as a cub, and who became as a child to them, whom the Adamsons loved, and who showed both Joy and George affection, a telepathic understanding, and indeed a love that was all but impossible between a lioness and two human beings, and yet existed. Elsa, who was raised to be tame, to all intents and purposes a large, immensely powerful but domesticated cat, sentenced to life behind bars or to death and then trained to live wild by Joy and George. Elsa, who had to learn how to live and fight and protect herself in a hostile environment, who had to go wild, but who never forgot, or forgot to love, her two human friends.

If, after all this, you are tempted to keep a lion about the house, remember that while the Adamsons may have conquered the savage beast with love, what worked for them in the African bush may not work for you—as a number of American pet owners, or their unfortunate neighbors, have discovered.

THE BEAST IN FACT AND FICTION

Fact and fiction blur when Elsa the real lioness becomes Elsa the star of television episodes no more true to life than those of the Six-Million-Dollar Man. Of course, creators of fiction about animals have complete license to humanize their characters, and, as in the case of *Watership Down,* it can have artistic merit. The trouble is that people often do not distinguish between fact and fiction. They fail to recognize, or they ignore, the fact that Bambi's life in the forest has no resemblance to the real struggle for survival in nature, and that Lassie the four-footed Good Samaritan is an actor in a drama, not a real dog faced with actual situations.

This sort of confusion interjects irrelevant considerations into man's dealings with animals. It encourages the owners of dogs, for instance, to make unreasonable demands on their pets, an attitude of "If Lassie can do it, why can't you?" It inspires emotional campaigns against the scien-

An illustration from a nineteenth-century magazine depicts the way in which the brown bear was once hunted in Russia.

tifically sound cropping of deer herds that otherwise would starve. Ed
Kozicky and John Madson, top conservation officials of the Winchester-
Western Company, took note of this problem in a paper presented to the
student chapter of the Wildlife Society at Louisiana State University.
Speaking of the way in which television has warped the true facts of life
in nature for an urbanized viewing public, they said:

> "Then came the miracle age of electronics. The outdoors could be
> brought into the living room through a picture tube, and Disney film
> productions lost little time in doing so. A vast Sunday evening audi-
> ence was riveted to the Disney version of wildlife. Starting with a
> proven formula for success—the humanization of wildlife with such
> cartoon characters as Bambi—the Disney studios went to depict
> Mother Nature as a kind old grandma who provides a peaceful and
> idyllic existence for her charges. Little mention was made of nature's
> stern realities—of the survival of the fittest, the constant struggle for
> food and cover, the rule of fang and claw. Many viewers began to feel
> that wild animals live in harmony in enchanted forests, a vision of
> freedom, peace and beauty that was missing from their own lives. In
> their new-found love of wildlife—whether real or imagined—they
> could not bear the thought of those wild creatures being hunted or
> trapped."

The false impression of nature described above is the one fostered
by the so-called humane organizations. A perfect example is a Christmas
card, issued in 1975 by the Humane Society of the United States. It shows
cats, a fox, and weasels all of which regularly kill and eat rabbits, with
two cunning bunnies—all of them bunched together in a cozy little
group. If the animals depicted ever could be gathered together in that
fashion—not that it ever would happen in nature—the result would be
not friendship but a red slaughter, first of the rabbits by their predators,
then among the meat eaters themselves.

The real animal kingdom is populated not by Bambi, Lassie, and
Peter Rabbit in pants, but by flesh-and-blood creatures much more
complex and fascinating than their humanized caricatures, and much
more intimately involved with man. They include the savage guard dog
in the hands of the wrong master, the lion which claws a careless visitor
at a zoo, and the elephant which must be destroyed because its feeding
grounds are needed for farmland. Among them, too, are the wolf, which
is the victim of both excessive love and unreasoning hate, the rat which
haunts the ghetto, and the venomous spider that has been granted a

year-round summer because of central heating.

These and the other animals that share the earth with humanity must be recognized for what they are if a balance is to be maintained between the interests of man and beast. By understanding the roles of animals in nature man can establish a sound, fruitful relationship with them, promoting their welfare as well as using them as a resource. Before this can come about, however, the real dangers posed by animals must be distinguished from the imaginary, and we must recognize the ways in which human actions can endanger animals, and in which they can imperil man.

2. MAN AND THE POISONERS: SNAKES

OF ALL THE DANGERS advanced by animals, none is more misconstrued than the threat from creatures which are venomous, those which can deliver a dose of poison by a bite or sting. Animals with this capability, especially if they creep or crawl, are viewed with universal dread, which sometimes is justified but is often undeserved or misdirected.

The loathing and terror inspired by venomous animals frequently are based on all the wrong reasons. This is partly because of attitudes discussed in the previous chapter, but it also arises from people's ignorance about the nature of venomous animals and the conditions that govern whether or not they endanger man. The confusion has enabled some of the genuine horrors among venomous animals to escape recognition, and has caused the persecution of some creatures which really are innocuous, and even beneficial.

Any damage done to man by venomous animals is purely in self-defense; not a single venomous animal preys on man or even remotely shows an interest in people as food. A man would be much too big a meal for even the largest venomous snakes, and they are the largest venomous animals of all. Most of the animals that can poison man, in fact, are very small and if not for their venoms could be easily killed with the bare hands. None of these creatures employ their fangs or stings against man unless he first triggers instincts that command them to protect themselves. This means that venomous animals do not go around searching for people to kill or injure, and are dangerous only if someone blunders into them or tries to handle or harm them.

Perhaps the most common misconception about venomous animals other than that they somehow are maliciously inclined towards man, is that they are universally deadly. Just because an animal possesses a deadly poison, however, does not make it a major mankiller or even dangerous to people. Some of the snakes with the most potent of all venoms kill very few people, while others whose poisons are much less powerful cause the deaths of thousands of humans. This is part of the reason that snakebite varies around the world from a minor nuisance to a real scourge. In the United States, for instance, only about a dozen people die annually from snakebite, while in Southeast Asia the death toll is in the thousands.

It is obvious that the variety and abundance of venomous serpents living in a region have a lot to do with whether or not snakebite is a serious problem there, but that is not all that matters. If it were, snakebite would be an extremely grim matter in several parts of the United States, which literally are crawling with potentially dangerous serpents.

A host of factors, related not only to the ecology and behavior of snakes, but to the social and economic conditions of the potential victims, determine whether or not a region has a severe snakebite problem.

Most of the 300,000 people bitten annually by venomous snakes around the world, and almost all of the 30,000 to 40,000 victims who die, live in tropical and subtropical lands where people habitually walk barefoot. Moreover, most of the regions where snakebite is common are within the range of venomous snakes that get along very well in the world of man, even to the point of entering human habitations. Life-style—human and reptilian—has a profound influence on the frequency of snakebite and the number of deaths that result from it.

Snakes have a jaw construction that permits them to swallow relatively large prey. Here, a rattlesnake swallows a jackrabbit.

THE CHEMISTRY OF DEATH

Of the 3,000 different kinds of snakes, only about 200 are venomous,
possessing not only poison but a means of getting it into the victim. Snake
venom, a clear yellow, viscous liquid, is produced in glands that are
similar to those which make saliva in other animals.

Most snakes have the kind of glands that can produce venom, and
evidence is mounting that many more of them than previously suspected

manufacture it, although they lack the fangs to deliver it. A few people have been mildly poisoned after being bitten by the feisty water snakes of the genus *Natrix,* common in most parts of the country, and in November 1975, an eleven-year-old boy in Camavillo, California, was severely poisoned when a supposedly harmless garter snake *(Thamnophis sirtalis)* bit his hand.

The boy saw the snake in the yard of his school and picked it up. So hard did the snake bite that the boy was unable to dislodge it. He walked into the school, where a custodian had to pry the jaws of the snake from the youngster's flesh with a screwdriver. A short time later, when the boy's arm began to swell and his shoulder turned black, both he and the snake were flown to the Los Angeles County-University of Southern California Medical Center.

The hospital maintains a consultation center on snakebite for physicians, and is the home base of one of the world's leading authorities on treatment of venomous bites, Dr. Findlay E. Russell. He verified the swelling was caused by venom. Once the boy recovered—only a matter of a few days—Russell held a press conference to discuss the case. As a result of the publicity, at least nine other people from different parts of the nation reported to Russell that at various times they or someone in their families had a similar experience.

From the evidence it appears as though garter snakes may produce poison and that in rare cases where they cannot let go after biting, some of the venom may seep into the wound. So unusual are these circumstances, however, that they cannot be considered dangerous, especially since they normally hardly penetrate the skin.

Perhaps venom is a common property of many harmless snakes as well as those species with the right kind of teeth to use it effectively. It takes a groove or channel in the teeth to carry enough venom to a wound to cause serious poisoning. Some snakes with channels in their teeth, however, lack fangs of sufficient size to penetrate deeply enough into human flesh; other serpents have teeth that are of the appropriate size and design, but which are set in the rear of the jaw, and are difficult to bring into play. Thus the ability to produce venom alone need not make a snake dangerous to humans.

Most snake venoms, nevertheless, are extremely powerful poisons containing a witch's brew of ingredients that play havoc with the body.

Near the bite, the venom actually begins to digest the victim's flesh. By the time a venomous snake swallows its prey, which is consumed unchewed and whole, the digestion of the meal is already under way.

Although gruesome to contemplate, this action of snake venom illustrates that its primary function is to help the snake get its meals rather than to defend itself. Very often, in fact, venomous snakes do not discharge poison when they strike people. About twenty percent of the people bitten by venomous serpents in the United States escape serious consequences for this reason, and many of the so-called miracle cures of snakebite probably work because the victims never were envenomated in the first place.

Snakebite victims who are not so lucky, however, can be in for a very rough time because the poisons manufactured in the venom glands of serpents rank among the most toxic materials known to man. Cobras and rattlesnakes, for example, inject their victims with a poison more than 30,000 times as potent as strychnine. Not for nothing was cobra venom among the deadly poisons the United States Central Intelligence Agency has been accused of squirreling away for possible assassination attempts.

SNAKEBITE IN THE UNITED STATES

Even in the United States, with its enormous public-health bureaucracy, it is extremely difficult to gather sufficient information on snakebite cases to produce an accurate picture of the problem, other than that about 8,000 people are bitten each year but few of them die. A few public-health researchers have attempted it, however, and from such studies the following generalizations can be made.

The incidence of snakebite rises with warm weather, which is logical, for that is when large numbers of both people and snakes are moving about. From a peak in midsummer, the number of snakebites shrinks to almost nothing by the middle of winter. Men and boys are twice as likely to be bitten by venomous snakes as women and girls and nonwhites slightly more than whites. Most of the people bitten are under twenty years of age, chiefly teen-agers and preteens.

The safest parts of the country are Alaska, Hawaii, northern New

England, and the upper Midwest, which lack venomous serpents. Texas, North Carolina, Florida, Georgia, Mississippi, and Arizona, on the other hand, have a high rate of venomous snakebite.

In any assessment of snakebite in the United States, exception must be made for zoo personnel and others who regularly come into contact with snakes. About a third of all venomous snakebite cases in the land involve zoo keepers or people with dangerous snakes at home. Virtually all of the ten cases which occur in an average year in New York City, for example, fall into this category.

The chances of recovering from a venomous snakebite are increased immensely by the presence of good medical care and facilities and the ready availability of antivenins. These are serums, usually prepared with a horse serum base, which are used as antidotes for snake venoms.

Antivenins vary according to the chemistry of the venoms they are supposed to counteract, and many large hospitals commonly stock several different types. If a hospital lacks the right antivenin for a patient, physicians often find it at zoos and similar institutions, which maintain a varied stock of such serums. A listing of the antivenins available in this country and where to get them in emergency is kept at the Oklahoma City Zoo.

Several zoos also have established emergency procedures with police and ambulance services for speeding serum to people who need it in a hurry. In 1973, when a teen-aged Philadelphia boy was bitten by a pet cobra he had hidden in his parents' basement, serum was rushed to the Albert Einstein Medical Center in Philadelphia from the Philadelphia Zoo to save the boy's life. The same year cruisers from New York and New Jersey police departments relayed serum from New York City's Staten Island Zoo to suburban Ridgewood, New Jersey, for a high-school teacher bitten by an Asian saw-scaled viper. The teacher had been observing the snake in a cage at his home.

Serum alone is not always the answer to snakebite, and other means of treatment, such as suctioning venom from the wound, often are necessary. One of the key problems in treating snakebite, according to the experts, is that it is so rare most physicians lack sufficient experience to deal with it. Sometimes nothing works. In 1964 the director of the Hogle Zoo in Salt Lake City died the day after he was bitten by an African puff adder, even though physicians treated him with serum flown to Salt Lake City from San Diego by Navy jet, and tried both heart massage and a tracheotomy to save him.

Part of the problem in treating venomous snakebite is identifying

The western diamondback rattlesnake of North America is one of the world's most venomous serpents.

the species of the snake responsible so the right type of antivenin can be administered to the patient. In this country, the task is not too difficult, because rattlesnakes of one type or another account for the major portion of snakebites.

THE PERILOUS PIT VIPERS

Fifteen species of rattlesnakes, divided into innumerable subspecies of interest only to taxonomists, inhabit the United States and bordering areas of Canada and Mexico. They include the nine-foot diamondbacks, among the world's most dangerous snakes, and the pigmy rattler *(Sistrurus miliarius),* only a foot long, with venom that at worst might prove fatal to a small child. The others range between these two extremes in both size and menace.

Rattlesnakes belong to a large group of serpents called pit vipers because of a pitlike structure between the nostril and eye that enables them to sense the heat given off by warm-blooded prey. The nerves in the pit are sensitive to as little as one-five thousandth of a degree of heat from two feet away. This natural heat finder helps rattlesnakes track the small mammals that are abroad after dark, when vision plays little role in hunting.

The other pit vipers living in the United States are the cottonmouth *(Agkistrodon piscivorus),* a chunky, tough-tempered water snake as dangerous as some of its rattlesnake relatives, and the shy, mild-mannered copperhead *(A. contortris).*

Pit vipers are highly advanced snakes in terms of evolution, and have awesome fangs, an inch long in some species. The fangs of the pit viper are doubly dangerous, for as well as being unusually long they are hollow and punch like a pair of deadly hypodermic needles.

When not in use the fangs lie back in the jaw, out of the way. Once the pit viper goes into action, however, it erects its fangs, a movement permitted by the arrangement of the bones in its jaw. The fangs pivot forward and up, so that they stab almost horizontally at the victim as the strike knifes home. Snakes such as cobras, which lack such efficient fangs, sometimes must strike several times, and a few venomous snakes even have to chew their poison into the victim to get the job done. The pit viper, on the other hand, needs to strike only once, if it hits its target.

THE SPEED OF A RATTLESNAKE'S STRIKE

It is not impossible for a man—or a mouse, for that matter—to sidestep the strike of a rattlesnake, for the speed at which the snake launches its attack is far from blinding. Some years ago Walker Van Riper of the Denver Museum of Natural History measured the speed of a striking rattler and found its head moves at about eight feet per second.

That is fast enough, of course, but in the light of a comparison made by Van Riper it cannot be considered overwhelming as many people believe. Van Riper calculated that his own untrained left hand moving in a boxer's jab traveled at 18.1 feet per second. Having been an amateur boxer, and a second and trainer for both amateurs and professionals, I can vouch for Van Riper's assertion that the jab of a skilled boxer moves much faster than he was able to punch. A quick-fisted prizefighter therefore, can jab with a speed almost three times that of a striking rattlesnake.

With a little practice, it is possible not only to parry the jab of a man who is fast in the ring, but to evade it by a slip of the head. Carrying out the comparison between the boxer's jab and rattler's strike, this means that a man who is quick and alert has a good chance of getting out of the way of an angry rattlesnake, even after the snake has begun its move.

Usually, moreover, the rattler signals its intention to attack by vibrating the string of horny buttons that tip its tail, and give the snake its name. On hearing this sound, the best course of action is not to run, but to freeze and attempt to locate the snake's position. The buzz of a rattle indicates that a strike is imminent, but if the snake is left alone it may not follow up with an attack.

Warned by the rattle, a man armed with a stick can kill the snake without too much difficulty. A physician friend of mine did it while hiking in the mountains or North Carolina. As he recalled the incident, he was striding along a rocky path, walking stick in hand, when he heard the rattler's buzz. Seeing the serpent coiling just a few feet away, he instinctively smashed it with his stick. The snake, a timber rattlesnake (Crotalus horridus) was five feet in length. Today the physician says he is sorry that he killed the snake, but that he reacted unconsciously, out of fear.

TIMBER RATTLERS

The timber rattler is probably the rattlesnake most often encountered by people ignorant in the ways of venomous serpents because its range extends into the populous northeastern states where, for the most part, it is the only rattlesnake. Extirpated from most cities and suburbs, it nevertheless survives not far from New York City, even within sight of the Manhattan skyline. When people from the cities head for the peace and quiet of the hills, they occasionally come across this large rattler.

The problem is that many people who lack experience with venomous snakes, or any snakes at all, either become unnecessarily frightened when they see a rattlesnake or, worse, unduly careless. I once stopped my car on the Blue Ridge Parkway in Virginia's Shenandoah National Park where several other tourists had gathered around a big timber rattler, apparently struck by a car. The blow probably had been glancing, for the snake, about five feet long, seemed to be recovering, and did not appear damaged. Even so, several of the people who had crowded around the creature as it lay on the pavement stood casually a couple of feet away. Considering that even a dead snake can bite through reflex action, their actions were extremely foolhardy.

"TAKE UP SERPENTS"

The timber rattlesnake is commonly used by the fundamentalist Christian snake-handlers of the southern Appalachians to show their trust in divine faith and healing. These people take literally the passage in the Gospel of St. Mark which states in part, "In my name . . . they shall take up serpents . . . it shall not hurt them."

If the timber rattlesnake were as aggressive as some of its relatives, the membership rolls of these sects would be severely depleted. As it is, the men who handle them usually escape being bitten, although once in a while a snake does jab its fangs into one of the worshipers. Undoubtedly in many of these instances the snake's occasional tendency not to pump venom when striking defensively contributes markedly to the congregation's faith in God. When a handler does get a full dose of poison, however, he usually is carted off before the authorities, which frown on such activities, can arrive. If the victim dies, the congregation attributes his misfortune to lack of faith.

In 1974 a worshiper at one such service in rural Tennessee tempted fate to its utmost by handling, not a docile timber rattlesnake, but a vicious eastern diamondback *(Crotalus adamanteus)* as he danced about singing hymns. The rattlesnake sank its fangs into the man's wrist. He

Fred Blair, who conducted a snake handling demonstration at the Jungle Habitat safari park in New Jersey, shows how to milk a rattlesnake of its venom.

danced about singing for a while longer, but then collapsed, and was quickly carried from the church by friends.

THE DANGEROUS DIAMONDBACKS

America's two species of diamondbacks, biggest venomous snakes in North America, almost always turn up on lists of the world's dozen or so most dangerous snakes. The eastern species, which reaches a length of eight feet, prowls sandy pine woodlands from North Carolina to Louisiana, seldom straying from within 100 miles of the coast. The western diamondback, *(C. atrox),* is just a shade smaller than its eastern cousin, and ranges from Texas to the border country of Arizona and California. It is generally acknowledged as the venomous snake that bites more people than any other in the country.

Between the two of them, the diamondbacks claim most of the lives taken by venomous serpents in the United States, because in addition to their size and aggressiveness, they pump large quantities of highly toxic venom into their victims.

Fred Blair, a veteran snake handler who directs a reptile show at the Jungle Habitat safari park in New Jersey, has been bitten by both species. An eastern diamondback struck him in the wrist while he was handling it during an exhibition, and a western diamondback bit him above his boot top while he was collecting snakes in Texas.

Blair experienced the tremendous pain and destruction of skin and flesh at the site of the puncture that is typical of rattlesnake bites. The venom of the diamondback also attacks the red blood cells and the nervous system. The latter action apparently was responsible for the numbness in Blair's tongue and lips which he felt after the western diamondback sank its fangs into his leg. So serious was this bite that Blair was hospitalized for several weeks and forced to walk with a cane for three months after leaving the hospital bed.

Even in cases as severe as diamondback attacks, however, the chances of a victim's recovery are increased by a quick but calm reaction to the event. Near Fort Myers, Florida, a few years ago the effective response of a fifteen-year-old youth saved a companion from the potentially fatal consequences of an eastern diamondback's assault. The snake struck while the thirteen-year-old victim and his three friends were collecting reptiles in a swamp. The fifteen-year-old had the presence of mind to make the bitten boy lie down and attempted to remove the venom from the wound with a Boy Scout snakebite kit.

Meanwhile, the two other boys in the group ran for the nearest telephone, which was a half hour away. Once there, they called the sheriff's office, but the two hundred searchers who responded could not find the bitten boy in the thick vegetation of the swamp, even with the aid of a helicopter. When help failed to arrive, the fifteen-year-old hoisted his stricken friend onto his shoulders, and lugged him to a house two miles away. The owner of the house put the boys in his car and rushed the bitten youngster to a hospital, where he was successfully treated.

SOME OTHER RATTLERS

Along with the diamondbacks, the western rattlesnake *(C. viridis)* ranks high on the list of American serpents most frequently implicated in snakebite. This is not so much because it is aggressive—it is, in fact, the snake carried by the Hopi Indians in their snake dance—but because it has an exceptionally wide range geographically and ecologically. This serpent, whose color varies considerably, lives in almost all habitats except desert in all of the states from the Great Plains to the Pacific. People in this vast region probably encounter it more than any other rattlesnake, thus increasing the chances of mishaps, although many of the humans who come across this snake are outdoorsmen at least somewhat acquainted with rattlesnakes.

When it comes to dangerous rattlesnakes, however, no place in the land, in fact on the globe, can match the southwestern corner of the United States which is the home of at least a dozen different rattlers. This so-called rattlesnake belt has a virtual monopoly on several highly dangerous serpents, worst of which is the Mojave rattlesnake *(C. scutulatus),* whose venom is more toxic than that of the diamondback. This creature, experts believe, has venom more potent than any other rattlesnake but one, the neotropical rattlesnake of Mexico and South America. The Mojave rattlesnake may be responsible for some of the attacks on people attributed to the western diamondback, for the bites of the two species are very similar and are easily confused.

Among the other rattlers of the rattlesnake belt are the speckled

rattlesnake *(C. mitchelli),* which is known for its willingness to fight rather than flee, and the sidewinder *(C. cerastes)* so named because it sidles over the ground with its body in an S curve. Notoriously quick and agile, the sidewinder often is difficult to see when its light brown body is half-buried in the desert sand. However, the sidewinder seldom injects enough venom to kill a man. Two other rattlesnakes of the southwest also pose a particular hazard because they blend so well with their surroundings. These are the tiger rattlesnake *(C. tigris)* and the twin-spotted rattler *(C. pricei).*

Fortunately, most of these snakes inhabit wilderness far from heavy concentrations of human population, or else the United States might have a much more serious snakebite problem. This could well be the case, for instance, if the Mojave rattlesnake ranged over the same territory as the timber rattler or the small pigmy rattlesnake.

Recent statistics on population show, however, that the western and southeastern states are the nation's new growth areas. Unquestionably this means that more people will be moving into prime rattlesnake country, with a resultant rise in contact between man and serpent.

AN INVASION OF RATTLESNAKES

Increasing encounters with rattlesnakes are especially likely in Florida, which has become the country's fastest-growing state. Vast areas of palmetto scrub and marshland, favored by one type of rattler or another, are being turned almost overnight into housing developments, populated largely by newcomers who, in the words of one Floridian, "call the exterminator if they see a tree frog on the window." Doubtless many of these new residents have little inkling that when they move into some of these subdivisions they may be fleeing the burglars and muggers of northern metropolises, but settling down in the heart of rattlesnake country.

During the summer of 1975, one subdivision near Miami was invaded by scores of pigmy rattlesnakes, which frightened homeowners so

Few pit vipers, such as this Pope's pit viper, inhabit southwest Asia, but most live in the Americas. Like the majority of pit vipers, the one shown here is quite venomous.

badly that they dug up precious shrubbery in attempt to eliminate cover for the reptiles. All summer long, however, only one person was bitten by the little serpents, which are so docile that even I have handled them in the field. The victim—if one can call him that—was a sixteen-year-old boy bitten on a finger, who experienced no serious symptoms.

The range of the pigmy rattler and its habitat preferences coincide largely with those of the eastern diamondback. An invasion of a neighborhood by diamondbacks similar to the incursions on the Miami area subdivision by pigmy rattlesnakes might have far more grim consequences. Such an event may never occur, of course, but the odds are good that in the next few years Florida will have an increase in incidents involving people and diamondbacks.

RATTLESNAKE ROUNDUPS

Common sense dictates that rattlesnakes should be avoided, but some people, such as the Appalachian cultists already mentioned, avidly seek them out. Notable in this respect are the participants in annual "rattlesnake roundups" sponsored by business and service clubs such as the Jaycees in several small towns across the country, especially in the southwest. Immensely popular with spectators, the roundups result in the capture and death of thousands of rattlesnakes, some of which are skinned alive before gawking audiences.

During the roundups men and boys fan out over the countryside armed with snake sticks and cans of gasoline, which are poured into rattlesnake dens to roust out their tenants. The snake hunters seldom are bitten, not only because many of them are quite experienced at their pursuit, but also because the roundups typically are held in early spring, when the weather is cool and the snakes still sluggish from winter dormancy. An old trick in handling snakes is to keep them cool, thus slowing their metabolism and keeping their reactions and movements torpid.

The snake collectors do the rodent populations of their areas yeoman service, for by cleaning out rattlesnakes, they remove one of the most serious threats to the proliferation of rats and mice. The snakes, writhing in sacks, are lugged back to public enclosures and tossed into arenas and pits in front of marveling men, women, and children, who pay admission for the privilege of viewing the serpents. Most of the reptiles are decapitated, skinned and sold as meat, either raw or fried. The amount of snake flesh sold at these roundups is substantial. Snake hunters at a roundup in Walnut Springs, Texas, during March, 1975 brought in 832 rattlers weighing a total of more than 1,000 pounds.

Among the dubious thrills which draw people to the roundups is the chance to see snake handlers risk good health by performing feats of derring-do with the captured rattlers. Sometimes the handlers are bitten, as was the case at the Walnut Springs fest when a man who tried to perform "the kiss of death" with a serpent was struck in the lip. He survived, however, after treatment at Parkland Hospital in Dallas.

COPPERHEAD AND COTTONMOUTH

While rattlers of one type or another account for about 90 percent of the venomous snakebites in the United States, their cousin the copperhead is believed to bite more people than any other single species, despite its mild disposition. The reason for this seeming contradiction is that copperheads thrive even in populous areas, and, in fact, until a few decades ago they even survived in New York City.

Adapting to a variety of habitats, including marshes, woodlands, and rocky hillsides, the copperhead ranges across North America from Massachusetts to Mexico, but is absent from peninsular Florida. Although many of the "copperheads" people see really are harmless species, the three-foot snakes turn up with regularity in suburban backyards and woodlots. Copperheads strike with considerable speed once fully aroused, but they are so lethargic that it takes considerable prodding to provoke them. There are cases of copperheads failing to strike even when stepped upon, which is easy to do because the snake's brown markings blend well with fallen leaves.

Children playing in abandoned shacks and farm buildings commonly are victims of copperhead bite. As a child, former Vice President of the United States Alben W. Barkley was bitten by a copperhead while he crept under a small building in search of an errant chicken.

Fortunately, the venom of the copperhead is of low toxicity, not powerful enough, most experts agree, to kill a healthy adult under normal conditions.

A neighbor of mine, who came to the United States from Great Britain ten years ago but has lived in our rural New England town only a short time, was bitten twice in one summer by copperheads. He did not see either of the snakes that struck him, but they had to be copperheads for if either of the serpents had been a timber rattler, the only other venomous snake in the area, my neighbor would have suffered much more than he did.

On both occasions he was removing part of a huge brush pile the previous owner had left near his home, which is surrounded by rocky ledges and oak woodland. The first snake bit him on the shin, and because the bite did not penetrate deeply, my friend did not seek medical aid. He felt only slight pain, and his lower leg reddened somewhat, but that was the extent of his discomfort.

The second time was more serious. He was bitten at the base of one of his fingers. Both of the snake's fangs penetrated his flesh, but he put off seeing a doctor, thinking this bite would be no worse than the first. He was wrong. His arm began to swell and pain increased sharply. Even so, he held out rather stubbornly for four hours, until he decided he needed medical help. He was taken to a hospital emergency room, and says he received "an injection of something," which probably was antivenin, for the swelling soon began to subside and he was able to return home. A study of copperhead bites made shortly after the beginning of this century, when snakebite treatment was not nearly as refined as it is today, reported that of ninety-seven copperhead bites investigated, only five were fatal. Two of the fatalities were youngsters aged six and nine years, neither of whom received much in the way of treatment. The other fatal victims, adult males, also failed to receive medical attention, stiff belts of whisky being the attempted therapy.

When man and copperhead meet, the chances are that if a fatality occurs, the snake will be the one that perishes. Copperheads normally are so slow to react that they are easily crushed with stick or stone. A friend of mine who lives atop a rocky ledge near the Connecticut River regularly dispatches copperheads which sun themselves in his back yard and reports they do not even attempt to defend themselves.

The copperhead's closest kin, the cottonmouth, is another kind of critter. Belligerent and highly venomous, the cottonmouth is a rugged

The coral snake of the southern United States is highly venomous but so docile that it often does not strike even if handled.

beast, which can reach a length of more than five feet. Cottonmouths are exceptionally heavy-bodied snakes; I have seen them with a girth as large as a big man's arm.

The cottonmouth is a creature of the southeastern states and the lower midwest, and is largely aquatic in habit, although on occasion it strays into uplands. Its name comes from the white interior of its mouth, which is revealed when the snake is angry and hisses. When disturbed, the cottonmouth readily gives battle, striking viciously and injecting its enemy with venom that causes horrendous destruction of skin and flesh at the site of the bite.

Cottonmouths thrive in the marshes and bayous of Louisiana,

where the Cajuns living there call them "congos." From time to time unwary fishermen are bitten by this species, but because the cottonmouth generally lives off the beaten track, many of the humans who encounter it are outdoorsmen familiar with the snake, and therefore well versed in how to avoid becoming its victim.

When I was growing up in New England, many of my friends referred to the common brown water snakes of the region as "water moccasins," another name for the cottonmouth. These snakes, which belong to the genus *Natrix*, resemble the cottonmouth in several respects —dark brown color, affinity for water, and a willingness to stand and fight. However, *Natrix* snakes are not dangerous.

RED NEXT TO YELLOW

Aside from the pit vipers, the coral snakes pose the only other serious threat to man from venomous serpents in the United States. Two of these small, brightly colored snakes inhabit the country, the eastern coral snake *(Micrurus fulvius)*, which ranges from North Carolina to Texas, and the Arizona coral snake *(Micuroides euryxanthus)* of the southwest.

Relatives of the cobras, coral snakes secret themselves under logs, boards and rocks, and are particularly shy animals. They possess what biologists call "warning coloration;" especially vivid markings which, as is often the case in nature, go along with a creature's ability to wage some form of chemical warfare. (The skunk is a prime example of an animal with this trait.) Coral snakes are banded with rings of scarlet and black, separated by yellow. Some harmless species mimic this warning coloration but not perfectly, for the bands are not arranged in the same sequence. It is easy to confuse the patterns of coral snakes and their harmless mimics, however, so it is a good idea to remember the adage, "Red next to yellow will kill a fellow."

People who keep this saying in mind will be warned by the bright colors of the coral snake should they happen to see one. But for the unwary, the attractive hues of the serpent can have the opposite effect from that intended by nature. Coral snakes look so appealing that people who do not recognize the danger they pose tend to pick up the little creatures. This is especially true of children, and there are many reports of children found playing with coral snakes. I have been told of one incident in which a youngster handled a coral snake for an hour before his mother discovered it.

The gila monster is very venomous but will not go out of its way to attack man. This gila monster is merely trying to get into the man's shadow, out of the sun. The big lizard lives in the southwestern United States and Mexico.

Coral snakes are remarkably docile and often do not respond to handling by striking, which is fortunate for their venom is quite toxic, more so even than the poison of the diamondback. Even when a coral snake does strike, moreover, its fangs are so small they often do not penetrate the skin. This seems particularly true of the Arizona coral snake, which has not been linked to a single human fatality. The Eastern coral snake, however, has killed a number of people, and it is estimated that about ten percent of the approximately twenty people bitten yearly by this species perish. This estimate may be low, however, for one study of twenty cases in which people were bitten showed that four of the victims died.

BEADS AND A BULLDOG GRIP

The snakes evolved from the lizards, about 100,000,000 years ago, and so it is not surprising that some lizards, at least, also have a venomous bite. There are, however, only two such species, the gila monster *(Heloderma suspectum)* of the southwestern United States and Sonora, Mexico, and its larger cousin, the Mexican beaded lizard *(H. horridum)*. Both are characterized by a squat, chunky body, a massive head, and a hide of black and yellow-orange or pink scales which look like beadwork.

The gila monster, particularly, has the reputation of being a savage little brute, and indeed it is. This foot-long terror prowls the desert in search of bird eggs, nestlings, or small mammals to eat. It has a bulldog bite so savage that it does not need its venom to dispatch its prey. The venom, produced by glands in the lower jaw, is a defensive weapon and very powerful.

Ducts from the venom glands of the gila monster channel the poison to the bases of the teeth, where the potent liquid pools between the lower jaw and lip. When the gila monster bites, it clamps down with its vicious teeth and literally chews the venom into the flesh of its opponent.

The gila monster's manner of poisoning its victim has been graphically described by Charles M. Bogert, retired curator of amphibians and reptiles of the American Museum of Natural History. Writing in the magazine *Animal Kingdom,* Bogert noted: "When a gila monster . . . bites it hangs on with unbelievable force. The venom is not driven under pressure, however, as it is with the more specialized snakes. It is merely drawn into the wound by capillary action."

Despite its savagery, the gila monster is so dull and sluggish that it cannot be considered dangerous to humans except—and this is a

The green tree viper is one of several of this venomous group living in Africa. Like other arboreal snakes, the tree viper blends well into the branches and leaves.

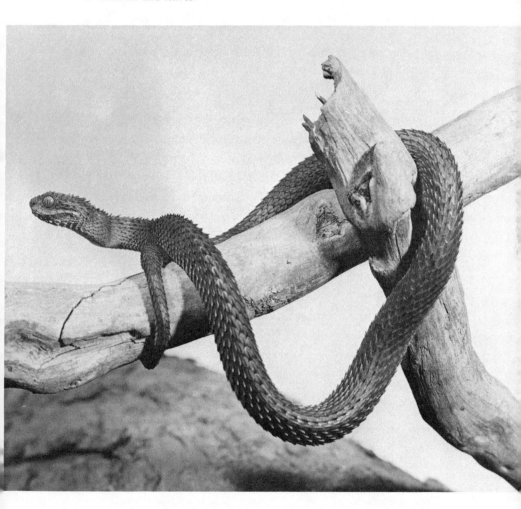

critical exception—people who tamper with it. Studies of the case histories of thirty people bitten by gila monsters since 1879 show that most of the bites resulted from human indiscretion. Of the eight victims who died, several were bitten after they tried to handle the lizards as a joke. One hunter was bitten fatally when he blindly brushed from his chest a gila monster which had crawled on him as he slept. The reptile clamped its jaws down on his wrist, and the man died a few hours later.

AVOIDING VENOMOUS REPTILES

The sure way to avoid being the victim of a gila monster is to heed its brilliant warning coloration and leave it alone. It is only a bit more difficult to avoid venomous snakes, even when walking in an area where they abound, if you follow a few simple rules.

—Watch where you put your hands and feet, and where you sit down.

—Do not tramp through high grass or brush without wearing protective boots, and keep trouser legs rolled down. It should go without mentioning that one should not wear shorts under such conditions.

—Be especially careful in areas where snakes are likely to be hidden, such as woodpiles, old buildings, and rocky ledges. If a log is in your path, step on it—not over it—for a serpent may be on the other side.

—In cottonmouth country, do not wade or swim where these snakes are commonly seen. Cottonmouths also may hide under beached boats.

—Take particular care at night, as rattlesnakes and cottonmouths often hunt by dark.

—Stay clear even of dead snakes. Several people have been bitten by dead snakes whose bodies have responded by reflex action.

—If you see a venomous snake, move away from it carefully. The striking distance of the snake is less than half the length of its body, so even a very large diamondback cannot reach you if you are a couple of yards away. No serpent in the United States will pursue a human. The snake's main instinct is to get away.

—If you hear a rattle, freeze and attempt to locate the snake before you take action.

Lest these precautions frighten readers, I should mention that in years of field work in prime snake country, in the United States and abroad, the number of venomous snakes I have encountered can be counted on my fingers, with a few digits to spare.

IF BITTEN . . .

If the odds go awry and you are bitten by a venomous snake, however, follow the advice of the American Medical Association. Incising the fang marks and suctioning the venom from the cuts is helpful only within a half hour after the attack. After that the venom has spread in the body. A tourniquet above the bite may help. Remember, however, that tourniquets can cause grave circulatory problems.

"The most important act following snakebite," says the A.M.A., "is to get the victim to a hospital or doctor as quickly as possible. New studies have shown that the antivenin is most effective within four hours of a bite, the earlier the better. It is of less value if delayed for eight hours, and of questionable value after twenty-four hours."

SNAKEBITE IN EUROPE

Snakebite is even less of a problem in Europe than it is in the United States, although its extent is difficult to determine because comprehensive figures on snakebite cases are lacking in many regions. Centuries of intense human activity—farming, urbanization, and industrialization—have made much of Europe untenable for dangerous snakes and, in fact, for most wildlife. Moreover, only a few species of venomous snakes are native to the European heartland, and most of these are no more deadly than the American pigmy rattlesnake or copperhead.

A close relative of the copperhead, the Asiatic pit viper *(Agkistrodon halys)* edges into easternmost Europe at the northern shores of the Caspian Sea. Other than this border species, all of the venomous snakes in Europe are vipers. These serpents differ from the pit vipers only in the lack of the heat-sensitive pit which the latter possess.

Of the seven vipers in Europe, only one species has a truly wide range, but it occupies more territory than any other serpent in the world.

This snake, the European viper or adder *(Vipera berus)* lives from England to the Pacific coast of Asia and from the fringes of the Arctic to northern Spain, Italy, and Greece. It is the only snake living north of the Arctic Circle.

Several thousands Europeans feel the stab of the adder's fangs each year, but very few of them die from the bite of the foot-long snake. During this century fewer than ten people have died from snakebite in England, where the adder is the only native venomous serpent. One of the victims was a young girl who perished not from the toxicity of the venom but because she was allergic to the horse serum used to make the antivenin administered to her. Following this tragedy, English physicians ceased using antivenin to treat adder bites. This policy had a grim result. Antivenin was withheld from another little girl bitten by an adder, and she died. American snakebite experts say the serum probably would have saved her life.

The two cases just mentioned, which occurred several years ago, illustrate the confusion that exists in the medical profession about the treatment of snakebite, particularly in places where doctors have little experience with the problem.

Normally the bite of the adder is so mild, however, that many victims do not even require hospitalization. Figures from Sweden indicate that only 12 percent of the more than 1,000 Swedes bitten each year by adders go to the hospital. While an exact tally of deaths from adder bite in Europe is impossible to obtain, it is probable that in western Europe, at least, less than 100 people have perished from adder bite since the beginning of the century.

LAND OF DEADLY SNAKES

More than half of the 130 species of snakes in Australia are venomous, and many of them are among the most terrifying reptiles in the world. They include thirteen truly dangerous species such as the savagely aggressive tiger snake *(Notechus scutatus);* the brown snake *(Demansia textilis),* which strikes its victim repeatedly; the heavy-bodied death adder *(Acanthopis antarcticus);* and the ten-foot taipan *(Oxyuranus scutellatus),* which sometimes attacks humans without provocation and injects twice as much venom as any other Australian serpent.

Despite this line up of killers—and there are many more not named here—Australia records only about as many deaths from snakebite each year as the United States. This may seem paradoxical, even allowing for the higher percentage of fatalities in Australia, but it is not. Part of the reason is that Australia, like most other parts of the world where snakebite is a minor problem, has a westernized society. Few people tramp about the bush unshod, and much of the population lives in highly mechanized, industrialized urban areas free of wild animals such as venomous snakes.

But Australia's low death toll from snakebite also is linked to the nature of the serpents themselves. The taipan serves as an example.

THE TERRIBLE TAIPAN

The taipan is undeniably one of the world's most dangerous snakes. So fast does this giant serpent move that it can strike a man several times before he can think of getting away. Its half-inch fangs have been known to penetrate even shoe and sock, and it floods the wound with a huge quantity of venom. Like other large, highly venomous serpents, the taipan carries enough poison to kill several adults.

Although the taipan usually tries to avoid contact with humans there is a well-authenticated case in which one of these snakes made an unprovoked, fatal attack on a woman as she walked home from a movie. More commonly, the victim of the taipan has forced an encounter with the snake, as in the following incident.

In July 1959 snake collector Kevin Budden of Sydney was searching for serpents in the bush near Cairns, Queensland. When a taipan slithered from a pile of rotting vegetation, he pinned it to the ground and grasping the snake behind the head carried it to his car, where he had left his collecting bags. As Budden tried to bag the snake it bit him on the thumb, sinking its fangs deeply and holding on. Budden's companions came to his aid, and the snake was dislodged. However, the stricken man refused to allow his friends to kill the snake, instructing them instead to get it to the Australian Commonwealth Serum Laboratories. Scientists needed taipans to study their venom, Budden knew, and he decided that the snake that had bitten him should be used for this purpose.

The next day Budden died, the usual fate of people bitten by the taipan. Few Australians, however, ever see a taipan, much less become victims of one, because this snake lives in isolated parts of northeastern Australia, far from most human habitation. Even within its scattered range, moreover, the taipan is very rare. Its existence was not even known until 1867, when one was killed in Queensland. Not for more than a half century after that did scientists get their hands on additional specimens. Two were caught on the Cape York Peninsula of Queensland in 1923.

The isolation and rarity of the taipan make it no threat at all to most Australians despite its dangerous nature. The Taipan can be considered a menace only potentially. The same is true, although to a lesser degree, of the tiger snake. It has venom even more powerful than that of the taipan, but also lives away from most human population centers. Because it is more abundant than the taipan, however, the tiger snake accounts for a few more fatalities.

Most fatal cases of snakebite in Australia are the work of the brown snake, not because it is particularly antagonistic towards humans, but because it is both dangerous and relatively common. Brown snakes thrive in certain grain-growing areas, and occasionally bite field workers. The chances of recovery from the bite of the brown snake, however, are much greater than from the strike of a taipan or tiger snake.

SNAKEBITE IN AFRICA—A SURPRISING SITUATION

From the Mediterranean to the Cape of Good Hope, Africa is the home of a wide variety of venomous snakes, including at least one that many people consider the most dangerous in the world. Africa also has vast numbers of people living under primitive conditions in areas where venomous snakes are abundant. Snakebite should be a major public-health problem in Africa, but it is not, although more people die from snakebite in Africa than in places such as the United States and Australia.

There is no way to get accurate statistics on deaths from snakebite in Africa, but experts on the subject accept a total of 1,000 deaths annually as a fair estimate. South Africa is the only African nation with a reliable system of reporting cases of venomous snakebite, and snakes there claim about a dozen lives each year. Based on studies completed several years ago when Kenya was under British rule, that country has about the same death toll as South Africa.

Exactly why the snakebite toll is so relatively low in Africa is difficult to say, in fact, it is something of an enigma, especially when the deadly character of many African snakes is considered.

THE WORLD'S DEADLIEST SNAKE

The deadliest snake in Africa—and many authorities believe in all the world—is the black mamba *(Dendroaspis polyepis)*, an unusually slim, extremely agile serpent, that can reach fourteen feet in length, but is no wider than the butt end of a pool cue. It is one of four species of mambas that live throughout much of Africa. The others, while not as deadly as the black mamba, are almost as unpleasant to encounter.

Judged the quickest of all snakes, the mamba can travel over the ground at a speed of seven miles an hour, much faster than a man can run. It strikes like lightning and can deliver a load of venom so toxic it could kill ten men. People who are bitten by the black mamba are almost certainly doomed to die, often within a few hours. Even antivenin is not much good. Of seven black mamba victims treated at one South African hospital during a seven-year period, all died.

In South Africa, the mamba is known as the "shadow of death," an indication of how people there regard the graceful but dreadful reptile. South Africa is the source of many horror stories about the mamba. One tells of a farmer who found a mamba in his home and tried to catch it in a butterfly net in order to sell it to a foreign zoo. Since like most venomous snakes mambas generally seek to escape rather than strike, the serpent darted for the door of the house, but the farmer injudiciously tried to intercept it. Thwarted in its escape bid, the mamba struck quickly and fatally, then slipped out of the house to safety.

Another report describes how a mamba fell from a tree limb on a man who was riding horseback through the brush during an antelope hunt. The snake bit him on the elbow, and he died two hours later. A Zulu who was bitten on the shoulder by a mamba entwined in some branches died only *ten minutes* after he was struck.

These cases illustrate not only the potency of mamba venom, but the major hazard posed by mambas. They spend considerable time in the brush and trees hunting birds, and their slender bodies blend so well with the branches that people sometimes blunder into them. Surprised at close quarters, the mamba often reacts by striking before it races away.

BOOMSLANG

In addition to mambas, Africa is the home of another deadly tree snake, the boomslang *(Dispholidus typus),* a five-foot-long serpent which, like the mamba, is difficult to detect in the branches. The boomslang is one of the snakes which has its fangs set in the rear of its mouth, so it must grab on to its victim and chew with determination to introduce venom.

If the boomslang strikes at a fleshy part of the body, such as the thigh or buttocks, the snake has difficulty employing its venomous fangs. But if it manages to grab a finger or arm, the bite can easily be fatal, for its poison is as toxic as a mamba's. In 1957, the famed zoologist Karl P. Schmidt of the Field Museum of Natural History in Chicago, succumbed a day after he was bitten by a small boomslang.

The circumstances surrounding the death of Schmidt, who was sixty-seven years old at the time, show how easily even an expert can make a fatal mistake when handling venomous serpents. The snake had been sent to Schmidt by a local zoo in the hope that he could identify it. While a colleague held the snake safely behind the neck, Schmidt examined it and discussed the possibility that it was a boomslang. As he talked Schmidt absentmindedly reached for the snake and grasped it so far behind the head that, as he took it, the animal was able to twist around and sink one fang into his thumb.

The wound bled profusely and the scientist attempted to remove the venom by suction. Because the snake was a young specimen, and only one fang had penetrated his finger, Schmidt was not overly concerned, even when he experienced nausea on the train going home. By evening his gums were bleeding, and during the night he vomited, but by morning he felt well enough to telephone the museum and say he would be at work the next day.

Then his condition worsened. After lunch he vomited again, and shortly experienced difficulty in breathing. His wife telephoned his physician and an emergency squad, which took him to the hospital. By the time he reached the hospital, about 3:00 P.M., he had died.

CRADLE OF COBRAS

Cobras, which conjure up some of man's worst fears of snakes, originated in Africa, and the greatest variety of species live there. To many people the sight of a cobra rearing up with hood outspread symbolizes all that is mysterious and deadly in the world of reptiles. The snake seems to be contemplating the death of its victim. Actually the cobra is trying to position itself at the right angle for its downward strike, which is not particularly quick, and in fact is slower than the strike of the rattler. Some snakehandlers of considerable experience and steely nerve are able to grab a cobra in mid-strike.

Cobras and mambas belong to a group of snakes whose fangs bear an enclosed groove to carry venom. Unlike the vipers and pit vipers, however, the cobra cannot raise its fangs, which are so short they sometimes fail to penetrate clothing of moderate thickness. The strike of the cobra is not nearly as effective as that of the vipers, and it often must bite several times to get the job done.

This is not to say that cobras should be treated lightly, for the bite of virtually all of them can be quite deadly. Among the African cobras that potentially are the most dangerous are several varieties with a predominantly black coloration that range through most of the continent. Some confusion exists as to the exact number of species and names of these dark-colored cobras, but the typical form is *Naja melanoleuca*, the black cobra. As will be explained later in this book, the black cobra may have made the United States its adopted home.

The black cobra is a creature of the wilds and generally avoids man. I know African game guides who have spent years afield and during that time have seen only one or two of these snakes. I was lucky enough to encounter one—more than eight feet in length—while driving along a dirt track in southwestern Kenya. The snake, its muscular body glossy in the morning sun, stretched across the road, with its tail in the brush at one side and its head almost reaching the other. I stopped the car and leaned out of the window, a safe distance away, to photograph the snake.

The bushmaster of the American tropics is one of the largest venomous snakes. Its bite can be deadly, but it usually lives deep in the forest far from people.

The moment I moved, so did the cobra. With a violent hiss as loud as steam escaping from a heating pipe, the snake launched its body in the air—almost four feet above the ground—and hurtled into the brush across the road. I wanted a photograph badly, but not enough to charge into the brush after the snake, so we parted company at that point.

Another of the black cobras is Gold's cobra *(N. goldii),* a West African species that lacks a hood. Slender and active, resembling the black mamba in form and habit, Gold's cobra has the reputation of attacking with little provocation. The famed reptile expert of the Bronx Zoo, Raymond L. Ditmars, testified to the snake's savagery in a 1925 article about his problems with a batch of Gold's cobras that arrived at the zoo from Africa.

"It comes right at you repeatedly," wrote Ditmars, "not in a mere hysterical rush, but with intention to bite." Ditmars compared the attack of Gold's cobra to that of the mamba, and speculated that some of the deaths attributed to the mamba really were the work of the cobra.

The spitting cobra *(N. nigricollis),* still another dark-hued species, is feared not so much for its bite as for its ability to squirt streams of venom more than a dozen feet. The venom jets from the orifices in the snake's fangs with such precise accuracy that the snake can hit a man in the eyes. The venom can cause permanent blindness. A snake related to the cobras, the ringhals *(Sepedon haemachates)* of southern Africa, also spits venom. A captive ringhals once was observed spitting five times in five minutes, indicating that the serpent carries a substantial supply of venom. An article in a 1914 issue of the *Bulletin* of the New York Zoological Society termed the ringhals "one of the most diabolical members of the order of reptiles," and reported one incident in which a ringhals allegedly pursued a missionary for fifty yards through the bush. The snake's persistent pursuit of the clergyman might have been proof of its diabolical affiliations, but more likely it was merely a demonstration of the way cobras sometimes defend their nesting territory.

COBRAS, MAMBAS, AND MAN

Despite the great fear inspired by African cobras and mambas, and their deadly potential, they are responsible for only a minority of snakebite cases in Africa. The chief reason is that, like the cobra I met on the road, these snakes will beat a hasty retreat at the approach of man. Moreover, the cobra's habit of rearing before striking not only telegraphs its intentions, but reveals its presence in the bush. Many African cobras will make themselves known when humans are several yards distant, and if left alone will settle down and slip away.

The only African cobra that is known to kill a substantial number of people is the Egyptian cobra (N. haje), It is a blackish snake that is believed to be the "asp" which killed Cleopatra. The Egyptian cobra is more of a mankiller than its relatives because it gets along well in close proximity to people and abounds in areas with large human populations, such as the Nile Valley. The species has been collected on the outskirts of such a large city as Nairobi, Kenya.

This Egyptian cobra, which lives in the Middle East as well as Africa, reaps an advantage from its human neighbors because it feeds on the mice and rats that live alongside man. In Israel the range of the Egyptian cobra has spread in the past twenty-five years as new areas of the Negev Desert have been opened up to agriculture, and rodents have thrived on the new farms.

THE MANKILLER

The snake responsible for the most bites and fatalities in Africa also is common in agricultural regions. The puff adder (Bitis arietans) is a thick-bodied, sluggish viper which has a wide range south of the Sahara. It shuns only the most arid desert and steaming jungles.

The puff adder has all of the attributes that make a snake a major mankiller. While its venom is not as powerful as the poisons of cobras and mambas, the puff adder delivers a heavy dose with typical viperine efficiency, and injects more than enough venom to kill a man with a single bite.

What makes the puff adder truly dangerous, however, is that it does not flee when man approaches it. Instead, it hunkers down in an attempt to escape notice, which makes it easy to step on.

Untreated, the bite of a puff adder is often fatal, but antivenin substantially reduces the odds of death. It also is almost certain that African bush doctors using folk remedies treat large numbers of puff adder victims each year. Most such cases are not reported, which muddles estimates of the snakebite situation in Africa.

Even allowing for many unreported cases, the number of deaths due to venomous snakes in Africa is remarkably low, especially when compared to the death toll in Southern Asia.

WHERE SNAKEBITE IS A SCOURGE

Each year in India and Southeast Asia more than 25,000 people, perhaps several thousand more, die from the bites of venomous snakes. The reason is simple. Nowhere else do so many people live at close quarters with such an abundance of venomous serpents. Numbers alone make the risk of unexpected encounters between man and snake higher in southern Asia than in any other part of the world. In addition, the odds are further increased, by the fact that several dangerous Asian snakes regularly visit or even inhabit places where they are likely to meet people. Some of these reptiles make a habit of prowling through human dwellings, or through rice fields where bare-legged people are at work.

As is the case elsewhere, however, some Asian snakes with very foul reputations actually pose very little threat to human life, because they live away from humans or because their aggressive tendencies have been overrated. The best example of this is the king cobra *(Orphiophagus hannah)*, which is often given the undeserved label of the world's most dangerous snake.

To be sure, the king cobra can be dangerous—extremely so—and at a maximum length of eighteen feet it is the longest venomous snake. Moreover, on rare occasions the king cobra may pursue humans, but only, it seems, in defense of its nesting territory. This infrequent behavior on the part of the snake has added to its notoriety, but it is not indicative of its usual pattern. Most of the time the king cobra is shy, even docile. A big king cobra discovered on a Singapore golf course failed to resist capture by two men who thought it was a nonvenomous python.

Meetings between king cobras and people are uncommon, however, because the species is not at all abundant. Moreover, because it feeds exclusively on other snakes and lizards, the king cobra is not drawn to human dwellings by the rodents which attract some other venomous snakes.

The Asian cobra *(N. naja)*, on the other hand, is an avid hunter of rodents especially in the evening and early morning prowls through towns in search of them. This species also feeds on frogs, and as a result frequents rice fields where the amphibians abound. Its feeding habits bring the Asian cobra into contact with man more than most other venomous snakes, and according to most estimates, it kills more people than any other serpent. Ironically, however, the Asian cobra is unaggressive to the point of timidity and strikes only if it feels cornered.

Another Asian snake that turns up around houses and in rice fields is the five-foot Russell's viper *(Vipera russelli)*. Unlike the cobra it is rather feisty and defends itself vigorously. It rivals the Asian cobra as a man-killer in much of its range, which stretches from India to Indonesia.

Throughout this same region the kraits, stout-bodied relatives of the cobras, also menace human life. The threat stems not from the disposition of the kraits, for they are unusually docile. These serpents are dangerous because they are extremely active by dark. They frequently roam through village streets and even into dwellings, and react to the approach of a human in much the same way as the African puff adder. When a krait senses someone coming, it does not flee but lies low, making it easy to blunder into the snake on a dark path or street. Once a person is bitten by a krait he is in serious trouble, for kraits have venom more potent than the poison of cobras or mambas.

The worst of the lot is the Indian krait *(Bungarus caeruleus)*, with venom so toxic that only a couple of milligrams of it can kill a man. In nine cases investigated by scientists during one study of krait bites, eight of the victims died. Even when treated with antivenin, a person bitten by the Indian krait has only a 50 percent chance of surviving.

If kraits were more belligerent, they might take even more lives than they do; as things stand, they kill almost as many people as the Asian cobra, and without doubt kraits constitute at least as much a hazard as Russell's viper.

The snakes mentioned in the preceding paragraph are not the only serpents that take a considerable toll of human lives in Asia, although they kill by far the most people. Among the other serpents responsible for a large number of bites are various vipers and pit vipers found in wooded areas. They seldom venture into human settlements or grain fields, but make life unpleasant for tea pickers and rubber tappers who work in the woods.

Snakebite will remain a scourge in southern Asia as long as social and economic conditions there remain so poor. Rodent control, availability of footwear, and access to antivenin would go a long way towards cutting the toll, but the masses of people in most of southern Asia have slight chance of seeing any of these things. I have no statistics regarding the availability of antivenin to support my belief that few Asian snakebite victims receive it, except in Thailand, which since 1923 has operated an institute in Bangkok which produces almost 30,000 units of antivenin yearly. However, in places such as southern India, even people who are relatively well off economically cannot obtain the basic antibiotics to treat disease. How easy is it, then, to get antivenin? In addition, it has been proven that when antivenin is administered in time to people bitten by the Asian cobra, the survival rate is better than 90 percent. Yet the cobra kills thousands of people every year. This fact speaks for itself about how few victims are properly treated in Asian countries.

SNAKEBITE IN LATIN AMERICA

Second—but not at all close to southern Asia in the number of snakebite deaths—is Latin America. Here as elsewhere, the situation is hazy, but according to a World Health Organization survey, the origin of most snakebite statistics in this book, about 4,000 people perish yearly south of the border because of venomous snakes. Mexico reports 200 deaths annually. Brazil may have as many as 2,000 snakebite deaths a year, although that number may be decreasing because of better medical care.

Most of the venomous snakes of the American tropics are pit vipers. Unlike so many venomous snakes of Asia, the American pit vipers generally do not enter villages or homes, so their victims often are farm or plantation workers who encounter them in the forest or fields. Occasionally the snake responsible for a serious bite is not a pit viper but one of the several species of large coral snakes that inhabit the region. While I was in Trinidad at the tropical research station of the New York Zoological Society some years ago, a coral snake killed a teen-age sugar cane cutter, but such mishaps are rare.

Of all the Latin American snakes the one that kills the most people is a six-foot pit viper known scientifically as *Bothrops atrox*. It has a confusing variety of common names, including *"terciopelo"* and *"Barba*

Amarilla," as well as fer-de-lance, although the true fer-de-lance *(B. lanceolatus)* lives only on the island of Martinique.

The *Barba Amarilla* is one of the most common venomous snakes in the New World, ranging from southern Mexico to the interior of Argentina. It is not a snake of the forest but invades sugar-cane fields and other cultivated lands, which together with its potent venom, long fangs, and nasty disposition make it so much of a mankiller.

Several other members of the genus *Bothrops* also are high on the list of dangerous Latin American snakes. Sixteen members of this group live in Brazil alone, contributing immensely to the size of the death toll in that country. Among the other bad customers in the genus besides the *Barba Amarilla* are the jararaca *(B. jararaca),* the jararaca pintada *(B. neuwiedi)* and the jararacussu *(B. jararacussu),* all of which are somewhat similar in appearance, at least to the layman.

The only rattlesnake in South America, the neotropical rattlesnake *(C. durissus)* is the most venomous of all pit vipers. Ten milligrams of its venom is believed sufficient to kill a man, and if untreated a victim of this snake has less than a 50 percent chance of living. The neotropical rattlesnake, which at the northern end of its range kills many people in Mexico, grows almost as large as the diamondbacks, but is much more dangerous. Besides having considerably more toxic venom than its diamondback relatives, the neotropical rattlesnake often strikes without the coiling so characteristic of other rattlers, and emits little in the way of a warning rattle. People who live in some parts of this serpent's range call it the "breakneck snake," thinking that its bite breaks a man's neck. This notion arises from the fact that the snake's victims often snap back their heads while suffering the racking spasms that are caused by its venom.

The biggest pit viper of the Americas is the bushmaster *(Lachesis muta),* a creature with a massive body that can be almost a dozen feet in length and exceedingly large fangs. Whether or not the bushmaster is a serious menace to man is the subject of some controversy. Documented cases of people bitten by bushmasters are rare, but many people, including many physicians experienced in tropical medicine, believe that this is because bushmaster victims die so quickly that they cannot reach medical help. A Latin American physician who had worked in Panama for many years once told me, before I was heading into bushmaster country, "If a bushmaster bites you, just sit under a tree and take it easy, for in a few minutes you will die."

If bushmasters were there, however, I never saw one, except in my mind's eye. That—in fact—is as close as most people get to the bushmaster, even in the heart of its range, for it is a creature of forest fastnesses. Human activity such as timbering or cultivation sends the bushmaster deeper into the jungle. Moreover, even where conditions favor it, the bushmaster is not abundant, so the chances of surprise meetings between these serpents and people are very slim. This fact—rather than the sudden death said to result from the touch of bushmaster fangs—is the reason why so few bites by the big pit viper ever are reported.

THE SNAKES TO FEAR

From this survey of the snakebite problem around the world, a conclusion can be drawn about the snakes that are most to be feared. Size, toxicity of venom, and aggressiveness are not always indicative of whether a snake seriously menaces human life. More often than not, the serpents that cause the most human misery are not particularly large or at all aggressive, although some of them are highly venomous. The truly menacing serpents are those with reasonably potent venom which get along well alongside man and, in many cases, even flourish because of human activity.

FRIENDS AND FOES

Because any discussion of snakebite naturally focuses on the harm snakes do to people it should be stressed that serpents also perform an invaluable service for man. The number of rodents that snakes destroy balances out the damage they do to humanity. Snakes not only contribute to reducing the depredations of rodents on crops and foodstuffs, these reptiles also save countless humans from some of the horrible diseases which, as we will read in a later chapter, are spread by rodents. When the Asian cobra prowls buildings after dark, it may threaten the lives of people who live in them, but at the same time it is exterminating rodents that can spread plague. The cobra, so feared by man, is a vivid example of how an animal's relationship with mankind can have both harmful and beneficial aspects, and how even creatures that can kill man can also benefit him.

3. MAN AND THE POISONERS: INSECTS, SPIDERS, SCORPIONS

PEOPLE SWAT OR RUN from bees, wasps and hornets, and crawling things such as spiders and scorpions inspire almost instinctive fear. While many of these anthropods can make life unpleasant and even dangerous at times, they cause horror far out of proportion to their actual menace. The spiders and scorpions, which are feared most are far less of a threat to human life, in terms of fatalities, than bees and other flying venomous insects.

BEES IN OUR LIVES

Drop for drop, the venom of a bee, wasp, or hornet is as powerful as that of many dangerous snakes. So little poison is injected when one of these insects stings someone, however, that the reaction usually is restricted to the site of the sting, which as most of us know can be very painful. For people whose bodies are extrasensitive to the venom, however, the results can be fatal. Allergic reaction to a bee sting can send the victim into shock, trigger convulsions, and cause his death in a very few minutes.

Despite its fearsome look, the tarantula is not dangerous to man. It is quite docile, and its venom does not have a serious effect on man.

Every year a few dozen Americans perish in this way. Figures from the United States Public Health Service for a period from 1957 to 1960 showed that bees and their relatives killed 127 people during that time.

Unpublished vital statistics of the United States also provide an idea of the scope of the problem. They show that in 1966 twenty-four people died from bee stings and sixteen people perished from the stings of wasps and hornets. The death toll of that year was larger than most. More representative was 1954, when twelve people died from bee stings and sixteen people from the stings of wasps and hornets.

Virtually all people who are hypersenstitive to insect stings, however, can protect themselves by going to a doctor and undergoing a series of immunization treatments. If received on a regular basis, injections of serums made from extracts of insect venoms can confer resistance to stings on an allergic person.

The sting of a bee differs from that of a wasp or hornet—in all cases only the female delivers the punch—in that it is a defensive weapon. Wasps and hornets use their stings defensively, but also to get food. They kill hosts of caterpillars, beetles and other insect pests, a service which often goes unrecognized.

The bee is even more valuable to man. Since time immemorial, bees have sweetened human existence with their honey, but that is not the key to their significance. The real value of bees to man is that these buzzing insects are the chief pollinators of flowering plants critical to human life. From fruit trees to soybeans, plants that permit human society as we understand it to function, depend on bees as pollinators. Without bees, flowering plants might not have become the dominant plants on earth, and very possibly in their absence humanity might not have evolved.

SUPER BEES: SUPER DANGER?

Thus far, this discussion of insect stings has covered only situations in which one or at most a few stings are suffered by the victim. If a man were the target of a large swarm of these insects, and they persisted in their assaults, the results would be extremely serious, even fatal. Most bees, wasps, and hornets seldom attack victims in this way, however, so this sort of incident has not been considered a real problem.

That is, it has not been a problem until quite recently. A new strain of highly aggressive super bee has appeared in South America, and attacks *en masse* with such savagery that it seems to have killed many human victims. Moreover, as news reports in print and on television have warned, this super bee is working its way north towards the United States, and may cross our southern borders in a decade or so.

The new bee is in a sense a man-made monster, for it arose through human agency. It originated in 1957 after some African bees which had been brought to a laboratory in Brazil escaped, and their queens crossed with local bees to produce the new, and reportedly savage strain. The new strain attacks twice as fast and in far greater numbers than the normal bees.

The African bees had been brought to Brazil because they were thought to be better suited to living in the American tropics than the bees already established there. Scientists hoped to breed some of their good qualities into the local bees. Like most other honeybees in the Americas, the local bees were descended predominantly from a European strain, which while it flourished in temperate regions was less successful and produced less honey in warmer parts of the New World.

The new crossbreed, now called the "Brazilian bee," inherited not only the African bee's liking for warm climate but its unusual aggressiveness. In 1974 a nest of African bees forced the evacuation of a village in Kenya. Like their African forebears, the Brazilian bees defend their nests savagely, regularly swarming after people and animals that come near. Moreover, they not only attack other creatures, but other bees as well. They have killed the local honeybees and taken over colonies throughout Brazil.

Many scientists believe, in fact, that the new honeybees are extending their domain over much of tropical South America. Now the Brazilian bee seems to be moving north, toward Central America and beyond.

The Smithsonian Institution Center for Short-Lived Phenomena has been keeping tabs on the Brazilian bees, and in April 1975 issued the following bulletin:

> The present edge of the Africanized bees' distribution in South America is French Guiana. The populations in this area are sparsely distributed and have low densities relative to the densities found in

similar habitats within the Amapa Territory of northeast Brazil, where the race has been established for a longer time (3-8 years). Although it was reported in 1972 that the Africanized bees were traveling northward to Central America at a rate of approximately 320 km. per year, their pace has slowed as they spread through the Amazon basin. The bees appear to be moving at a more rapid pace over the coastal savannahs than in the interior rain forests of Brazil. The pattern of movement suggests that the Africanized bee is better adapted to the drier coastal habitat. Lack of resources of the inability to adapt to the rainy climate are likely to be limiting the population density and rate of spread in the interior forests. The coastal route being taken by the Africanized bees is longer; consequently it will take longer for the bees to reach Central America than had been predicted earlier.

Whatever its rate of travel, the Brazilian bee seems destined to reach the borders of the United States within the next several years. If it does thrive in dry habitat, then perhaps it will find southern California and parts of the southwestern states to its liking. Alarm over an invasion of the United States by the bee has prompted the United States Department of Agriculture and National Academy of Sciences to look into the problem.

It could be extremely serious, for if reports from South America are to be believed, the Brazilian bees menace people and livestock. Some reports claim that as many as 300 people have been killed by the bees.

These reports may be exaggerated, but a report from the Center for Short-Lived Phenomena warns that "The Africanized bees can be extremely aggressive and tend to attack in large numbers when disturbed. An unprotected person or animal could easily be killed by the massive stinging . . ." The report went on to cite the deaths of three men and a child in northern Brazil attributed to the bees during 1974.

Some scientists challenge whether the Brazilian bees are as bad as reputed, however, and question whether all deaths attributed to them are their fault. Dr. Harald Esch of the University of Notre Dame, who has observed the bees in Brazil, says on this subject: "All attacks by bees in Brazil are automatically blamed on the African hybrid," he said. "If an attack is reported the hybrid is said to be in the area. But even European bees, the kind introduced earlier in Brazil, are aggressive when not handled properly."

Esch's point was that perhaps many of the attacks blamed on the Brazilian bees were the work of local honeybees handled unskillfully.

Any story as sensational as one about killer bees is bound to suffer from exaggeration, but if the Brazilian crossbreeds respond as rapidly and savagely to human approach as their African ancestors do, they pose considerably more of a threat than other honeybees. And if they continue to move north, as they probably will, the Brazilian bees will enter the southern United States, although the cooler climate of North America no doubt will bar an extensive invasion of the nation. There is hope, too, that as years pass continued crossing with other honeybees will dilute the savage instincts the Brazilian bees have inherited from their imported ancestors. Only time will tell, however, whether or not the bees from Brazil are indeed killers which owe their existence to man.

SPIDERS AND SCORPIONS—REAL AND IMAGINED DANGERS

Like Little Miss Muffet, many people have an unreasoned fear of spiders, which for the most part are shy small creatures seeking to do nothing more than stay out of sight and consume huge quantities of insects. All spiders bite and inject venom, for this is how they kill and consume their prey, but only a handful of the more than 30,000 different kinds of spiders in any way threaten man. At most, spiders kill only four or five people yearly in the United States. The fangs of many spiders are too small and weak to penetrate human skin, and the venom of many of those that can has little effect on man.

The latter is true of some of the largest—and to the minds of many people most frightening—of spiders. This group includes the giant bird-killing spiders of South America, which have a leg-span as big as a dinner plate, and the hairy creatures commonly called tarantulas. These spiders can bite painfully, but the pain results from punctures by their large fangs, rather than from their venom. Many of them, however, especially the tarantulas, are remarkably docile. Mexican boys often keep tarantulas on strings, as pets, and I have handled the big spiders a number of times without any problems.

Despite the fact that the bite of a tarantula is no more dangerous than that of a toy poodle, the fallacy persists that they are horribly deadly. So much fear does the tarantula inspire that a security dog agency in California rents the spiders to merchants who use them to frighten off burglars. A San Francisco jeweler whose shop was the repeated target of break-ins placed one of the spiders in a display window at night, with a sign warning: "This area is patrolled by tarantulas." His troubles with thieves ceased. Actually, if a burglar had attempted to grab jewelry from the window, the spider would have scurried for the nearest crack or cranny.

NOT SO MERRY WIDOWS AND DANGEROUS RECLUSES

Although at least fifty species of spiders in the United States have been involved in bites on people, the only spiders to be feared in the United States belong to just two groups. Best known of these is the black widow *(Latrodectus mactrans),* which has a worldwide range in the tropics and temperate lands with a moderate climate. In the United States the range of the widow spans the country from coast to coast as far north as Oregon and New York.

The black widow is only one of four "widow" spiders inhabiting the United States, the most widespread of which is the northern widow *(L. variolus),* which ranges from northern Florida to southern Canada, and all across the country except for the southwestern states. The other two spiders in this group live only in Florida. The red widow *(L. bishopi)* builds its small cobweb only amidst the stiff leaves of the palmetto in the central and southern parts of the state. The brown widow *(L. geometricus)* is not a native but a tropical species somehow introduced into Florida.

Only the female widows, which are about a half inch long, bite; the males do not even feed, but function only to reproduce. Widows use their minuscule fangs against man only in extreme circumstances: you must virtually crush one before it attempts to defend itself.

Because widows are secretive creatures, they seldom encounter humans, except when they sometimes live in trash piles, dumps, and in the wells of privies. It is in the privy that this little spider and man most often meet, and most of the black widow bites reported in the United States occur there.

The honeybee can be a mortal enemy of people who are sensitive to its sting. For these people a simple sting can mean death.

Men are the usual victims of the black widow because they engage in outdoor pursuits more than women, and more often resort to using outhouses. Two-thirds of the bites are on the buttocks, thighs, or genitals.

The bite of the black widow usually produces a stabbing pain which often vanishes within a few hours. By then, however, the victim may have other problems ranging from severe cramps to coma, depending on the severity of the bite. The bite of the widow is not fatal to healthy adults, but it can kill a child.

The other dangerous spiders living in the United States are the brown spiders, which like the widow are fragile creatures a half inch in length. Several different varieties of brown spiders live in the southwestern states, but the member of this group that is most widespread and has received considerable notoriety in recent years, is the brown recluse *(Loxosceles reclusa).*

The recluse formerly lived only in the southern and south-central states, but its range has spread in scattered fashion across the land. The sole reason for the spread of the recluse is man. There are few better examples of how human activity can turn an animal that poses little or no threat to man into a real danger to people's welfare.

The dispersal of the brown recluse has been made possible by two things that are part of the "good life" as lived in the United States—centralized home heating and the increased mobility of most Americans. The recluse is very sensitive to cold, but across the southern tier of the nation winters are mild enough to permit its survival. There, under purely natural conditions, it lives outdoors beneath rocks and logs, and virtually never encounters man.

Farther north, however, the living habits of the recluse change. It becomes a house spider, finding the solitude it needs in closets, attics, and cellars. In doing so, the recluse creates the conditions under which it can come into conflict with people. Women cleaning house and performing other domestic tasks are the most frequent victims of the spider.

Even indoors the recluse could not survive farther north than the border states in homes lacking modern heating systems which send warmth into every corner of the house. The advent of centralized heating and the ability of most Americans to afford it broke the ecological barrier that northern winters had placed before the recluse. The fact that the recluse often creeps into clothes or packing boxes that are taken along when people travel did the rest.

Not until the 1950s, when the recluse began to turn up around the country with some frequency, was its bite recognized as dangerous. The bite of the recluse—also called the fiddleback because of the distinctive dark marking—kills tissue around the wound. Eventually a circular dollop of flesh with a circumference equal to that of a half dollar turns purple, then black, and sloughs away, leaving a deep hole.

The venom of this spider effects the kidneys and destroys blood cells, and in a half dozen rare cases has caused death. Generally, however, the bite is not fatal, although certainly painful and unpleasant, and can leave a lasting scar.

No wonder then, when swarms of recluses began to turn up in the buildings of various Illinois institutions, in the 1960s health officials became alarmed. On one occasion, a building at Eastern Illinois University was closed until the spiders could be exterminated. In Matoon, Illinois, the high school was closed for several days in 1968 when hundreds of the spiders were discovered in lockers and in other parts of the school.

Perhaps because the publicity from such incidents made people

The black scorpion of the southwestern states is dangerous. This one is in a defensive position with its young aboard its back.

aware of the recluse, citizens began to report finding it in increasing numbers, from Connecticut to California. About this time, while writing a news syndicate feature on the recluse, I happened to meet a utility company repairman in Bridgeport, Connecticut who had just been bitten on the hand by one of the spiders while in the basement of a public housing project. The residents of the project were almost exclusively black, and many of them traveled back and forth from the southern states, so it is highly likely that the recluse had arrived in Bridgeport this way. As far as I know, this incident, which as I remember took place about 1970, was the first report of the recluse in New England.

Some time before that—no one knows exactly when—a much more dangerous South American relative of the recluse had been established in the basement of Harvard University's Museum of Comparative Zoology. After the basement population was studied by scientists, it was destroyed. However, this species *(L. laeta)* could again be an unknowing hitchhiker to this country in someone's baggage, and like the recluse could take advantage of the year-round summer provided by America's overly heated homes.

It may be, however, that the range of the recluse could shrink in the immediate future. As the price of home heating fuels has increased, room temperature in many American homes has been lowered, and many people have shut off the heat completely in little-used parts of their dwellings. The cold-sensitive recluse may suffer most from this state of affairs.

SCORPIONS

Scorpions are no threat to people in the United States, except perhaps in the southwest, where two species belonging to the genus *Centruoides* can sting most unpleasantly. The sting of *C. sculpturatus,* native to Arizona, is especially painful and has at times killed very young people.

Elsewhere in the world, a few scorpions can be extremely dangerous. The species *Leinrus quignestriatus* of the Middle East is a menace to people who work and live on farms. It was the object of an eradication campaign in Israel, where kibbutz residents made sweeps of their areas to destroy the small creatures. The campaign has been so successful, according to Professor Aharon S. Shulov, the venomous animal expert of the Hebrew University in Jerusalem, that around many of the cooperative settlements it takes hours to find a single scorpion. Only a few years ago, Shulov says, a collector could find several scorpions in the desert around many kibbutzim. The use of pesticides to control agricultural insects also has decimated the scorpions, according to Shulov.

The most dangerous of all scorpions are those of a group (genus *Androctonus*) living in North Africa. One of them *(Androctonus australis)* has venom as toxic as a cobra's. If not treated, the victim of this creature can die in a few hours.

MAN, ANIMAL, AND ACCIDENT

Since most people do not knowingly place themselves within striking range of venomous animals, the great majority of deaths and injuries caused by these creatures result from pure chance. They are accidents in the truest sense, surprise encounters sought by neither man nor beast. Sometimes the conditions that produce these encounters are generated by human actions, but not deliberately. The man who packs a spider with his bags and moves from Missouri to New York does not purposely cart a brown recluse along with him.

When people deliberately handle venomous creatures, however, either for legitimate purpose or out of idiocy, the nature of the encounter between man and animal changes completely. The situation that develops is not natural and is full of the ingredients of conflict. The animal cannot flee or hide, but is put in a position in which it is forced to react defensively in a way that can harm man. When an animal bites or stings someone under these circumstances, the attack might not be expected by the victim, but it is no accident. The victim has made the animal attack him, for, compelled to defend itself by instinct, the animal has no choice.

In his relationship with all sorts of animals, man often commits deliberate acts that change innocent creatures into killers. Such acts are not necessarily evil, inhumane, or against nature. They are part and parcel of the way man lives, for better or worse.

4. HUNTER AND HUNTED

ACROSS THE VAST expanse of the African savannah nothing moves but the brown grasses and the thorny branches of the acacia scrub, stiffly rustling in the warm wind. Suddenly, on the knife edge of a horizon that had been empty only a moment before, a figure appears, as if by magic. Quickly the figure assumes the shape of a man, tall and slim, his only garment a togalike robe that ripples behind him as his strides eat up the distance. In one hand he carries a spear, longer than he is tall, a third of its length a keen metal blade that glints in the East African sun.

The man is a Masai, one of a haughty race of warrior cattlemen who roam the plains of Kenya and Tanzania, ignoring as best they can national boundaries and pressure to settle down. The Masai stride through the bush with an arrogance born of the certainty that they are its rulers. "The Masai fear no wild animal," an African friend once explained to me as we watched a young warrior glide by and vanish into the head-high grass.

Every so often, to the consternation of game wardens, the Masai set out with their long spears to demonstrate the truth of my friend's assertion. Armed with spear, shield, and traditional short sword, the Masai seek out confrontation with the supreme predator of their land, the African lion.

Lions sometimes raid Masai herds, but protecting their cattle is not the only reason why the Masai seek battle with the big cats. They kill the king of beasts for reasons of the spirit as well as expedience, the same combination of motives that probably prompted ancient man to slaughter the great cave bear. Meeting the lion in combat testifies to the courage of the Masai, and is an honor sought by every warrior.

Government wildlife authorities have tried to curb the killing of lions by the Masai except when they can prove they are losing cattle to the cats. An attack by lions on a herd is all the excuse the Masai need to take on as many of the tawny predators as they can find. Not very long ago, after lions raided the herds of one village in southwestern Kenya, the warriors killed eleven of the big cats before game wardens could arrive to verify the loss of cattle.

The risks entailed in matching blades against the fangs and claws of the lion are obvious, and many Masai men bear the scars from such encounters with extreme pride. The Masai lion hunts resemble a well-known inlay depicting a Mycenaean lion hunt in ancient Greece, about 3,500 years ago. Like the Masai, the Mycenaeans fought the lion with long spears while they protected themselves with large body shields. There may be more than coincidence here, for some scholars have suggested possible links between the cattle tribes of East Africa and pre-Homeric Greece.

On the other hand, cultural bridges may have nothing to do with the fact that warrior peoples in more than one part of the world have sought glory by killing lions with spears. All over the world, probably ever since man became fully human, hunters have risked their lives against animals for reasons that are intangible. The motivation, as we have seen, may be an abiding need to ease a whisper of doubt, deep in man's soul, that he is not, after all, the master of his world. Man may court danger in the shape of a wild beast to reassure himself that he can survive in nature; or perhaps by meeting the beast on its own ground the hunter seeks the comfort of knowing that like the animal he is part of nature, and is not alone.

MAN-MADE MENACE

Even when man hunts for reasons as practical as filling his belly, however, he can foment violent confrontations with animals which, while wanting nothing more than to get away from him, can do him great harm. Rather than fight man, even large, powerful animals usually attempt flight but if there is no other way out they may launch counterattack.

Hunting is one of the ways man uses animals to his advantage—exploits them, if you will. Actually, all of the ways man uses animals, whether as pets, for entertainment, or as subjects of photographs, constitute exploitation in one form or another; and all can entail a certain amount of peril for man, along with their benefits. Hunting always has been dangerous, but as we shall see, the reasons for the danger have changed.

MAN THE HUNTER

Since his beginnings, man has been a hunter. The instinct to hunt other animals goes back to his prehuman origins. Evidence for this assumption has been provided by our closest living relative, the chimpanzee. Scientists have observed bands of chimpanzees fanning out over the African savannah, surrounding the young of monkeys and antelope, and killing them for food. Baboons, which also kill and eat small animals, even have kidnapped and killed human babies from women while they worked in the fields. These hunts, anthropologists believe, parallel those that took place in Africa millions of years ago when our half-ape ancestors left the safety of the trees to search for red meat on the open plains. Some scientists believe, in fact, that the cooperation among members of a band that hunting game demands fostered the evolution of the human species.

ICE AGE SLAUGHTER

Even before the rise of our own species, *Homo sapiens,* primitive men were working in concert to kill large, dangerous animals such as mammoths and wild oxen. As the cave bear remains in Europe indicate, Neanderthal man—who may or may not have been akin to us—could tackle the largest carnivore of his day.

The most ruthlessly efficient big-game hunters the world has ever known, however, were men of modern type, who arrived on the world scene as the last ice age was waning. They were the ancestors of the American Indian, members of hunting bands who followed the herds of game from Asia, across a bridge of land exposed by a lowered sea level to Alaska. Exactly when man first arrived in the New World remains unknown, but it was at some point during the last ice age, at least 25,000 years ago.

The aboriginal Americans were such expert hunters that they may have exterminated the last of the ice age wildlife, such as mammoths and the giant prehistoric bison. Scientists are coming to accept this theory, which has become quite plausible in the light of certain archaeological discoveries.

The finds are of weapons, such as stone spearheads and arrow points, which not only are beautifully made, but must have been quite deadly. Among them are large spear heads called Clovis points, named after the community in New Mexico where, in 1926, they were first found. Since then other Clovis points have turned up from coast to coast, proof than the hunters who made them had populated the continent.

The Clovis points are fluted: they have a channel in the middle of one side, which is assumed to have facilitated attachment to a wooden spear shaft. Recently, however, two Canadian scientists have developed evidence that the weapons which bore the Clovis points were more complex than had been believed, and were so deadly they could have hastened the extinction of mammoths and other ancient game. The fossils left by giant North American ground sloths, for example, cease at the point in time when the ancient big game hunters arrived in their habitats.

The newly recognized advance in ice-age weaponry was discovered by Larry Lahren of the University of Calgary, Alberta, and Robert Bonnichsen of the Archaeological Survey of Canada. For several years archaeologists had puzzled over the function of slender bone shafts, about ten inches long, found in some of the sites where the Clovis points have been unearthed. Lahren and Bonnichsen examined both the points and shafts and came up with a novel idea. The bone shafts, they suggest, were lashed at one end to the fluted points, and the other to a wooden spear shaft.

When the spear was thrown at a mammoth or other animal, the

point and bone "foreshaft" were imbedded in the beast, but the wooden shaft could be yanked free by the hunter, who could then arm it with another stone-tipped foreshaft, and launch it again. While it would have been difficult for a man to lug several complete spears on a hunt, carrying one wooden shaft and several foreshafts would have been no problem.

Many hunters of the western frontier considered the bull bison as dangerous as the grizzly bear.

The latter arrangement provided the hunter with a new dimension of Stone Age firepower.

The use of such weapons, together with mass slaughter techniques such as driving herds over cliffs, may have been responsible for the disappearance of the ice-age animals of North America by 6,000 years ago. The skill of the hunters was probably only one of the elements of the extinction of the big game. Changes in climate, such as a decrease of rainfall, probably played a part. But if the game already was in decline, the Clovis hunters apparently finished it off.

THE HAZARDS OF HUNTING

Even when armed with such sophisticated weapons, however, the ice-age hunter was taking his chances. The giant bison of the time, which weighed a ton, had horns with a span of several feet, and the mammoths surpassed the bulk of the largest modern elephant. Assuming that these creatures defended themselves like their living relatives, many of the ancient hunters, in the Old World and the Americas, must have lost their lives during the chase.

On rare occasions people have found archaeological sites which testify to the hazards faced by the prehistoric hunter. In the Middle East, scientists who opened one Neanderthal grave found the skeleton of a man holding the jaws of a boar. It is easy to speculate that the boar killed the man during a hunt, then was in turn killed by the hunter's companions, who later placed the trophy head to rest with him. Prehistoric rock paintings from Tanzania show spearmen facing a charging elephant, which thunders down upon them, ears outspread and tusks thrusting. Several paintings on the walls of European caves show tense confrontations between wild cattle and hunters. The Lascaux cave in France is the site of a painting that portrays a man who seems to have been killed by a wounded bison.

BEWARE THE BISON

Bison and other large wild cattle are perfect examples of animals that normally ignore man or try to evade him, but when hunted can be explosively dangerous adversaries. Many people who have never seen an American bison *(Bison bison)* at close quarters believe it is a plodding creature as inoffensive as a common steer. This impression is fostered by the fact that the bison were so easily slaughtered during the great massacre of the western herds in the last decades of the nineteenth century.

Before some 60,000,000 American bison were destroyed in the senseless decimation of the western herds, this species probably was the most abundant large mammal on earth. The very size of the herds, coupled with the way bison stampede when panicked, made them extremely vulnerable to hunters with rifles who had only to fire into the packed masses of animals as they thundered over the land. Besides, many bison hunters took virtually no chances, shooting the animals from cover or even from railroad cars.

Actually, in circumstances other than those just described, the bison ("buffalo" is a less precise name for the creature) acts more like a fighting bull than a steer. This applies not only to the bull bison but to the cow, particularly in defense of her calf. Martin S. Garretson, who was secretary of the American Bison Society, the organization which led the effort to save the species, contended a cow bison's maternal fury equaled that of a sow grizzly bear.

A large bison bull can stand six feet high or more at the top of his shaggy hump, while the females measure only a foot or so less than that. From its wet, dark snout to the tip of its sloping rump the bison is twice as long as it is tall, with a weight of up to a ton. The huge head of the bison, which looks even larger because it is mounted on massive shoulders, is topped by a pair of crescent-shaped horns tipped with points of stiletto sharpness.

Despite its ponderous size the bison can wield its weapons with the finesse of a master swordsman, slashing and hooking in a manner much like that of the Spanish fighting bull. The skull between the horns reaches such a thickness that it is reputed to stop a .30-caliber rifle slug. This, of course, is not the purpose for which such massive bone structure evolved; it is really an adaptation which comes into play during the rutting season, when bull bison battle head to head, battering and shoving one another furiously, trying to gain an opening for a vicious horn thrust.

Few other animals threaten an adult bison in the wild. The only animals which preyed on the bison herds of the past were the grizzly bear and packs of timber wolves, but neither bear nor wolf always emerged victorious.

When attacked by a grizzly or by wolves, bison form a ring, young in the center and bulls outermost, facing the enemy with a phalanx of threatening horns. Once the ring of horns formed, the hunt was virtually over for the predators, for it was an impregnable living fortress.

Bison can be dangerous even if they do not intend harm. Strange sounds and sights can trigger a stampede, which sends the huge animals rumbling overland at a speed of thirty miles an hour. During pioneer days stampeding bison sometimes demolished wagon trains. The plains Indians utilized the bison as a weapon by taking advantage of this fact and stampeding the animals into the wagons of pioneers.

DEATH ON THE FRONTIER

Bison enjoy rubbing their hides against trees, and, when available, utility poles—a habit which used to disrupt communications in the West, for the bison bowled over many a telegraph pole. Before bison were exterminated in the woodlands of the Eastern states, this manner of scratching their hides almost resulted in the death of a Pennsylvania pioneer. He barely escaped with his life when bison literally rubbed down his cabin. The frontiersman had made the mistake of building his home near a salt lick which drew the bison in large numbers.

Pennsylvania was the scene of what probably was the last bison hunt in the northeastern states, an event which happened after frightened bison killed a pioneer's wife and children.

The tragedy, which occurred during the final week of the eighteenth century, resulted directly from human interference with the natural migratory cycle of the bison.

The American bison was not only an animal of the western plains but of the eastern woodlands. In addition to the great western herds, about a half million bison ranged the Appalachian states from western New York to Alabama. During the summer these woodlands bison separated into small groups which spread out over the northern end of their range, feeding mostly in upland meadows. As winter approached, the bison would gather and follow the Appalachians southwards over paths used for centuries.

The opening up of the Appalachian frontier during and after the American Revolution changed all that. Migration along the traditional trails became a march to slaughter as the bison were shot and killed by waiting settlers. Eventually, as farms and settlements were built along the trails, the small summer herds were cut off from the migratory pathways, and imprisoned in the islands of wilderness that remained in the hills.

One by one the little groups of bison were exterminated, either by the guns of the settlers or by starvation, as, especially during the winter, the limited range left to them failed to support them. By the end of the century, it is now believed, only one small herd of a few hundred bison remained in the northern part of the range.

The herd found refuge in the rugged hills of central Pennsylvania, where green ridges running diagonally from northeast to southwest form a rampart more than 100 miles long. Winter on the ridges is as rugged as the rock that forms them and the last winter of the eighteenth century was particularly severe. Cut off from their lush southern pastures, the bison foraged in the mountain fastnesses, but before the winter was even a few weeks old, the animals were starving.

Forced from the mountains by hunger, the bison sought food on the settlers' farms, which was tatamount to a death sentence for the animals. The settlers had barely enough feed and hay for their own livestock, and even if they had a few hundred animals of the size and temperment of bison were not particularly welcome on anyone's doorstep.

On December 29, 1799, the herd appeared near the one-room cabin of a man named Samuel McClellan, who promptly killed four of the bison. Frightened, the herd lumbered off towards another farm, where they trampled outbuildings and devoured a winter's supply of hay. McClellan, who had arrived upon the scene, and members of the farm household fired into the snorting, steaming animals, felling several more to the snow-covered ground.

Again the famished, frightened animals turned, this time back the way they had come. They rumbled towards McClellan's place, where they stopped, wild-eyed and snorting, a heaving mass of shaggy bodies churning about in bestial confusion. Within McClellan's cabin, his wife and three small children huddled, screaming in fear of the huge animals outside the wooden door.

McClellan, hearing the screams but out of ammunition, rushed among the bison and drove his woodman's knife into the lead bull. Like a locomotive running wild the bull bolted, heading straight for the cabin door with the herd behind him. Blindly the bison followed their leader, packing the cabin with their massive bodies, crushing everything within, including the helpless mother and her children.

Frantically, the settlers ripped down a wall of the cabin, and, like

The African buffalo carries some of the world's most impressive horns. This helmet of horn is said to be able to stop a bullet.

a flood tide from a burst dam, the bison poured out, fleeing into the forest.

Bent on vengeance, the settlers followed the herd, intent on killing every one of the bison. On the last day of the year, and of the century, the hunters found the bison stranded in deep snow, bogged down and unable to move. With guns and knives, the frontiersmen brought to an end the last bison of the northeast, in a bloody preview of the much greater slaughter that would follow in the new century.

Although a stampeding herd of bison can wreak horrible destruction the rampage is blind, not directed at anyone in particular. Quite the opposite is true when an individual bison is out to get someone. Like a skilled streetfighter, the animal will maneuver unobtrusively for position, waiting for the right moment to launch its attack, or when pursued it may flee, only to whip around and gore its pursuer. I once was in a paddock with a big bison bull that deliberately tried to edge between me and the only exit. Each time I turned toward the bull, he stopped, but as soon as my glance shifted, he would begin to maneuver again, keeping his eyes on me all the while.

Martin Garretson, in his classic book *The American Bison,* warned readers, "There is no time, either on the range or in the corral, when a man working with bison does not have to be on his guard . . ."

Cowboys who herd bison in roundups at some of the western bison refuges back up Garretson's claims. They advise anyone who happens to be unhorsed by a bison to lie on the ground and freeze, for the bison rely more on scent and hearing than eyesight.

Even bison that apparently are tame cannot be trusted, according to Garretson, whose book was published in 1938. He cited an incident in which a Nebraskan who had a pet bison was gored when he turned his back on the beast.

Also according to Garretson, a game rancher in Idaho had reared a bison bull and trained it to carry him on its back. One day the animal killed him. When dealing with bison, Garretson says in his book, "Nothing can be taken for granted."

Cowboys herd bison into a pen at the Wichita Refuge in Oklahoma. This job is dangerous because the bulls often turn and charge the horses.

CUSTER'S CLOSE CALL

Garretson's advice goes double for people who hunt bison in the open. Bison hunters of the Old West who pursued the shaggy beasts on horseback had to use mounts trained to avoid the bison's slashing charge.

Even with an expertly trained horse, it was a risky way to hunt. General George Armstrong Custer almost never reached his appointment with destiny at the Little Bighorn because he erred Bighorn while hunting bison from a horse. A decade before the battle and his death, Custer was chasing a bison only to see the creature whirl, lower its horns, and counterattack. In most unsoldierly fashion Custer panicked, shot his horse, and was dumped on the ground. The bison, as if disgusted at such an undignified encounter, dropped the attack and left the scene.

BISON HUNT IN CONNECTICUT

A few years ago hunters in the small Connecticut town where I live were called upon to stop a marauding bison bull which was savaging homeowners' shrubbery. The bull had escaped from a fenced pasture in an adjoining town where a wealthy man had for many years kept a few dozen bison. The beast wandered about the countryside, which is heavily wooded, emerging from the forest to feed on shrubs.

Three local woodsmen set out to track the bison. For the better part of a day they stayed on its trail until, in the afternoon, they saw the animal on a rise near a reservoir. Sensing its pursuers, the bison lowered its head and charged them. They fired, striking the bull twice. Although hit by two slugs the bull did not fall, but instead turned his charge and lumbered off with the hunters in pursuit. After galloping for a few hundred yards the bison stopped, and the hunters fired again, this time killing the animal. What probably was the first bison hunt in the history of Connecticut had ended. The bison was picked up with a crane, placed on a truck and returned to its owner who had it butchered and distributed its meat to his friends.

THE FADING GLORIES OF DANGEROUS GAME

Although American bison are commonly called "buffalo," this name more properly applies to the true buffalo of Africa and Asia. The African buffalo *(Syncerus caffer),* which can weigh up to 1,500 pounds, is reputed to be one of the most dangerous of all big-game animals to hunt. Some authorities claim that it has accounted for the lives of more hunters than any other creature in Africa.

Any discussion of the dangers of big-game hunting, particularly in Africa and Asia, must necessarily focus on the past. The glory days of hunting big, dangerous game animals are over—the danger and hardship have all but vanished with the passing of the true wilderness.

Earlier in the century a hunting safari in Africa could be a rugged and risky undertaking. The country was barely explored, communications were primitive, travel difficult, and tribes unfriendly. Today one can motor out into a carefully managed game preserve, hunt without working up a sweat, and then retire to a shower and cocktail—all under the supervision of a guide whose job relies as much on his ability to mix a martini as it does making sure that his clients are exposed to not the least amount of danger.

Moreover, the decline in numbers of many species has prompted their removal from the list of lawful game animals. Not only is it illegal to hunt the tiger in India, for example, but it also is a violation of United States law to bring the pelt of an endangered species such as the tiger home with you. Increased public awareness of the plight of many kinds of wildlife also has made big-game trophy hunting a less fashionable avocation than it once was—although when hunting is conducted according to sound wildlife management rules, it does not contribute to the extinction of wildlife. The fading interest in big-game hunting is reflected by the fact that many African hunting guides now generate most of their income by leading photographic safaries, often with elderly women as clients.

This is not to say that stalking and killing game as savage and powerful as the African buffalo is always the safest way to spend one's leisure time, but with the proper firearms danger is not essential to the experience and usually results only because of someone's blunder. A physician friend of mine who is a dead shot had a very close call with a buffalo in Kenya because his gun bearer made a mistake and handed him the wrong weapon. My friend had crept to within easy range of a very large buffalo, then had reached back for his favorite rifle. Instead, his bearer handed him another weapon, which unknown to all had been fired back at the camp. Taking careful aim, the physician pulled the trigger, only to hear the loud metallic click that signified the chamber of the rifle was empty. It was a very trying moment. Fortunately for my friend, when the buffalo heard the hammer strike home, it decided not to charge, but trotted off in another direction.

That you never know what to expect from a buffalo was demonstrated for me a few years ago while I was encamped in a tent near a game lodge in Kenya. One night I was awakened by sound of an animal cropping grass under the tent fly, on the other side of the canvas a few inches from where I lay. Before going to bed I had seen several zebras nearby, so I assumed that my visitor was one of them.

The creature continued to feed, keeping me awake but I did not protest until it leaned into the side of the tent and threatened to roll me out of bed. So I whacked it through the canvas, until it moved away. The next morning I looked around and saw tracks that looked suspiciously large, so that night when I returned to the tent I peered under the fly, switched on a flashlight, and had my suspicions confirmed. Staring back at me was a buffalo.

Since the animal seemed not at all concerned, I decided not to worry either, and retired, leaving it to its nocturnal foraging. The next night the buffalo—whether or not it was the same one I cannot be sure—returned again. I was growing rather used to the visits until one morning, when I went outside, I saw that a neighboring tent had been reduced to wreckage by a foraging buffalo.

In order to get at grass under the edge of the tent a buffalo had hooked the bottom with its horns, overturned it, and flipped it over, along with the two beds and furniture within. Canvas, beds, dressers, and bedclothes lay in a heap amidst snapped tent ropes. Fortunately the tent had not been occupied.

ARMOR OF HORN

The horns of the African buffalo are the most impressive of any carried by wild cattle. Spanning a full yard from tip to tip, they curve downward from the skull and then upward like a pair of longshoreman's hooks placed handle to handle. They are flattened at the base into a thick boss which covers the entire front of the skull, and is said to be thick enough to stop a bullet. That is not the purpose for which the buffalo's armor of horn was intended, however, but rather to protect the bulls as they bang heads while fighting over females in the mating season.

Buffalo are native to much of Africa south of the Sahara. Their size

Another of the huge wild cattle is the guar, or seladang, of southern Asia. It has been known to backtrack and charge hunters. Unless molested, however, it will not go out of its way to bother people.

and color varies according to the type of habitat in which they live. The biggest buffalo are the black animals that live on the savannahs in the southern part of the continent. These creatures can reach a weight of 1,500 pounds and stand five feet high at the shoulder. The smallest buffalo inhabit the forests of central Africa. They are reddish in color and only about half the size of their huge southern relatives. Where forests and plains meet, buffalo herds sometimes are composed of both types, with a variety of shades and sizes between the two extremes.

ASIAN WATER BUFFALO

The wild Asian water buffalo *(Bubalus arnee)*, which reaches its largest size in India, can weigh several hundred pounds more than its African counterpart. The buffalo of India is more than six feet high at the shoulder, and has huge, sweeping horns which can measure six feet long on the outside curve. The smallest Asian water buffalo, called by the name *tamarau* on its native Mindoro Island, is only a third as large as the Indian variety. The *tamarau,* however, has a bad reputation, and people who live in country inhabited by this small buffalo keep out of its way. Some zoologists regard it as a different species from the larger buffalo.

The Indian buffalo is extremely rare in the wild, although the domesticated form of water buffalo has been bred in many parts of the world. Domestic buffalo, which lack the huge horns of the wild variety, are common sights throughout southeast Asia, and in parts of Latin America, Italy, and Australia.

Because only 2,000 Indian buffalo survive, they are protected. In the past, when they were more numerous, they were considered fair game, and had a very fierce reputation. Acting alone, or more often in concert as a herd, the buffalo have killed many tigers. Indian buffalo also seem extremely intolerant of tame riding elephants, which appear to invite the wild cattle to charge. A few years ago an Indian forestry official told in the *Bengal Journal of Natural History* how he had surprised a cow buffalo and her calf while riding through the forest on elephant back. The cow behaved in typical fashion. On seeing the elephant, she lowered her huge horns and charged, sending the elephant lurching away in fright.

ATTACKS BY ANTELOPE

Antelopes are generally regarded as inoffensive, gentle creatures, whose only defense against hunters is to flee. This certainly is true of the smaller kinds of antelopes, such as gazelles, but some of the larger members of the antelope tribe are very able to take care of themselves, against other animals as well as man. Among the most courageous fighters of all the antelopes are members of the genus *Oryx,* which have horns that are either straight like lances or curved like the Saracen scimitar. Oryx, particularly the South African gemsbok, are known to fight lions to a standoff, fencing and jabbing at the big cats with their long horns. Somali tribesmen used to hunt the oryx of their region on horseback, and there are documented reports of the antelope turning on their tormentors and goring them. Edward Arnold, a big-game hunter of the last century, wrote of how he was charged by an oryx under similar circumstances. Arnold had shot the antelope in the foreleg, but it was able to flee from him. Mounting his horse, the hunter gave chase. Suddenly the antelope swerved and aimed the points of its horns at Arnold, who narrowly escaped being gored by quickly turning his horse aside.

The roan antelope *(Hippotragus equinus)* and the stately sable antelope *(Hippotragus niger),* both related to the oryx, can be equally dangerous. When wounded, the roan will charge its hunter, and because of its size—600 pounds—and power, it is treated with great care by professional hunting guides.

HOLDOVERS FROM THE ICE AGES

Many stories are told about the dangers of hunting rhinoceros, but although these huge animals can pulverize a man with ease, they are overrated as mankillers. All five species of rhino remaining in the world are dull-witted primitive survivors of the ice ages, and all are threatened with extinction, particularly the two smallest types, which live in Sumatra and Java, and perhaps Indochina. The great Indian rhinoceros *(Rhinoceros unicornis)* also has almost vanished and lives only in a few sanctuaries in India and Nepal.

The two species of rhinoceros in Africa, the white *(Ceratotherium simum)* and the black *(Diceros bicornis)* are in somewhat better shape in terms of survival, but even their situation is rather precarious.

Like almost all other large wild animals, the rhinos have suffered severely from destruction of their habitat. Just as deadly to the rhino as the loss of the needs to survive is the belief of many Asians that rhino horn ground to a powder acts as an aphrodiasiac, and commands a huge price on Oriental markets.

The gemsbok of southern Africa is the largest of the oryx antelope. It sometimes kills lions with its horns.

The black rhinoceros has claimed several human victims. Attacks on humans often are the work of rhinos which have been wounded and left by hunters. This rhino is in the Bronx Zoo, New York City.

Some zoologists believe that rhino horn attained its sexual significance because of the awesome reproductive energy of the Indian species. When the male great Indian rhino mates, he copulates for about an hour, ejaculating almost by the minute during that time.

Because rhino horn is such a highly saleable product, poachers have decimated rhino populations in both Africa and Asia. The horns they obtain by the slaughter are shipped to the Far East and sold in Chinese medicine shops in Hong Kong and other large cities.

The number of horns on a rhino differs according to species. The two African rhinos carry a pair of horns, both very long. The Indian species, whose bodily is heavily armored with overlapping plates of thick hide, has only one small horn, virtually useless as a weapon. However, the Indian rhino has huge canine tusks in its lower jaw, and when necessary can slash an enemy to pieces with them. Normally, the Indian rhino is shy and flees from man. Captive specimens become so gentle that zoo keepers regularly enter enclosures with them. For some reason, like the Indian buffalo, the one-horned rhino sometimes charges riding elephants, which it has been known to disembowel with its tusks.

The huge white rhino, which at five tons in weight is second only to the elephants in size among land animals, is a gentle giant, but when substantially provoked will charge a man.

Herbert Lang, a mammalogy curator at the American Museum of Natural History a half century ago, wrote an account of hunting the white rhino. One of the massive, square-snouted animals was so timid that it ran off on hearing the click of a camera shutter, Lang reported.

Lang's report, which appeared in an issue of the New York Zoological Society *Bulletin,* told of two rhinos killed by his party in the Belgian Congo. One of the beasts charged when a member of the safari crept up on it to take its photo. As the rhino plowed through the grass, an African hunter who was with Lang hurled his six-foot spear into the animal's side, evoking an enraged squeal from the creature. The blade of the spear penetrated a half foot deep into the rhino's ribs, and the ponderous animal plunged away through the undergrowth, with blood spurting from its nostrils. The rhino presumably died in the bush.

The second rhino was shot, but not brought down, so Lang and his companions went after it into the high grass. As they pushed through the grass, the wounded animal suddenly loomed up ten feet away and charged Lang, who took to his heels with the rhino pounding after him. Lang's African aide courageously tossed a camera in the charging beast's face, but it bounced off without diverting the animal's attention.

With the rhino jabbing its two horns at his heels, the mammalogist sprinted into a cluster of trees. The rhino followed and became tangled in the undergrowth. Just then another member of the party ran up and blasted away at the behemoth from close range. Mortally wounded but still fighting, the rhino tore free of the tangle, then dropped. However, it gained its feet again and ran for several yards before it finally fell dead.

The black rhino, which is smaller but more truculent than the white, is deemed the most dangerous of all its kind. It can be very disconcerting to suddenly see one of these one-ton creatures suddenly loom out of the high savannah grass or scrub, sniffing the wind, nostrils wide and ears outspread, its dull mind seemingly considering whether to charge. Indeed, black rhinos have charged safari vehicles, overturning them and bashing them and their passengers about the plains. Biologist Iain Douglas-Hamilton, whose studies of the ecology of the African elephants has brought him wide acclaim, was trampled and badly hurt by a black rhino.

Douglas-Hamilton, a slim bespectacled Scot who takes considerable risks to get close to the subjects of his field studies, tells of his harrowing experience in his book, *Among the Elephants.* Douglas-Hamilton was walking through an area of thickets near Tanzania's Lake Manyara with his mother, who was visiting him, and a game ranger. Earlier in the day they had seen two rhinos browsing in the area, so knowing that most animals flee from the sound of humans, they shouted loudly as they moved through the thickets. Suddenly a rhino burst out of the brush almost on top of Douglas-Hamilton. He shouted to warn the others, then ran, with the rhino behind him.

As the young scientist fled through the brush, a strap on his sandal broke and he fell on his face. The next moment the rhino thundered over him, leaving him battered, but alive. As a result of the trampling, which he was lucky to survive, Douglas-Hamilton spent several weeks in bed with a badly injured back, his muscles ruptured and seized up so tightly he was unable to walk.

Other scientists, game rangers and explorers have been charged by black rhinos for no apparent reason. A Swiss zoologist Rudolf Schenkel was tossed by a rhino in the Tsavo National Park of Kenya, but when the scientist crawled under a half-fallen tree, the rhino ambled away. A few years ago a black rhino charged and killed a woman who had shot it with a slug too small to kill it.

Despite incidents such as these, most of the time the black rhino is an easy target for a hunter with a modern rifle, or in the case of a poacher, with a poisoned arrow.

The rhino's eyes are rather myopic, and while the beast hears well, it usually needs to get a whiff of something to tell what it is. Many of the seemingly aggressive approaches that rhinos make to people in the bush merely are attempts to catch their scent. Once a rhino gets a sniff of the human species, however, the chances are that it will head off for another neighborhood rather than attack; but rare is the person who will calmly stand still and wait to see what happens.

A hunter armed with a rifle has little to fear from even the black rhinoceros, but by leaving a wounded rhino to wander in agony, a hunter can transform an animal that only mildly threatens man into a monstrous mankiller that will attack humans on sight. Even rhinos which have never been wounded are unusually aggressive in places where hunting pressure is intense. Woe to anyone who happens across a rhino with a rifle slug buried in its body, or a poacher's poisoned arrow festering in its flesh. These are the rhinos which may be responsible for many of the so-called unprovoked attacks upon people. The rhino described above, which was shot with a bullet of too small a caliber, ran off after killing the woman who wounded it, but the next day reappeared, chased a motorist from his car, and killed him.

TOUGH AS TWO TIGERS

For sheer savagery and raw animal courage when cornered by hunters, however, no animal—not the rhino or even the African buffalo —can match the awesome ferocity displayed by the wild boar *(Sus scrofa)*. From India to the American Appalachians, the wild boar occupies a revered position in hunting lore because of the fearless tenacity with which it battles to the last for its life.

Indian shikaris, a vanishing breed of hunting guides, have a saying that sums up the nature of the boar. The wild boar, they say, is tough enough to "drink at a river between two tigers." That about says it for this agile, highly intelligent ancestor of the domestic pig, which has been exported from its native range in Eurasia to hunting preserves in many other parts of the world.

The ancient Greeks, who made boar hunts the subject of legend, hunted the boar with an iron-tipped spear whose shaft was equipped with a pair of crescent-shaped blades which projected forward like the horns of a bull. The purpose of the blades was to prevent the boar from writhing down the spear shaft toward the hunter after the creature was impaled.

Such a precaution testifies to the respect the Greek hunters had for the way in which the boar persevered in its raging attack, even as it was dying.

British army officers in India were particularly fond of "pig sticking"—hunting boars with lances from horseback. Being mounted, however, was no assurance of safety from the boar's slashing charge. Wild boars, which can reach a maximum weight of more than 300 pounds, have been known to kill even camels and tigers with their razor-sharp

canine tusks and can easily slice a riding horse to ribbons.

The tusks, two in each jaw, grow continuously and are honed to a deadly edge as the upper pair rubs against the lower. All four tusks, even those in the upper jaw, point upward. In a brawl the boar slashes up and to the side with these vicious weapons, which can slit a man open in a twinkling.

The unflinching courage of the boar is exemplified by an authenticated story from India about a boar which had earned the emnity of farmers in one district by devouring their crops. Tired of the boar's depredations, which had lasted for several years, one of the farmers decided to put an end to the creature. One night, when the fields were illuminated by the cool light of the full moon, the farmer armed himself with a bow and arrows and stationed himself atop a huge boulder to wait for the boar.

As usual, the boar emerged from the dark shelter of the forest and made for the farm plots. Once in the open the shaggy wild pig made an easy target, illuminated by the bright moonlight, and the farmer greeted the creature with a rain of arrows.

Pierced by several arrows, the boar turned and charged the source of its troubles, but could not surmount the rock to get at the farmer with its tusks. The boar raged repeatedly against the sides of the rock like a storm battering a sea cliff, but the farmer remained beyond the animal's reach and sent arrow after arrow into the brute's body.

Finally, sorely wounded, the boar crawled away, dragging itself towards some bushes alongside a nearby road. By dawn the boar had reached the shelter of the bushes, but when the tormented beast saw several bullock carts approaching down the road it hauled itself to its feet and charged them. As it reached the carts the boar suddenly dropped to the dusty roadbed and died before the eyes of the terrified drivers. When the boar was examined, the drivers discovered that an arrow had skewered its jaws together, so it was in effect weaponless for its last charge.

Larger than the black rhino, the white rhinoceros has a more docile reputation. It is the second largest land animal living today.

THE BOAR OF THE APPALACHIANS

The fact that the boar can be dangerous to man and a threat to agriculture has not stopped people from artifically extending its range. The species has been introduced by man in places as far apart as New Zealand and eastern North America. A small population of wild boar inhabits the central part of New Hampshire, and a sizable number of these creatures roam the Great Smoky Mountains of western North Carolina and eastern Tennessee. Both groups descend from boars imported into this country for game preserves.

The boars of New Hampshire owe their origin to animals which escaped from a preserve when a fence around the hunting area was destroyed by the disastrous New England hurricane of 1938. By the end of World War II, the progeny of the escapees had spread throughout the central part of the state. State authorities, alarmed at the claims for crop damage that were being filed because of the boars, authorized hunting of the animals, and most were killed. I remember as a boy in Connecticut

An 1887 depiction of a hunt for feral pigs, or razorbacks, in Arkansas shows that domestic pigs gone wild are as aggressive as their relative, the wild boar.

seeing a photograph in a local newspaper showing a New Hampshire woman, rifle in hand, standing next to the strung-up carcass of a boar she had shot when it charged her.

Authorities in the southeast, unlike those in New Hampshire, have tried to increase the number of boars in their region, for the boar has become a popular game animal there. (The meat of the boar is more tasty, to my mind, than domestic pork.) Tennessee in particular has undertaken a substantial program of managing its boar population, which has quite a story behind it.

The origin of the wild boars of the Great Smoky Mountains is sometimes disputed, but the official version goes like this:

In February 1908 the Whiting Manufacturing Company of Great Britain purchased a large tract of land in the mountains of Graham County, southwestern North Carolina. Soon after the purchase, the British firm permitted George Gordon Moore, an American investment adviser, to establish a game preserve on the tract, around a mountain called Hooper Bald. Moore intended to entertain wealthy clients on the preserve with wild boar hunts.

Before he could import boars, however, Moore had to fence the area, a task which was completed by 1912. In April 1912, fourteen young boars from the Ural Mountains of Russia arrived by railway express at Murphy, North Carolina, twenty-five miles from the preserve. The animals—eleven females and three males—were loaded aboard ox-drawn wagons and hauled to Hooper Bald, which took three days and the life of one of the female swine.

The other boars were liberated on the preserve but almost as soon as they were freed they managed to root their way out of the fence. Although the boars could come and go as they pleased, most of them stayed in the 500-acre tract within the fence, although occasionally they forayed out into the neighborhood.

For a decade the animals were left virtually alone, and they reproduced, until as many as 100 boars inhabited the preserve. Meanwhile, Moore had abandoned the preserve and given it to his foreman, a man called Cotton McGuire, but he could not maintain the operation either, so called an end to it and prepared to leave the area.

Before leaving, however, he decided to stage a grand boar hunt and invited several friends with their dogs to take part in the affair. The boars proved more than a match for the hunters and their hounds. Only two boars were killed, but a dozen dogs were casualties. Several of the hunters escaped the tusks of the boars only by scrambling up trees.

During the melee, most of the boars went through or under the fence and headed into the mountains, where they quickly became established. As the years passed the boars—called "wild hogs" in the parlance of the southern mountains—spread westward into Tennessee, and because the land was wilderness—largely national forest—they prospered. Today about 2,000 wild hogs inhabit the forests of southeastern Tennessee and southwestern North Carolina, and many more roam game preserves in the region.

HOG HUNTS

Hog hunting in the southeastern mountains provides some of the most exciting and hazardous big-game sport in the nation. It is no sport to try alone and requires the cooperation of several men and dogs. The "hog hounds" are of motley origin but share a common characteristic —toughness. "A hog hound needs to be a fearless individual and possess great stamina," advises a report on wild hog management and hunting by the Tennessee Fish and Game Commission.

Among the breeds tough and mean enough for the job are black-and-tan and bluetick hounds, the Plott hound, bull terriers, wolfhounds, and Airedales. The hound breeds usually are used to find and track the prey while the terriers move in when the boar is brought to bay and worry it until the hunter arrives.

The "fighting dogs" that tackle the cornered boar usually work as a team, often in pairs. One dog snaps at the head of the hog while the other rips at its flanks. This way the hog is kept off balance, as its whirls first to meet one attacker, then the other.

Before the hog is brought to bay, however, it may engage the dogs in a running battle over many miles of countryside. Hogs have been known to go for thirty miles or more leaving bleeding and whimpering dogs in their wake. The Tennessee Fish and Game Commission report advises hunters to get to the scene as soon as possible after the dogs have cornered the hog and kill the hog before it dispatches the dogs.

However, the report warns:

This can be a dangerous task because a hog bayed by dogs will usually charge a man on sight, and an adult boar possesses weapons capable of inflicting severe injury. Hunters have been lacerated and badly bruised on occasion and several men have been "treed" for hours when caught unexpectedly or unarmed.

The true wild boar of the Old World has been introduced in the southern Applachians, where it is a valued big game animal.

Sometimes men hunt hogs not with a pack of dogs but with only one, a rare, highly prized variety called the "catch dog." The catch dog must be a fearless, rugged brute. It hunts alone, silently trailing the boar to its lair, creeping close enough to tackle the hog with a sudden rush. The dog's goal is to sink its teeth into the hog before the hog realizes it is under attack, and to hold the quarry until the hunters arrive. Few dogs are capable of this feat.

THE BALANCE OF POWER

American boar hunters generally dispatch their quarry with .30-caliber rifles, or shotguns firing rifled slugs. Assuming that the hunter can handle his weapon the firepower of either the rifle or shotgun can stop the charge of the most enraged boar. Modern firearms have weighted the odds heavily in favor of the hunter even against the most dangerous big game. As Arctic explorer Vilhjalmur Stefansson noted earlier in this century, even the great grizzly bear of the Arctic barren grounds has "no more chance against a man with a modern rifle than a fly has against a sledgehammer."

This is not to say that all danger has been eliminated from hunting animals such as the African buffalo, wild boar, and grizzly bear. When the hunter's index finger squeezes the trigger, it not only fires the gun but initiates a confrontation between animal and man which could conceivably end in his death. Usually, of course, it does not. Firearms give the hunter so much of an edge that real danger only arises when the hunter makes a mistake, usually in judgment.

The late Olaus J. Murie, famed naturalist and conservationist, stressed this point in an article he wrote about grizzly bears *(Ursus arctos)* in a 1957 issue of the magazine *Animal Kingdom,* magazine of the New York Zoological Society. Most hunters who are killed or injured by grizzlies, Murie said, are victims of their own ignorance of the bear's capabilities. Too many hunters try to shoot grizzlies at close range, he explained, forgetting that even when fatally wounded a big grizzly can cover twenty yards in its last furious charge.

Murie, who killed several grizzlies for the Smithsonian Institution's National Museum, noted that he quickly learned to shoot these huge beasts only from a distance, and never from their downhill side, for that is the direction in which they tend to make their last rush.

The naturalist, who was one of the leading figures in the Wilderness Society for many years, also cited an example in which a hunter ill-advisedly followed a wounded grizzly into the brush while his hands were mittened and his rifle over his shoulder. The bear suddenly reared up in front of the ill-prepared hunter, slamming him with its powerful paws and raking great gashes in his head and arms. Knocked flat, the hunter was in mortal danger when a companion, who had been a short distance behind, arrived and shot the bear.

THE PERILS OF SHOOTING BLIND

Among the worst mistakes that any hunter—of big or small game—can make is to shoot blindly before he identifies his target. All too often the target is another hunter, a domestic animal, or a wild animal other than the one bargained for. It is a mistake that even the experts have made. Carl Akeley, whose exploits as a hunter of African animals for great museums brought him world renown before World War II, almost paid with his life for this fault in judgement. Returning to camp after a day of shooting on the East African plains, Akeley glimpsed a shadowy form behind a bush.

"I then did a very foolish thing," Akeley later wrote of his experience. "Without a sight of what I was shooting at, I shot hastily into the bush."

The snarl of a leopard that answered Akeley's shot told him the identity of the beast in the bushes. Fearing that he had wounded the leopard, and knowing that in such a state a leopard fights to the finish, Akeley, who was accompanied by an African helper, decided not to track the creature in the lowering darkness. His idea was to return to his camp, spend the night, and then track the leopard the next morning.

Akeley started for camp, trudging through a deep gully in the last light of the day. Suddenly, twenty yards away, he saw the leopard crossing the gully and, although he could not see well enough to aim, began firing at the spotted cat. His first two shots blasted into the sand behind the leopard but the third slammed into the beast, killing it—or so Akeley thought.

The African who was with Akeley began to chant a victory song as

the two men headed for the leopard. The cat, however, was far from dead. In the darkness, Akeley heard the cat snarling and spitting, and realized that the beast was after him. Frantically working the bolt of his rifle, Akeley discovered that the weapon's magazine was empty. He inserted another cartridge and prepared to deal with the leopard, when from out of the gloom it hurtled at him, aiming for his throat.

Apparently because one of Akeley's shots had crippled the leopard's right hind foot, the cat's aim was off, and its fangs missed the hunter's throat, sinking into his right arm instead. His rifle sent spinning by the impact of the leopard's body, Akeley fought for his life as the cat tried to disembowel him with its hind claws. However, because the cat was off target its rear legs had straddled Akeley's body, so the creature could not employ its talons to rake out his innards.

As the cat chewed into his right arm, Akeley grabbed its throat with his left hand, forcing it to loosen its grip enough so he could work his arm free, bit by bit. At the same time he managed to roll over so he was atop the leopard, his right hand in its mouth, left hand squeezing its throat. Forcing his elbows into the animal's armpits so its foreclaws could not reach him, Akeley kneed the beast in the chest as hard as he could. To his joy he felt a rib break under the leopard's spotted skin, so he kneed the beast again until it stopped struggling.

Barely able to stand, Akeley called to the African who had been watching the battle with horror. The leopard had begun to stir, and Akeley realized if it regained its strength, he was in no shape to continue the fight. He took the African's knife and plunged it into the leopard, killing it.

Covered with grime and blood, his clothing in shreds and arm mangled, Akeley dragged himself back to camp. His arm was so badly mauled than when antiseptic was pumped into it the liquid flowed out of the numerous punctures made by the leopard's teeth.

Akeley's battle with the leopard happened on his first trip to Africa. During succeeding treks into African's forests and plains he had other close calls, including one, described in the last chapter, which brought

At the climax of a boar hunt this hunter in the Tennessee mountains takes aim. His accuracy must be good or he will be in mortal danger, for a cornered boar is a fierce adversary.

him even closer to death's door than his combat with the leopard, shot so foolishly in the dusk.

SAVED BY PUNCH

Early in the century a British army major had a similar wrestling match with a big cat, in this case a lion, only to be saved by a copy of the venerable British humor magazine *Punch*. The officer, P.H.G. Powell-Cotton by name, had shot a big, black-maned lion, to see it vanish into a patch of brush. The major and other members of his hunting party tried to provoke the lion into reappearing by tossing sticks and clods of earth into the brush. The tactic worked, and the lion charged, straight towards the major. Aiming his double-barreled big-game rifle at the tawny form hurtling towards him, Powell-Cotton fired twice, but failed to stop the cat. Reaching back for another rifle from his gun bearer, the major grasped only air, for his gun bearer had fled.

Powell-Cotton tossed his empty gun at the lion and ran, but in a few bounds the beast caught him, knocked him on his face, and dug in its claws. The lion's claws, however, shredded not flesh but the pages of the venerable British humor magazine *Punch,* which the major had folded in his pocket. Before the lion could do any further damage, one of the expedition's porters picked up a stick and bravely began to club the beast. Inspired by his bravery, other porters joined in and pummeled the lion enough to distract its attention until an African militiaman accompanying the safari shot the animal.

Sport hunting of the big cats has dwindled, because like most large predators, tigers, leopards, cheetahs, jaguars, and even lions are increasingly imperiled by man's activities, chiefly destruction of habitat. In the case of the lion, at least, well-managed sport hunting could lead not to the downfall of the species but to its preservation, a possibility that will be discussed in the final chapter.

General Custer of Little Big Horn fame is shown in this old photograph with a grizzly bear he has killed. The grizzly was the creature
most feared by frontiersmen as well as by the Indian tribes of the
Old West.

CONQUEST BY THE SPEAR

When man stalks the big cats he is challenging the master hunters
of nature at their own game. If the human is armed with hand-to-hand
weapons, like the Masai lion hunters, the rules are totally different than
when the weapons are firearms. Even if one is apalled by the killing of
wild animals, it is not difficult to admire the supreme courage it must
take to face animals such as the lion with only a blade.

The Masai, as pointed out earlier, are one of the few peoples left who regularly hunt the lion in this manner, although the custom may not survive much longer. I have not witnessed a Masai lion hunt, but a young man of the tribe explained to me how the kill is made. Here is the way he described it:

Usually several warriors make up the hunting party, although sometimes a single hunter pursues the beast. If a lone hunter makes the kill, he must bring back the ears and tail of the lion as proof of his victory. Each hunter carries his spear in his right hand and large body shield of cowhide in the left. The traditional Masai short sword, about two feet long, hangs encased in a cowhide scabbard on the hunter's right hip.

Once the lion is brought to bay, the hunters attempt to spear if from a distance. "If the lion is a coward," I was told, it is killed in this way. "But if the lion is brave," the young Masai told me, and charges, the hunters meet it with the sword. A warrior who still is holding his spear when the lion charges shifts it to his left hand, which also holds the shield, and takes his sword in his right.

Braced behind their shields, the warriors hack and stab at the lion. If a man goes down he crouches, attempting to get as much of himself under his shield as possible, while his companions assail the lion from all sides. Turning from one man to another, the lion is stabbed from all quarters and, ringed by flashing blades, cannot escape.

When there is need, a single Masai can be a match for the lion. Author Marguerite Mallet, whose book *A White Woman Among the Masai* was published in 1923, when lions were much more abundant than today, tells how one young warrior dispatched one of the huge cats single-handedly. The lion had crept up upon an elderly Masai herdsman and was savaging the old man when the warrior arrived on the scene. Lacking a shield, the young man wrapped his left arm in his blanket, and using it to ward off the lion's claws and fangs, drove his sword down the creature's throat. The herdsman, although severely mauled, survived to display his scars with great pride.

TIGER MAN

The spear was the trademark of South America's legendary "tiger man," Sasha Siemel, who from 1923 to the 1950s hunted the biggest cat of the New World with only that weapon.

Siemel, a Latvian adventurer who had emmigrated to the Mato Grosso wilderness of Brazil, earned his nickname for killing jaguars, the powerful spotted cats which are called *"tigres,"* or "tigers" in Latin America. The jaguar is a stocky, heavily muscled beast, immensely strong, of legendary ferocity, and at its maximum weight of 350 pounds, larger than some lions or tigers. Native to California until a century ago, the jaguar now is rare north of the Mexican border, but still is common in some areas of Central and South America.

Reputed to be the most ferocious of all big cats, the jaguar regularly preys on animals as large as tapirs, and even caymans, the aggressive tropical relatives of the American alligator. Jaguars also sometimes kill domestic livestock, which has earned them the enmity of South American ranchers.

Siemel, the "tiger man," was essentially in the business of predator control and was hired by ranchers to dispose of the spotted cats. Using a variety of weapons, Siemel killed at least 200 jaguars, but he achieved celebrity status because of the 30 or more big cats that he spitted on his spear.

The spear consisted of a foot-long blade mounted on a sturdy shaft six feet in length. Just behind the blade was fitted a crosspiece to prevent the weapon from penetrating so deeply that the cat would be able to reach the hunter with its claws.

Siemel's technique, which he learned from the Indians of the Mato Grosso, required tremendous strength of both will and muscle. It hinged on knowing exactly how a jaguar attacks when cornered—like a thunderbolt, suddenly, in a furious headlong rush climaxed in a mighty leap upon the victim.

The proper use of the spear turns the jaguar's own fury against it. Bracing the butt end of the spear in the ground the hunter must meet the jaguar in mid-leap with the point of the weapon, to impale the creature. Then, as the cat writhes on the metal blade above the hunter's head, he must flip the animal over and pin it to the ground.

Small wonder that as the story of Siemel's combats with jaguars was spread by newspapers and magazines he became something of an international celebrity, particularly since only a few years ago there was little public sympathy for predatory animals, nor understanding of their role in maintaining the balance of nature.

Today there is wide recognition that even big, savage predators are valuable members of the wildlife community and that many of them are in danger of extinction and thus need protection. Campaigns by agricultural interests to destroy predators draw considerable fire from conservationists and animal lovers, and many predators are now protected by law.

THE QUESTION OF HUNTING

With the rise of the environmental movement the preservation of endangered species has taken on all the trappings of a major public crusade. Fashionable women have put aside their leopard coats. Bumper stickers proclaim: "Save the Whale." Voters demand that their legislators protect the wolf. Wildlife conservationists, who for years were taken seriously only by one another, now can rally millions of people in behalf of one species or another. Such broad public interest in wildlife has worked wonders, but it also has been accompanied by an appalling amount of confusion as to just what conservation of wild animals is all about.

A substantial number of Americans, mostly residents of urban areas, have come to believe that banning legitimate sport hunting of species which are in no way imperiled is somehow the way to save endangered wildlife. These people fail to recognize that sound wildlife conservation means not only saving imperiled species from vanishing, but also managing species that are in a healthy condition and using them as a natural resource. Included in the proper utilization of some of these species is regulated sport hunting.

Adding to the confusion is the fact that many people who say they are against hunting unwittingly lump all forms of hunting together in their minds. They make no distinction between abuses of wildlife such as poaching and uncontrolled market hunting, and legitimate taking of legal game by law-abiding sport hunters.

There are instances in the past, however, when hunting in the name of sport has contributed to the decline of wildlife, but it never has been the sole cause of the extinction of a species. Hunting for sport played a part in the slaughter of the American bison, although it alone would not have caused a substantial decline in the herds. Big-game hunters— mostly kings, princes, and army officers—shot thousands of tigers in

India during the British colonial rule, but this is not the main reason why the tiger is endangered. The plight of the tiger has been created by commercial hunting for the fur trade, and even more by the destruction of the habitat it needs to survive. A good gauge of just how much effect sport hunting has had on the disappearance of wildlife is the fact that only two of the thirty-two extinct varieties of birds native to the fifty states ever were hunted for sport.

Actually, in the fifty years since the beginning of modern game management in the United States, the populations of most animals hunted for sport have increased. At the turn of the century only 500,000 white-tail deer remained in the entire nation. Today this heavily hunted species numbers almost 10,000,000 animals, and according to some estimates even more. The 250,000 elk in the United States today are five times the number that existed in 1910. Wild turkeys have risen from 100,000 birds in 1952 to more than 1,000,000 today, and are hunted in more than half of the states.

Proper wildlife management dictates that only animals which are

An illustration sketched in 1888 showed what the artist envisioned as the perils of elephant hunting. Today most of the danger has been eliminated from hunting big game.

biologically surplus may be harvested by hunters. When this principle is followed, as it is in the United States, sport hunting cannot lead to the extinction of any game species.

Sport hunters, moreover, have been a major force in combating the most serious peril facing wildlife—the loss of habitat. A bullet or trap may kill individual members of a species but if the habitat required by the species is eliminated, all of its members will vanish. By saving land for game, hunters have kept it for other animals as well.

For most of this century, hunters were the heart of the conservation movement, and furnished many of its early leaders. Theodore Roosevelt, a founding father of modern conservation, was a hunter. So was George Grinnell, who helped found the nation's first Audubon society, and Gifford Pinchot, first head of the United States Forest Service.

The sporting-arms industry, which naturally has a high stake in seeing that hunting remains in a good light, stress that hunters contribute vast amounts of money to wildlife conservation. And it is true. Since 1934 the federal stamps that must be purchased by anyone who hunts migratory waterfowl have brought in more than $130,000,000 for purchase and lease of wetlands, the nation's most threatened wildlife habitat. The wetlands preserved by the waterfowl stamp program provide a home for fiddler crabs, savannah sparrows, herons, muskrats, and all sorts of other animals besides game birds.

Over the years hunters also have paid almost $2,000,000,000 to their states in license fees, virtually all of which have been spent on conservation and outdoor recreation—not just for hunters but for swimmers, campers, bird watchers, and the rest of the population.

If sport hunters in the United States deserve criticism, it is on two points. The first is that they fail to police their own ranks. Not long ago, in a state-owned waterfowl marsh at the mouth of the Connecticut River, one group of men shot a feral mute swan, a number of pigeons, and even fired a few rounds at a boatman who piloted his craft near their waterfowl blind. The marsh was crowded with other hunters, who roundly cursed the violators, but none of the other hunters made an effort to summon a game warden or the police.

The hunting establishment's other fault is that under the pressure of sportsmen, wildlife management agencies put too much emphasis on increasing the populations of game animals at the expense of other

The warriors of ancient Assyria were dedicated lion hunters. Nobles, princes, and kings of many other ancient Mediterranean cultures also sought the lion as quarry.

species. Increasingly, however, state fish and game agencies are paying more attention to nongame species that need help.

All in all, however, I believe that sport hunting is a highly positive force in American wildlife conservation. Other conservationists may not be as enthusiastic in their praise as I am, and they may have some justification, but no major conservation organization in the nation has taken a stand opposing legitimate sport hunting. Some conservation groups actively support hunting, while others take a fully objective stance, such as that of the National Audubon Society, which is so balanced in its outlook it is worth quoting in full:

> The National Audubon Society, since its origin at the turn of the century, has never been opposed to the hunting of game species if that hunting is done ethically and in accordance with laws and regulations designed to prevent depletion of the wildlife resource. We have made this clear repeatedly in official statements of policy and it remains an Audubon policy.
>
> Two points need clarification. First, we will advocate restrictions on hunting, including the complete closure of a hunting season, whenever

we are convinced that the welfare of the species involved requires it. We would be remiss in our responsibilities as a conservation organization if we failed to implement such convictions. On the other hand, those who have worked with us at close hand know that we insist on sound scientific information before deciding those issues.

Secondly, we do not advocate hunting. This is no contradiction, though some people seem to think it is. Our objective is wildlife and environmental conservation, not the promotion of hunting. We think lots of justifications for hunting are weak ones, and too often exaggerated for commercial reasons, and we do not hesitate to say so when the occasion calls for it. But this does not make us antihunting. We are pushing people to think more clearly about these problems.

Unlike the National Audubon Society, most of the groups that fan antihunting sentiment do not always base their positions solely upon scientific fact, and sometimes take stands based more upon emotion than biological reality.

A spokesman for the Friends of Animals, which is billed as a "humane conservation organization" described her organization's outlook on wildlife conservation for me when she said, "We don't subscribe to any form of wildlife management. We think the animals should be left alone." That kind of policy might work well in the Garden of Eden, but to keep hands off wildlife and let the chips fall where they may in today's world would cause the extinction—not the salvation—of many kinds of animals.

Another antihunting group which has prospered because of the confusion about legitimate hunting and its place in wildlife conservation is the Fund for Animals. Its founder, author Cleveland Amory, archfoe of hunters, advocates the establishment of a Hunt-the-Hunters Hunt Club. With what he attempts to pass off as humor, Amory suggests that people who dislike hunters should go out and kill them.

Amory and similar critics blur the issues involved in the question of hunting. They ride the crest of public indignation over the decline of rare species, yet vent their spleen on hunters who shoot nothing more endangered than a ringneck pheasant or white-tail deer. Meanwhile, the real roots of the problem—the human greed and thoughtlessness that cause the destruction of the environment—are lost in the uproar. What it all boils down to is that Amory and people like him think there is something intrinsically wicked about killing a wild animal.

That is their opinion, and they have a perfect right to it, but not to

Hunters in Nevada have treed a young mountain lion with their dogs. Where the lion is still common, management of it as a game animal affords a means of preservation. Elsewhere the species needs total protection.

force their morality down the throats of others. This, in effect, is what Amory is trying to do to the 20,000,000 Americans who hunt.

Personally, I find it curious that people who rage over shooting a buck can drool over a barbecued hunk of steer or chops hacked from the corpse of a cuddly little lamb. The contradiction smacks of placing wild animals on a higher plane than their domestic kin, as if the wild beasts were somehow superior. Or is it merely that the farther one is from the slaughterhouse, the easier it is to like steak?

Many misconceptions about hunting are indeed based on distance. Sentiment against hunting thrives in cities and suburbs, where a walk in the park is the nearest many people get to the woods. With one or two notable exceptions, for example, most of my friends who live near me in rural eastern Connecticut love to hunt. The majority of my friends who live in New York City and its environs think hunting is abominable, and I cannot convince them otherwise. I generalize, of course, but feel safe in asserting that as the distance from the farm and the open spaces increases, so does prejudice against hunting, or at least puzzlement at why some people need to hunt.

The impasse between hunter and antihunter is to some extent a measure of how much and what kind of contact people have with wild animals. Most naturalists, biologists, and zoologists I have met hunt, or if not, have no objection to people who do. People who blindly oppose hunting, on the other hand, very often have limited exposure to wild animals—perhaps only at the zoo, or when feeding squirrels in the park, for instance. The ranks of antihunters also are filled with people whose ideas about the way animals live in the wild have been colored by the antics of the humanized beasties of the boob tube.

No wonder they cringe at the thought of a deer being shot. They are saddened not by the death of an animal no more nor less noble than a cow, but by the murder of Bambi, dedicated father and husband.

Ironically it is the very animality of the deer—its fleetness, its exquisitely tuned senses, and the strength it exudes in the mating season —that is its true glory. Bambi pales besides the real animal, which the hunter knows far better than the animal lover. The hunter who must understand the way of the deer enough to stalk and kill it gains a deep appreciation for the qualities of the deer. By stalking, killing, and, hopefully, eating his quarry the hunter experiences wild animals in a way that is unique, and which I believe is the reason why so many professional biologists and conservationists are hunters. It is the only way I can answer people who ask me, "How can you be a naturalist and hunt animals?"

I thought about it one autumn morning when the air was so clear and sparkling that it seems as if the bare trees in the woods behind my home were made of crystal. The sky was a cold blue, as blue as I have seen it anywhere in the world. I had just stepped out the back door when, from beyond the trees, I heard the ringing cry of a Canada goose. As I looked up, squinting in the brightness, a flight of a dozen of the big birds brushed the treetops and, only a few feet above my roof, flared their wings as they braked for a landing in the pond across the road.

In the crystalline atmosphere of that early morning, caught in the dazzle of the new sun, the geese literally sparkled as they passed over-head—and I could hear the shivering whir of the wind on their outspread wings. I can truly say that as the geese passed overhead I marveled at their splendor and thanked God for creating them. Simultaneously, I had another reaction. I yearned for a chance to shoot one of the geese from the sky. As it was, the hunting season on geese was closed, and anyway, I had no shotgun in my hands, but I hoped deeply that when the season opened, the geese would come again.

If antihunters see my reaction as worthy of a Jekyll and Hyde, I submit it was no more schizophrenic than most of man's responses to the animals which share our planet and our destiny. My shooting of a goose is much more humane than the declawing of a pet cat. Moreover, the emotion the geese evoked in me was favorable in terms of the survival of their species.

How? I can explain only in this way:

The geese symbolize the wilderness, or whatever remains of it. Canada geese are prospering, and I have little fear they will vanish from the scene. Before they do, however, they may become fat semidomes-ticated fowl with greasy flesh, dulled instincts, and absolute dependence on handouts of bread and corn at ponds in city parks. The sight of the geese flying free in the sky inspires me to devote my efforts toward keeping wild places for wild things like them. Nature is giving way under the onslaught of man; every river running with the lubricious spewings of industry, every dredged-out marsh, proclaims the horror of that fact. But the geese refute that nature is already dead. As long as they are free to come and go in the autumn sky—and I am free to hunt them—I feel a little wildness remains in the world.

It is not the same for all people who love nature. Some persevere and are inspired to keep the faith by just watching. And that works for me, too, yet my commitment to keeping wild places and wild creatures is fueled even more when I hunt, for I feel a sense of participating in nature.

I have observed the magnificence of wild animals over much of the world and under many seas. I have listened in the darkness as the coughing rumble of lions rolled across the African landscape and have watched a tiger poised on a ridgeline above a herd of Sambar deer. I have watched in the Everglades as a bald eagle swooped low over a slough, where an alligator a dozen feet long slid through the water. My hunting has been confined to the narrow limits of the state of Connecticut, and the quarry has been no more exotic than deer and ducks. Yet never has nature seemed so precious as when I have been crouched in a soggy duck blind, listening to the stiff whisper of the brown *Spartina* grasses, watching a teal streak towards the decoys, and wondering if I will be quick enough to take it with a shot.

Why do I hunt? Because for all but the last few moments of our existence, our species has been a race of hunters. Because when man hunted for survival, he was as much a part of nature as the animals he killed, and I seek to recapture that niche. Because I feel the need to reaffirm my manhood. Because by hunting I prove that I am part of nature, and perhaps also, like the hunters of the cave bear, that I can cope with nature's challenge.

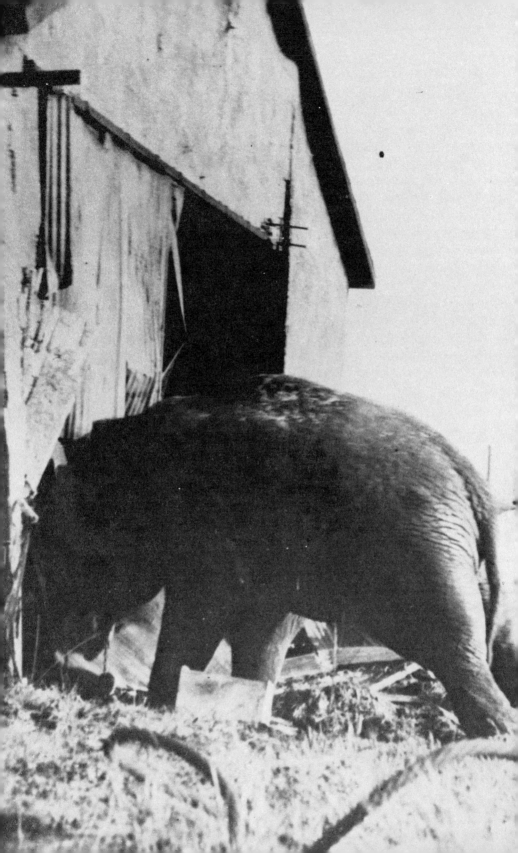

5. MAN'S OWN ANIMALS

LONG BEFORE THE END of prehistory, man used the knowledge he had accumulated as a hunter to establish the ultimate form of exploitation of the animal kingdom—domestication. Since then there has appeared an entirely new assemblage of animals; the product not of natural evolution, but of selected breeding planned and directed by man. These creatures created by man have but one reason for existing, to serve humans by providing them with food, doing their work, or pleasuring them as pets.

That man the hunter should have become the tamer of animals and eventually the creator of completely new species is not at all surprising in the light of hunting man's intimate relationship with his prey. After all, early man had to know enough about wild animals to successfully stalk and kill them. This fact was more than sufficient motivation to make the ancient hunter an expert naturalist, deeply cognizant of the ways of wild creatures and the patterns governing their lives.

Given the powerful human instinct for taking advantage of all that the animal kingdom offers, it is only natural that insight into the biology

"Tusko," a bull elephant kept in a shed in Portland, Oregon, escaped from his chains one day in 1931 and destroyed his former abode. He later calmed down and was rechained.

of animals sparked new ideas about how to exploit them. It was only a step from driving herds of game over a cliff to corraling wild sheep and goats in gullies or ravines, where they were easy to catch for the cooking pot. At that point, the prey became possessions and the hunter a herdsman.

Eventually another dimension was added to human control of animals as people learned to breed them for traits that were valued, such as heavy flesh or passivity. Man has designed his own animals, creatures whose evolution has been manipulated for human ends. The bodies and behavior of domestic animals have been shaped in ways that make them useful to man—they are biologically engineered, so to speak, solely for service to humanity. For no other purpose do these creatures exist.

Strong mutual interdependence links man and the animals that exist only because of him. Man breeds his animals, feeds them, cleans up after them, protects them, provides them with shelter and very often medical care. Many domestic creatures, such as the shivery little chihuahua and the fat, high-strung Angus steer, are travesties of their wild forebears, suited only to the world of man. On their own, without man's help, such creatures could not survive.

In turn, domestic animals have deeply influenced the evolution of human society. Once prehistoric man had domesticated animals, he rose above the animals in that no longer was he totally dependent upon the vagaries of nature for survival. No longer was he purely a predator subject to the law of the jungle, but he was able instead to exercise some control over nature in the form of his tame cows, pigs, sheep, and goats.

With meat, milk, and cheese available from domestic stock, men were released from the endless task of following game. While not responsible for the beginnings of urban life, domestication certainly encouraged it, especially in parts of the world such as the Near East, where climate, terrain, and presence of the right kinds of animals led to the establishment of the first towns and cities.

Starting more than 5,000 years ago, the use of draft animals vastly increased the expanse of land farmers could plow, provided power to drive machines such as grist mills, and eventually to transport for man as well as his baggage. Beasts of burden helped build cities, and later when assess, horses, and elephants were pressed into service for war, helped destroy them as well. Time and again, for example, new ways to use the horse—first to pull chariots, then under a single rider, and later with stirrups—shifted the balance of military power between nations and altered the course of history.

Domestic animals have proliferated until today there are somewhere in the neighborhood of 7,000,000,000 of them. Americans tend to think of them in terms of cattle, horses, cats, and dogs—there are at least 100,000,000 cats and dogs in the United States. Elsewhere in the world, however, a surprising variety of beasts have been yoked into human service ranging from llamas to elephants. The number of domesticated Asian water buffalo in the world alone totals 150,000,000 beasts.

Ironically, as the numbers of man's animals have increased, the wild creatures molded by millions of years of natural evolution are declining. Adaptations enabling them to survive under normal conditions lag behind the rapid environmental changes caused by man. Moreover, wild animals often suffer from the pressures of competing with man and his creatures. Overgrazing by the Masai cattle herds has turned lush East African pastures into dusty wasteland no longer capable of supporting game animals. Coyotes and eagles are shot and poisoned by sheepmen in the western states, allegedly because these predators take lambs. The world's last truly wild horse, *Equus przewalski,* goes thirsty in the Gobi Desert because nomads have taken over waterholes for livestock. Many wild creatures have been driven to the brink of extinction because of their domestic cousins.

DANGERS IN OUR MIDST

Domestic animals are so much a part of our life, in the city as well as on the farm, that we tend to take them for granted. The importance of the role they play in human society is often forgotten, and so is the fact that in creating domestic animals man has produced some killers without parallel in the wild. The ranks of domestic animals include the only creatures deliberately bred and trained by man to kill other men; one of the forms of domestication is the use of animals as weapons of war.

Under circumstances which are not uncommon, many kinds of domestic animals can be far more dangerous to man than wild beasts; many more people are attacked by dogs than by wild animals in America.

Like all other domestic animals, dogs are the creation of man but were bred from a wild animal, probably the wolf or some creature very similar to it. Thus we share our homes and streets with carnivores closely related to wolves; often as big, and sometimes trained to be much more vicious than the gray hunters of the wild ever are toward man. While most people who saw a wolf on the streets would either run from it or shoot at it, they accept dogs as a matter of course.

Thus people will not tolerate big, wild animals in their midst but readily live side by side with dogs, horses, and cattle, many of which have the size and physical weapons to do great harm. The potential danger of many domestic animals eludes most people and causes considerable misfortune, as does the occasional tendency of some domestic beasts to revert to the ways of their wild ancestors.

DANGER ON THE FARM

Domestic pigs, so close biologically to the wild boar that the two can interbreed, often show evidence of their savage ancestry. A domestic sow will fight viciously in defense of her young, and smart farmers tread carefully around piglets. It also is a good idea to keep an eye on small children if there are pigs in the barnyard, because they have been said to attack youngsters, ostensibly in order to devour them.

A bizarre incident in which pigs consumed a corpse that had been prepared for a wake occurred about 1912 in the mountains of southern Puerto Rico, near the town of Guayama. Many of the people who inhabited the mountains lived in houses made of thatch and palm built on stilts, below which lived pigs and other barnyard animals.

A man living in such a house had died and his family held a wake to mourn him. The body lay in a plain wooden coffin which was left inside one room of the house. As darkness fell, and rum was passed out freely among the men who had come to pay their respects, a candle was lighted near the coffin.

Rum continued to flow and before long it evoked memories of an old family feud. In short order a brawl erupted and machetes, which all the men carried in those days, began to flash. In the melée, the candle fell over and was extinguished, and the coffin was overturned so violently

The Greek general Pyrrhus used war elephants to defeat the Romans in southern Italy.

it crashed through the floor, spilling the body out into the midst of the pigs. Before anyone could discover the body, and drive off the pigs, they had eaten most of the corpse.

Trying to drive a hungry pig away from its dinner can be a risky job, as an Altamonte Springs, Florida, man discovered recently. A 265-pound hog that his neighbor kept as a pet wandered into the man's yard and began to root in a flower bed. The man grabbed a shovel, and tried to chase the hog with it, but the hog was not frightened. Instead it charged him, knocked him down, and bit his arm. After sheriff's deputies were summoned to the scene, the hog was impounded.

Like pigs, domestic cattle originated from a powerful, aggressive wild beast, the aurochs, a huge wild ox that once ranged from Britain south to northern Africa and all across Eurasia to the shores of the Pacific Ocean. Agile, with great horns, the aurochs had a reputation for fierce courage and immense strength. Long after it had been bred down into domestic cattle, the aurochs was hunted by medieval nobility, and its horns furnished drinking cups for kings and princes. Excessive hunting, together with the destruction of the wilderness it needed to survive, pushed the aurochs over the brink of extinction by the end of the Middle

Ages. The last of these huge oxen died in 1627 in Poland.

Aurochs blood lives on, however, in virtually all modern strains of cattle, although in the 7,000 years cattle have been domesticated most breeds have become mere shadows of their spirited wild ancestor. The spirit and savagery of the aurochs remains only in a few varieties, most notably the Spanish fighting bull.

To a varying degree, the bulls of any type of domestic cattle can be dangerous. This is especially true if they are not naturally hornless, or if their horns have not been removed. Dehorning a bull, particularly if it is kept in close quarters with people, can save lives, as it probably saved the life of my wife's uncle several years ago.

He was attacked and battered by a hornless Holstein bull while herding cattle towards a tick bath on his father's farm in Puerto Rico. When the bull balked at entering the bath, he prodded it with a stick, whereupon the animal turned and charged, slamming him against a barbed wire fence. Although shaken, he was not seriously injured; but had the bull carried horns, the episode might have been fatal.

Failure to dehorn a bull cost the life of a Scott County, Virginia, farmer in May 1975. The farmer, I.L. Stallard, Jr., was moving the bull, a 1,000-pound Hereford, from one pasture to another when the animal attacked him. No one witnessed the actual attack, but Stallard's mother heard her son scream and went to the pasture to see what had happened. She found her son on the ground, with the bull looming over him. The woman picked up a stick and drove off the bull, which Stallard had raised from a calf.

The bull had driven a horn deep into the chest of its victim, who was a large, powerful man used to handling the animal. The bull's thrust was so vicious it not only penetrated the chest cavity but pierced the aorta as well.

A few weeks before the incident, a friend of mine, who also farms in Scott County, visited with Stallard and advised him to dehorn his bull. Stallard said he did not want to pay a veterinarian to do the job.

TREED BY A BULL

The old saw about familiarity breeding contempt is right on the mark with respect to the way people in cattle-raising areas so often take bulls for granted, a fact brought home to me by two incidents in which I was involved in Puerto Rico. The scene of both encounters was a brush-bearded cliff that slants upward 1,500 feet from the sea near the town of Yabucoa, on the southeastern corner of the island. I often visit a beach colony which is perched near the base of the cliff, where heavy surf booms on beaches of red and black sand.

Although a winding narrow dirt road permits automobiles to travel up and down the cliff, the going is easiest on horseback, trail bike, or foot along paths that cut through the head-high brush beyond the beach houses. Many of these paths are made by cattle which neighboring farmers release to feed in the brush.

Seasonal streams that flow from the heights to the sea have slashed deep ravines in the face of the cliff. Sometimes several hundred feet deep, the ravines are filled to the lip with tangles of lush tropical growth that shelters a large variety of birds.

I went to the edge of one deep ravine to watch the birds early one morning a few years ago. With cameras and field glasses slung over my shoulders, I started down one of the cattle trails towards the bottom of the ravine. As I walked along I suddenly heard the drumming of hooves from the maze of greenery that blocked my vision of the trail below. Knowing that bulls as well as cows roamed free in the area, and not even wanting to bump into a running cow on the narrow trail, I turned, ran back up to the rim of the ravine and climbed on to a mango tree whose thick trunk jutted out horizontally over the small valley.

The hoofbeats came closer and in a few moments a large brown cow lumbered up the trail below my branch, then headed off into the brush. Feeling a bit foolish, I climbed down from the tree and turned back into the ravine. As I did, the bull which had been following the cow at a gallop came crashing up the trail. Reverting to the ways of my very early ancestors, I scampered up the tree again, cameras and field glasses swinging and banging together. The bull intent on its pursuit of the cow, pounded on by, not even looking up at me. Even so, I waited until I could no longer hear the creature plowing through the brush before I came down.

Not long after that, another bull wandered out of the brush and spent almost an hour terrorizing the beach colony by rampaging through its streets and people's yards. This creature was a huge black animal, with loppy ears and humped shoulders indicating it was part Brahma.

The creature appeared at dusk as we were loading the car and preparing to leave after a weekend at the beach. Looking about for a moment, the bull snorted and thundered down the street, lofting its ponderous bulk up and over the low fences around cottages, trampling through lawns, and across the porch of one of the houses. We scattered like the few other poeple who were on the street, and ran indoors, watching as the bull lorded it over the neighborhood for more than a half hour before returning to the brush.

RAMPAGE BY ELEPHANTS

The hazards of a bull on the loose in the streets pale before the havoc that can be created by an elephant running wild. Westerners sometimes forget that in Asia elephants of the species *Elephas maximus* have been domesticated for 5,000 years. Responsive largely to touch, either by hand or "elephant hook," the Asiatic elephant generally obeys its masters docilely but intelligently. If one of these creatures runs amok, the results can be catastrophic.

An example of an elephant rampage at its worst took place about forty years ago in Thailand (then Siam), when two tame pachyderms stormed through the streets of Bangkok. Both animals, which belonged to the Royal Elephant Stables of Siam, often appeared in ceremonial processions. The larger of the two, Thong Kham by name, was seized by a periodic agitation called *"musth,"* which is peculiar to male Asiatic elephants. In his fit, Thong Kham turned on a smaller stablemate, Siri Nan, who broke his chains and lumbered off into the streets. Thong Kham, also free, careened off in another direction.

Siri Nan wandered about, frightened and confused, until he crossed a bridge over a river in front of an exclusive school for girls. The weight of the elephant was too much for the bridge, and its timbers cracked, plunging Siri Nan into the water. Wedged between the pilings of the bridge, with his tusks jammed into the mud on the river bottom, Siri Nan was in serious trouble. Scores of people rushed to the scene to try and pull the elephant free, but imprisoned as he was by mud and the splintered remains of the bridge, he drowned before he could be rescued.

Meanwhile, Thong Kham was thundering about on more grisly

business. As the bull elephant lurched down the street an old man, perhaps somewhat deaf, failed to hear him coming. The elephant flattened the man, then stomped him to a bloody paste before moving on.

That Thong Kham had become a danger to the city was obvious, and a truckload of soldiers was dispatched to stop the bull. As the vehicle approached Thong Kham, he took the offensive. Ears spread and trunk in the air, the elephant charged head-on at the truck as the soldiers emptied from it and scrambled for their lives. The truck crumpled as the elephant piled into it, buckling its metal and dumping it upside down in his rage.

After demolishing the truck, Thong Kham turned and retraced his steps in the direction of the stables. On the way he smashed several homes, but after a few hours, quietly returned to his point of origin.

Although Thong Kham had started to calm down, he was now deemed a murderous menace to the populace, and sentenced to death. The elephant's keeper was ordered to poison bananas with strychnine

Elephants have been used in wars in Asia right down to modern times, as this old campaign photo shows. During the Indochinese conflict, the Viet Cong and North Vietnamese used elephants to carry supplies.

and feed them to the creature. Thong Kham consumed the bananas, and died.

THE EARLIEST TANK

The military potential of the elephant was recognized by generals thousands of years ago. Elephants were the first tanks, for in ancient warfare they served a function similar to that of armor today; the generals of ancient India fashioned their tactics around the deployment of war elephants.

The Indian armies were composed of four divisions—cavalry, chariots, infantry, and troop-carrying elephants. Ridden by lancers and bowmen, the elephants were shielded with heavy leather. Their tusks were tipped with spikes and sometimes the pachyderms even were trained to wield swords with their trunks, making them an altogether terrifying weapon.

Understandably, armies opposed to elephants for the first time tended to break and run at the sight of these animals. However, there was a catch to the effective use of elephants in war: once the opposition learned that elephants panicked easily, means of thwarting the beasts were quickly devised. Fire, concerted discharge of arrows, and mobile cavalry all served to counter an assault by elephant troops. Once burned, stung by a rain of arrows, or frightened by horsemen dashing among them and jabbing them with lances and swords, elephants were as likely to stampede through their own army as the ranks of the enemy.

THE ELEPHANTS OF PORUS

The famed Indian king Porus, a giant and a soldier who in defeat won the respect of Alexander the Great, deployed 200 war elephants when his army took to the field against Alexander in 326 B.C. The armies of the two leaders met at the river Hydaspes, now called the Jhelum, in northern India.

Porus ranged his elephants along the eastern bank of the river to block any attempt at crossing the stream by Alexander's forces. Alexander, however, sent troops far upstream, outflanking the elephants, and the battle was joined on the eastern shore of the river.

When the elephants charged into Alexander's army, his archers picked off their drivers, while his infantry frightened the masterless creatures by clashing shields together. Trumpeting in panic the elephants were useless to the Indians, and nullified as a weapon.

Porus himself fought from the back of a great war elephant. Renowned for his bravery and great personal strength, the Indian warrior nevertheless was captured and brought before his conqueror. Asked by Alexander how he should be treated by his captors, Porus supposedly drew himself up and declared, "Like a king," which, in fact, is what Alexander did.

ROMANS, PIGS, AND PACHYDERMS

A descendant of Alexander's line, the professional soldier Pyrrhus of Epirus, introduced the Romans to the horrors of fighting war elephants late in the third century B.C. Pyrrhus had come from Greece with his army to help Greek colonies in Italy curb the spread of Roman power. With only twenty war elephants, he almost accomplished that goal.

In a series of devestating battles his elephants smashed through the Roman lines, putting up the tough legionaries to flight. It was only a matter of time, however, before the Romans, like other soldiers before them, learned that elephants were not invincible.

During one engagement between the two armies, swine kept in the Roman encampment broke loose and rushed among the elephants. Frightened at the pigs scurrying through their ranks, the elephants bolted. This event so heartened the Romans that they later issued copper bars commemorating it. The bars of metal pictured an elephant on one side and a pig on the other.

Another story tells how the Romans took heart from the bravery of a young legionary who when faced by an elephant leaped at it and sliced away its trunk with his sword. Screaming in pain, the trunkless elephant turned and trampled through the Greek troops.

Despite such bravery, the Romans never gained the upper hand over

Pyrrhus. He was forced to disengage and return to Greece, however, because even in winning he had lost so many men that his victories were virtually meaningless. From this campaign more than 2,000 years ago, the term, "Pyrrhic victory" is derived.

WAR HORSES

No other animal has influenced the outcome of so many battles as the horse. The importance of the horse in battle is dramatically portrayed in Shakespeare's play, *Richard III*, when King Richard of England, unhorsed and beaten by Henry Tudor on the field of Bosworth, cries out, "A horse, a horse. My kingdom for a horse."

Long before the Middle Ages, horses employed in warfare had shaped the fate of kingdoms and even empires. Domesticated on the plains of southern Russia about 5,500 years ago, the horse was first utilized in war to pull chariots. Waves of Indo-European invaders who fanned out from the Russian steppes during the third and second millennia B.C. rode crude chariots through Europe and India as they supplanted the native peoples of those regions.

After 2,000 B.C. the horse-drawn chariot appeared in the Near East. About 1,700 B.C. nomadic invaders called Hyksos, or "shepherd kings," swept into Egypt on light two-wheeled chariots, crushed the Egyptian infantry, and established themselves in Upper Egypt for more than a century. The Hyksos were driven from Egypt only after the Egyptians mastered the horse chariot and its deployment in warfare.

It took another thousand years before the mounted cavalryman became a major force in battle, and again the new technique came from the Eurasian steppes. Scythian nomads developed the skills needed to ride horses and fight effectively at the same time. By now horses had been bred to a larger size than the ponies which first were domesticated, thus making the mounted warrior possible.

The invention of the stirrup, which occurred in the Far East and reached Europe around the sixth century, made the horseman supreme in battle for more than 700 years, until the longbow, firearms and other hand weapons were employed by infantry. Stirrups provided the stability and support that turned horsemen into armored knights.

A heavily armored knight needed a large, sturdy horse, which led to the development of the huge war horses of the Middle Ages. These horses probably owe their origin to powerful steeds bred by peoples such as the Parthians of Iran and the ancient Armenians; the horses apparently reached Western Europe through the Eastern Roman Empire.

The medieval war horse was more than transport. Knights trained their mounts to bite and kick at the enemy and at opposing mounts in the heat of battle.

THE DOGS OF WAR

When medieval armies entered the field, they often were accompanied not only by horses but by troops of vicious fighting dogs. Chiefly mastiffs or huge hounds and similar to the Irish wolfhound, war dogs were loosed upon both opposing soldiers and the canine troops of the enemy.

Mastiffs were sent from England to aid Charles V in his struggles with the French during the mid-16th century. The French countered with war dogs of their own. In one particularly vicious encounter the English dogs won the day and sent the French animals whimpering for cover.

The Spanish conquistadors carried war dogs with them to the New World. Cortez, the conquerer of Mexico, unleashed mastiffs trained to run down men and tear out their throats against his Indian foes. A painting now in a British museum shows Balboa, discoverer of the Pacific Ocean, watching and chatting with his men as Indians are savaged by a pack of dogs.

The use of dogs in war was not a medieval invention, for dogs, domesticated more than 14,000 years ago, have fought at man's side since ancient times. The Assyrians and Greeks set mastiffs against their enemies. The Romans organized their war dogs into special units, a fact perhaps recognized by Shakespeare in the play *Julius Caesar* when Mark Antony cries out over Caesar's corpse, "Cry havoc and let slip the dogs of war."

Unlike horses, dogs have continued to play an important role in warfare. Modern armies have used dogs as sentries, pickets, messengers,

A staged photo from World War II shows how dogs—in this case
a Doberman pinscher—were used to guard military bases.

and carriers of medical supplies. During World War I, Italian troops
stationed Maremma sheep dogs several hundred yards ahead of their
lines to warn of the approach of enemy troops. Both the German and
French armies had thousands of dogs with them in the trenches of the
First World War. The canines carried dispatches and medicine for the
wounded.

German shepherds and Doberman pinschers landed with the United States Marines during the Pacific campaign of World War II. On several occasions the keen senses of the war dogs warned American troops of enemy ambushes.

Dogs also saw action during the United States involvement in Indochina. In the Indochinese jungles the dogs encountered a hazard even more dangerous than enemy fire. Nosing about the undergrowth, the dogs were highly vulnerable to the many venomous snakes of the region. Several dogs were killed by serpents; one dog was fatally bitten when it shoved its handler out of the way of a snake's strike.

DOGS FOR A NEW KIND OF WAR

The nature of the war in Indochina caused a radical change in the type of dog used in combat, and for most military tasks. Until midway through the war in southeast Asia, the main type of dog utilized by the military was the "sentry dog," an animal trained to alert its handler of anyone's approach and to attack anyone but the handler. In 1958 the Sentry Dog Training Branch was established at Lackland Air Force Base in Texas to train dogs and handlers for all the services.

Sentry dogs are conditioned to attack by a process called "agitation," a program of controlled harassment during which the dog's aggressive tendencies are raised to a fever pitch. This is the standard method of training an attack dog.

Military dogs are not physically abused during agitation, which begins with a trainer's teasing the dog. A friend of mine in charge of sentry dogs at a Navy communications base in Morocco several years ago remembers how in one case the teasing worked too well. A German shepherd which was agitated while tethered broke free and with a single bite laid open the chest of the trainer, baring his ribs. German shepherds, favored as military dogs, have a tremendously powerful bite. A shepherd of 60 pounds in weight can exert a pressure of 400 pounds per square inch with its jaws, more than enough to crush a man's arm.

My friend recalls how a thief who had entered the base in Morocco to steal cable was bitten so savagely by a sentry dog that his leg was broken and so mangled it required more than 100 stitches to close his wounds. It took the dog less than a minute to do the damage.

For obvious reasons when the dog's training progresses to where it must be permitted to bite the agitator, he wears a heavily padded suit and a facial protector.

When an attack dog is after you and you are unarmed, the chances of coming out unscratched are so slight that there really is only one way to fight the animal. That is to sacrifice an arm, using it to take the dog's bite while you attempt to rip out its windpipe with the other hand before the shock of the bite fells you.

Today the Army and Marines still use some dogs of the sentry type in places, such as the boundaries of high-security military bases, where the only people likely to approach will be intruders with no right to be there. The sentry dog, in other words, is most useful for what military men call "static security," a situation where the lines between the dog and the potential enemy are well defined and not subject to change, and where there is little danger of it attacking an innocent person.

The fluid lines of the guerrilla war in Indochina, however, reduced the value of the sentry dog. Moreover, the sentry dog warns its handler by barking, which can prove disadvantageous in counterinsurgency operations where silence and stealth are at a premium.

The Air Force, which has the responsibility for the entire military dog training program, decided a new type of animal was needed, and evolved the concept for what is now known as the patrol dog. The overriding characteristic of the patrol dog is versatility. It can scout and track, detect the enemy but keep silent, work closely with people other than its handler without endangering them, and yet on the command of the handler, attack as viciously as the sentry dog.

The only breed trained as patrol dog is the German shepherd, not because it is the best scout, tracker, or attack dog, but because it can do *all* jobs reasonable well. It is aggressive but not vicious, big but not gigantic, and has two coats—an outer and inner—which make it adaptable to the full range of climatic conditions.

The major difference between the sentry dog and patrol dog is that the patrol dog is "controllably aggressive"; it initiates or halts attack instantly on command. The only exception to this rule is if someone assaults the dog's handler. In that case, the dog attacks on its own initiative.

Patrol dogs are so conditioned to command that they will halt an attack in mid-charge, and can be trusted around crowds of people, even youngsters; they are extremely useful for military law enforcement duties, such as escorting payrolls and patrolling a base housing area. At the same time, the patrol dog can perform the same jobs as a sentry dog. In an attack situation, the two types of dog are indistinguishable, except that the patrol dog can be stopped with just one word from its handler.

The handler needs only two commands to control the patrol dog's aggression. "Get him" triggers the attack; "out" stops it. The dog's unfailing response to the commands is developed during a twelve-week training course for both animal and handler.

At first, patrol dogs are agitated just like sentry dogs, but as training continues, the dog is given approval for halting the attack at his handler's command as well as launching it. This is the most difficult part of the animal's conditioning.

DOGS AGAINST CROWDS

Like the military, law-enforcement agencies use dogs for a variety of tasks, ranging from finding lost children to detecting caches of marijuana by scent. Police use dogs, chiefly German shepherds, to disperse mobs and demonstrations, a fact which became apparent to many Americans for the first time in 1963, when Birmingham, Alabama, police set dogs upon civil-rights demonstrators. News agencies transmitted photographs showing the dogs, fangs bared, straining at the end of six-foot leashes as they bounded at frightened people. Naturally, the photographs provoked considerable controversy about the use of guard dogs by police, a policy that minority groups have claimed is directed mainly at them. The same week that dogs were used to harry the Birmingham demonstrators, however, college youths massed for a high-spirited march on downtown Providence, Rhode Island, also were met with and dispersed by police employing guard dogs.

The sight of a big dog, snarling, with lips drawn back over curved fangs, is much more frightening to most people than even an armed policeman waving a billy club. Something about the dog strikes at fears rooted deeply in man's psyche, the human terror of the power of the beast, perhaps.

Almost any big, tough, guard dog can give a mob reason for pause, but a breed used by police in Germany also has a powerful physical impact—quite literally—upon crowds. This is the Rottweiler, a stocky, unusually strong animal whose ancestors were brought to southern Germany 2,000 years ago by the Roman legions. I know a considerable amount about these bull-necked creatures because I own one.

Weighing more than 100 pounds, but marvelously compact at the same time, the Rottweiler has served both as a guard dog and cattle herder. A Rottweiler assigned to guard a herd will pursue errant cows and by bounding sideways against their flanks, shove them back in the direction of the herd. A big Rottweiler is said to be able to knock a running cow off its feet in this manner.

This ability, together with the dog's aggressiveness—which shows up in its descendant, the Doberman pinscher—caught the fancy of German police about the turn of the century. A dog capable of knocking over a cow would have no trouble bowling over people, the police reasoned, and the Rottweiler was adopted for use in crowd control. Actually, the interest of police in the breed saved it, for the pure Rottweiler stock almost had vanished.

Typical of how police use Rottweilers is a story I was recently told of how two of the dogs broke up a crowd stoning an American army barracks in Germany a few years ago. Police were summoned to the scene and arrived in front of the barracks in a van. Using a bullhorn, the police ordered the crowd to disperse, while they brought from the van a pair of black-and-brown dogs on leashes. The mob paid no heed to the command, so police unleashed the Rottweilers, which stormed into the crowd.

"All of a sudden," says an American soldier who witnessed the incident from within the barracks, "people started going down." Springing first at one demonstrator, then another, the dogs went about their job with cool precision, and in moments had toppled several people to the ground. The members of the mob still on their feet broke and ran.

CANINE SECURITY

Many businesses and industries have taken a cue from the police and military establishments and use guard dogs to protect their properties. Dogs patrol lots where new automobiles are stored, industrial plants, and department stores. In some stores, security dogs are released to roam the aisles at night after closing; mere knowledge that somewhere in the building dogs are on the loose is enough to deter many burglars.

The large working breeds are the ones generally used for civilian security. German shepherds, Dobermans, Rottweilers, Bull mastiffs, Great Danes, Bouvier des Flandres, and several others all have the bulk, strength, and aggressiveness to handle the job.

Several such breeds are naturally protective because they were developed to guard livestock from wild animals and even human raiders. Some of them were also fighting dogs and, like the Bull mastiff and Rottweiler, have long been used to guard some men against others.

Years—even centuries—of breeding have made these dogs extremely protective of their master and people and property they associate with him. Someone who acts in a manner that the dog perceives as threatening to what is under its protection may find himself confronting a thoroughly aroused beast capable of inflicting serious injury or worse.

Dogs with strong guard instinct have little choice but to react the way they do, just as a sporting dog such as the Brittany spaniel instinctively points at game birds without being taught.

As a case in point, I have only to consider my Rottweiler. Before the dog was a year old, I learned that the owner of a guard breed always must keep his dog's instinct and capabilities to do harm in mind. I had invited some graduate students to carry on studies of bats in a marshy area near my home one summer night. After spending a few hours in the marsh, they returned to say good-bye.

Talking and laughing, they burst unannounced through the front door into the living room where my wife and I were sitting, with the young dog lying on the floor a few feet away; in a split second the dog underwent a frightening transformation. What had been a drowsy, relaxed pup exploded with a rumbling snarl and launched itself at what it believed were intruders. As the dog hurtled past me I managed to grab the thick collar around its neck and shouted a command for it to stop. The dog obeyed, although it continued to eye the students, whose ashen faces testified how close we had come to tragedy.

The episode demonstrates how quickly a dog like mine, good-natured most of the time, can become a menace. In most such cases, it

is not the disposition of the dog that undergoes a change. In specific circumstances all dogs—not only guard breeds—bite. The fact that they do so is part of being dogs. It is up to the owner to make sure that his dog is not exposed to the conditions that make the animal dangerous— the dog cannot be expected to avoid them.

Fortunately for me and my guests I learned this lesson at the cost of only a few moments' fright and an apology. One of the grim facts of life in the United States today is that many people are learning the same lesson at a much more expensive and painful price—even at the cost of human life.

THE DOG-BITE EPIDEMIC

The number of attacks on people by dogs has reached what public health officials consider an epidemic in the United States. Each year dogs sink their fangs into at least 1,000,000 Americans. This means that at one time or another one out of every 200 Americans can expect to be the victim of a dog bite.

The magnitude of the dog-bite menace emerges from the examination of studies made of the problem by various health agencies. A survey begun in 1971 by the federal Center for Disease Control shows that dogs attack more people by far than any other animals in the land. The center sampled several parts of the country for a year and came up with these telling statistics:

—Of 112,094 bites in the sample, 84 percent were inflicted by dogs.

—Of the remainder, cats were responsible for only 10 percent; rodents 4 percent; and skunks, foxes, and other wild animals, the remaining 2 percent.

The astonishing increase in dog bites has been documented in several urban areas. Until 1965, for example, the number of people bitten by dogs in New York City each year remained constant, at about 28,500

A vicious sentry dog stands guard over a Navy installation in Viet Nam.

victims. Starting in 1965, however, the toll of victims began to mount with frightening rapidity; by 1970, it had increased more than 30 percent, so that now about 38,000 New Yorkers require treatment for bites each year, at a cost of about $50 per victim.

During 1972 a total of 6,922 dog bites were reported in Baltimore, Maryland, which represents almost a 150 percent increase over the number of bites there in 1953. Another study, in St. Louis, indicated that one out of every fifty children in that city between the ages of five and nine years is bitten by a dog each year, and 10 percent of these young victims suffer wounds so serious they require stitching. Between 1960 and 1970, the dog bite rate in St. Louis, and in Washington, D.C. doubled.

As meaningful to me as these formal studies is a quick survey I made one morning in 1975 of 10 youngsters in a Sunday school class which I was teaching. Nine of the children either had been bitten by dogs, or had family members who had been victims.

Most victims of dog bite—and probably most fatalities—are in fact children, which makes the mounting incidence of bites even more grim. The case histories and studies to be cited later in the chapter will further clarify the dismaying extent of the problem and what contributes to it, but briefly, the causes of the dogbite epidemic are these:

—Americans have gone pet crazy. Half as many dogs and cats as people live within the nation's borders. Of the total, dogs number about 50,000,000.

—Many pet owners are either ignorant of the needs and behavior of their dogs, or simply do not care. The animals are often subjected to exceptional strain, or allowed to run free.

—A substantial number of dogs owned by Americans are large aggressive breeds, and not only is ownership of such breeds increasing, but many of these dogs are trained to attack.

—With an eye towards cashing in on the public appetite for large dogs, many breeders are mass-producing puppies with little regard for quality. The products of these puppy-mills often are nervous, ill-tempered and neurotic.

Figures from the American Kennel Club, which maintains the registry of the nation's purebred dogs, are very enlightening. During 1973 and

1974 and 1975 the twenty most popular breeds registered with the club included German shepherds, Doberman pinschers, Great Danes, Saint Bernards, and Siberian huskies, all large- to giant-size dogs. In 1974 alone dog owners registered 80,000 shepherds, 45,000 Dobermans, and 20,000 Great Danes. Remember, in addition, that the club records reflect in no way the vast numbers of large mongrels which populate the land.

Many of the people who own these big animals treat them like lap dogs, sometimes keeping them confined indoors or tied most of the day, or conversely, letting them range the streets untended. Permitting a dog, particularly a large dog, to roam the streets is the cardinal sin of a pet owner. It is estimated that almost all of the dog bites that occur are the work not of strays, but of family pets allowed to roam as they please.

Some other generalizations that can be made about dog bites do even more to sharpen the focus on the problem. Like snakebite, dog-bite rates change with the time of day and of the year. It stands to reason that the number of bites increases when more people and more dogs are on the streets, so the rate is highest in summer and during the late afternoon.

Not only are throngs of people traveling between home and work or school during the afternoon, but all sorts of dogs are receiving their daily exercise. Many pet owners on returning home for the day, either walk their dogs or open the door and let them roam. If the dogs have been confined for the day, they may be jumpy and nervous, and therefore more likely to bite.

Statistics show another interesting fact about dog bites, or rather the dogs that inflict them. Most of the dogs guilty of biting people are males. This point is extremely significant when coupled with the knowledge that many dog bites occur within a block or so of the dog's home.

How are these facts related? The answer lies in the territoriality of the male dog, who is quite possessive of the boundaries of the area it considers its own.

When the dog's owner walks it on the same route each day—or even worse, frees it regularly to run around the neighborhood—the dog eventually considers the area its territory, marked by its urine on bushes, utility poles, and fire hydrants. Each time the dog travels the route its protectiveness for its own turf is reinforced, and the chances increase that it will attack other dogs and people it considers interlopers.

If the dog happens to be small its bite probably will not be serious, except, as will be shown, if the victim is an infant. Perhaps as many as half of the dog bites in the nation are inflicted by large dogs, which has vastly increased the gravity of the problem.

Says Dr. Alan M. Beck, director of the New York City Bureau of Animal Control, and authority on the dog-bite problem, "We are being very casual about big animals that are potentially dangerous, especially with regard to children. When a dog as big as a Saint Bernard bites a child in the head, for instance, the teeth easily can penetrate the brain and cause death."

There is a certain prestige attached by some people to ownership of a big dog, as if the master somehow demonstrates his personal physical prowess by virtue of possessing the animal.

The rising popularity of big dogs, more directly results from the growing fear of crime in the streets and in the home, reflected by advertisements for large breeds that now stress their abilities as protectors in addition to their charm as pets. What the advertisements should also stress, but do not, is that even sound breeding and calm temperment are no guarantee whatsoever that a dog will not bite someone—and that the only way to be safe is to keep the dog under control at all times.

The problem is that too many pet owners either do not realize this fact or will not spend the time required to keep their pets both happily adjusted and under supervision. While a little dog left to its own devices is at worst a pest, a large dog on the loose—or for that matter rigidly confined without exercise—can be a menace. Almost anywhere you go, particularly in cities and their suburbs, large dogs abound, often ambling freely on the streets or else straining unhappily at the end of a chain or rope.

A veterinarian I know sums up the situation quite well: "The wrong people are buying the wrong dogs for the wrong reasons."

KILLERS FOR HIRE

The comment made by the veterinarian is even more cogent with respect to another trend in dog ownership, a frightening symptom of the times in which we live. Dogs trained for security—even full-fledged attack dogs—are increasingly available to the general public. Animals trained to kill people are casually sold or rented to anyone with enough money.

A team of public health officials in New York City, led by Dr. David Harris, associate director of the Mount Sinai Hospital in New York City, recently published a study of the dog-bite situation citing strong links between the growing incidence of attacks and the rise in ownership of large dogs, especially those trained for security.

The following paragraphs are taken from their study in the Bulletin of the New York Academy of Medicine.

> There is substantial evidence that there has been a change in the character of the canine population in New York City in recent years, with a trend toward large, feisty, and aggressive breeds. According to the American Kennel Club, poodles and German shepherds were the most popular pedigree breeds registered in the United States in 1970. However, because this register does not include mixed breeds, it does not give an accurate characterization of the canine population. A strong motivation behind the increased ownership of large dogs is their use for the protection of person and property from criminal assault. . . .
>
> Indirect evidence lending support to this hypothesis that there are more large, aggressive dogs in New York City can be drawn from an examination of the Yellow Pages of the city telephone directories. There has been an increase in the number of pets advertised in the Yellow Pages as guard dogs, trained to attack, for the five boroughs. Eight years ago advertisements for friendly dogs as pets were the only ones shown. Photographs of friendly poodles and terriers predominated. During the past few years this pattern of advertising has changed markedly; now several pages are devoted to advertisements of guard dogs. Pictures depicting growling German shepherds and boxers in aggressive attitudes predominate. Companies with such names as The House of Lethal Dogs and the We Bite Dog Academy are representative.

Firms offering to supply or train security dogs do in fact take up several pages in the yellow pages of New York City telephone directories. To a somewhat lesser degree the same is true of the directories for most other large cities. Los Angeles and Miami directories list at least a dozen security dog companies each. Atlanta, the home of a company by the frightening name of Bad Dogs, Inc., has more than a half dozen. The Detroit yellow pages list several, as do the directories for Philadelphia and St. Louis.

A telephone conversation I had with a large New York City security dog agency showed me how easy it is to obtain a killer dog. When I inquired about procuring a dog for protection a representative of the firm explained he could offer a choice of several breeds, including mastiffs, Rottweilers, Dobermans and German shepherds. He added that he would "make a marriage" of me and the dog, fitting the animal to my needs, but before he asked what they were, he offered to "bring a dog today."

Next he explained that the dogs provided by his firm had various capabilities. Some of them would guard me while I was "sitting at my desk." Others would protect me against muggers and assailants on the street.

Before the conversation was over I was offered a German shepherd slightly less than a year old that allegedly was of show quality but too aggressive for the show ring. It had been trained as a home protector for three months. Another dog was available immediately if I wanted it, the man said. It was not particularly suited to the home, he admitted, but was "more for the Mafia," the type of dog you might want "if someone was after you, like if you were a bookie or someone like that."

The price for such canine protection was $750 to $1,500 per dog.

Never once was I asked about my home situation, whether I had children or neighbors close to my home. Had I wanted a dog I could have had it by my side in a matter of hours, although in the hands of an untrained person, a dog conditioned to attack is a time bomb. Military dog handlers take 360 academic hours of training before they are graduated from the twelve-week patrol dog course at Lackland Air Force base.

People who want the ultimate in a vicious canine, however, can go to a number of breeders who are crossing wolves and dogs. A concern in Iowa, for example, offers in its catalog a wolf-German shepherd cross, which, the catalog warns, is a "one-family dog." The price is $225. Wolf-dog crosses, it should be noted, are extremely unpredictable and savage, sometimes even to members of the family.

A LITANY OF TRAGEDY

The generalizations and figures cited above are borne out in grisly fashion by accounts of attacks on people by dogs which I have gathered from newspaper articles and which have been provided to me by personal communications. In addition, I will relate a number of incidents which hit very close to home.

A survey of the back issues of almost any large newspaper reveals the frightening frequency at which serious dog bites occur, and the grim similarities that crop up in incident after incident. Here are a random few:

—On a Friday night in the autumn of 1975 a seventeen-year-old Mt. Perry, Ohio, girl was sitting in a chair at a neighbor's house talking with friends, when the family dog attacked her. The dog, a three-year-old Great Dane, suddenly lunged at the girl, without apparent provocation. It bit the teen-ager so badly she died some hours later at a hospital.

—During May 1975, a two-year-old boy died of bites from his family's German shepherd in Fort Worth, Texas. The dog, only six months old, usually spent much of the time chained in the back yard. Because the chain had broken, the infant's father had tied the dog with a rope. Straining at the rope, the dog, which had been given to the family by a friend, snapped it, and hurtled through the screen door of the family home. Once inside the dog attacked the two-year-old, picking up the youngster in its mouth and dragging him around the house. The boy's terrified mother fought the dog for her son's life and finally wrenched the youngster from the animal's jaws, just as the father, who had been outside, grabbed a rifle, ran inside and shot the dog. The boy died two hours later in the hospital.

—Early one morning in January 1975, a five-month-old girl in Kansas City was attacked and killed by her family's pet, a small mongrel which had just had puppies. The youngster's mother told police she had fallen asleep after being up with the baby until 4:30 A.M. while the father was out. The baby had been left on a mattress on the living room floor. When the father returned he found the youngster under a table, with the dog attacking her. Bitten on the groin and leg, the child was pronounced dead after an ambulance brought her to the hospital.

—In April 1974, the community of East Islip, New York, a suburb of New York City, was shocked by the fatal attack on a six-year-old boy by a Saint Bernard belonging to a neighbor. The death of the boy, Lawrence Calemmo, climaxed a sad series of seemingly harmless events, which began when the youngster was at school.

While at school Lawrence complained of an earache. The school nurse tried to reach his parents, but could not, so she telephoned a neighbor, Mrs. Roy Johansson, who lived across the street from the

Calemmo family and asked if she would come and get the boy. Mrs. Johansson brought Lawrence home, where he began playing in a den with her daughter, the same age as Lawrence. The family's St. Bernard was sleeping nearby in a corner.

As he played, young Lawrence ran past the sleeping dog, which suddenly vaulted to its feet and pursued him. Mrs. Johansson, in the kitchen, suddenly heard her daughter scream, and when she rushed into the den found the dog standing over the boy, who was face down on the floor. When Mrs. Johansson tried to pull the Saint Bernard off the

Marines with their sentry dogs are trucked to a base near Da Nang during the Viet Nam conflict.

youngster, the animal growled menacingly, so she ran into another room, grabbed her husband's shotgun, loaded it, and then fired twice at point-blank range into her pet.

The shots killed the dog but not before young Lawrence was fatally injured. The dog's teeth had punctured his skull and he died despite the efforts of physicians to save him.

Everyone who knew the boy and the dog were perplexed as well as shocked by the tragedy. The boy was described as well behaved, the dog as so gentle children could sit upon its back. Examination showed the animal was not rabid, nor, in fact, are most dogs which bite people.

For a time a rumor circulated that the dog had been stabbed in the ear with a ball-point pen, but when medical authorities dissected the animal's head no such evidence was discovered.

—Saint Bernards were guilty of at least two other serious attacks on children during 1974. In one, a four-year-old Indianapolis boy was killed. The victim of the other assault, a seven-year-old boy in Guilford, Connecticut, was not killed but was severely bitten on the face and neck. The dog, chained by the side of the youngster's house, jumped on him as he walked by. The boy's mother had just obtained the dog from an animal shelter, where it had been taken after biting a girl in another community only two weeks before. About that same time a Saint Bernard in Virginia ran out of its yard into a neighbor's and bit the face of a nine-year-old boy who was playing ball.

The increasing viciousness of the Saint Bernard breed was cited in an editorial in the March 1976 issue of the American Medical Association journal the *Archives of Surgery* which expressed alarm over the dog bite menace. Improper breeding in the past decade has made Saint Bernards "more vicious and unpredictable than ever before," the editorial warned.

Again and again, like a litany of tragedy, the same sort of reports appear in the news. A little girl is killed when a neighbor's golden retriever turns on her. Another girl is attacked and killed after she falls into a pen where two German shepherds are confined. A young boy dies from the bites of a pair of German shepherds, guard dogs, that have escaped from their enclosure. Another German shepherd on the loose attacks three boys, biting one so severely it takes 100 stitches to close his wounds. Police later say the dog broke free of its tether after some passing youngsters stoned it.

In any examination of serious dog-bite cases a number of parallels are likely to turn up. Often the dogs responsible have been roaming free. Some have been restrained, but for too long a period on the end of a chain or rope—sure to turn a big, active dog into a psychological mess. Some of the dogs have been allowed to mix with children in an unsupervised manner, although youngsters often unknowingly provoke dogs, and a small child is virtually defenseless against a dog larger than he is. In themselves, many of these things seem harmless, slight oversights or mistakes on the part of the dog owner or the victim, but they are the ingredients of calamity. Small children never should be left alone with dogs, even the family pet. By way of example, one day the eighteen-month-old son of some friends of mine crept across the kitchen floor after a beagle belonging to one of their neighbors, and pulled the dog's tail. The dog, usually an amiable sort, whirled around and bit the child on the face, causing wounds that had to be treated surgically.

THE HORROR COMES HOME

The terrible consequences of not keeping an eye on young children around big dogs was brought home to me a few years ago, when my six-year-old daughter was brought home, the left side of her face torn and bloody. As I look back now, what happened to my daughter stands as a perfect example of how a series of seemingly innocent acts can create a situation in which a dog is almost certain to harm someone. In this case, the injury was caused not by a bite but by the dog's claws, and the animal was not trying to attack my daughter, but merely to escape.

It happened in this way. My neighbor owned a small German shepherd, which was exceptionally active, and always on the move. That day the dog was within its doghouse, which in turn was inside a pen.

My neighbor's daughter, a few years older than mine, hit upon an idea for a game, using the dog. My daughter was to hold the animal in the doghouse while other youngsters hid dog biscuits around the yard. Then the dog would be released in hopes it would find the hidden tidbits.

As my daughter restrained the dog within the doghouse, the animal grew nervous, then suddenly bolted for the door, knocking my child down and scrambling over her in its bid for freedom. In the process, the dog's claws furrowed her cheek, ripping it deeply and narrowly missing the eye.

Our neighbor's son found my daughter, picked her up and carried her into the house. Even after a doctor had patched and sewn up her face, it appeared as if my daughter would bear deep scars from the wounds. Most of them healed, however, and the one deep scar that remained was made considerably less visible by plastic surgery at a later date. Today only a few fine lines remain on my daughter's face as reminders of the accident.

If there is any sort of lesson in what happened to my daughter it is that big dogs always are potentially dangerous around children. Moreover, never take for granted that a youngster knows enough to keep out of trouble with dogs. My daughter was accustomed to dogs, and in fact to many sorts of animals, because I was a zoo curator at the time. Even at her young age, she might have known better, but that was not the case.

ON BEING BITTEN

Many of the injuries people receive from dogs are the result of actions like my daughter's that provoke fear rather than aggression on the part of a dog. Unlike some of the seemingly deliberate attacks described above these encounters seldom if ever place people in mortal danger, but the results can be serious, as the harm suffered by my daughter demonstrates.

Not long ago I was bitten when I frightened an already thoroughly upset dog with a move that was undeniably stupid for someone who works with animals. The dog was a vizsla, a sporting breed which originated in Hungary, and I was trying to place it in a good home for a neighbor. Separated from its master, who was an elderly man no longer capable of caring for it, the animal had been in a kennel for several days, and was extremely nervous.

I had put the dog on the seat of my pickup truck, between my wife and myself, as I drove around to the homes of friends in search of a new owner for the animal. As I returned to the truck after stopping at one home, I vaulted rather quickly back into the driver's seat, startling the dog. It turned and snapped at the nearest available piece of flesh, which happened to be my right cheek. The moment its teeth penetrated my face, which fortunately was partially shielded by a thick beard, the animal jerked away from me, as if realizing that it had erred. Then it sat there, shivering with nervousness. All the while my wife was sitting right next to it, but it in no way threatened her, nor did it make any further moves towards me. As it was, however, there were four bleeding holes in my cheek, and I had to return the animal to its owner.

In no way could I blame that vizsla; the bite resulted only from my thoughtless action. It was obvious that the dog was not vicious, nor particularly high-strung, but only jittery because of its master's absence and exposure to a parade of strangers. Man—not dog—had added my statistic to the accounting of the nation's dog bites.

PERIL FROM PACKS

One of the most unsettling aspects of the dog-bite problem in addition to the way it has mushroomed is the tendency of free-roaming dogs to band together in packs. Dog packs range through both urban and rural areas with increasing frequency. Many of the animals in the packs come from the ranks of the country's 15,000,000 feral dogs, strays which have taken to the ways of the wild. But at least as many, and possibly more members of dog packs are pets on the prowl, dogs whose owners release them to wander rather than give them supervised exercise.

Feral or pet, when dogs band together in packs they quickly lose all semblance of domesticity, and endanger both other animals and people in their path.

Author and naturalist Roger Caras described the nature of dog packs in a speech at a conference held in 1974 in Chicago on the ecology of surplus pets: "There is always a little extra Doberman blood to sharpen the sense of attack; there is a beagle with a better nose; an Afghan, perhaps, with better eyes and greater speed; a shepherd with brains . . . they are imput no wild species can ever hope to match."

Packs of dogs roaming at will kill an estimated 175,000 head of livestock yearly, at an estimated cost of $7,000,000. Georgia, North Carolina, Pennsylvania, and other states with large deer population report sizable losses of deer to dog packs. The packs are particularly devastating in winter when they can run on the crust over the snow, while the deer bog down in it.

Deer are not the only creatures chased by dog packs in the forest. A friend of mine was riding his horse through a wooded part of a state park in eastern Connecticut one winter day when he suddenly realized a dog pack was after him. He urged his horse on through the snow, with the dogs yowling not far behind. The horse was a large, sturdy animal and was able to outdistance the dogs, but for a few moments it was close enough to give my friend a thorough scare.

Today the sentry dog is seldom used. The armed services instead train dogs like this one, which is aggressive only under the direct control of their handlers.

Packs of dogs are at least as common in urban areas—particularly in the slums—as they are in the country. St. Louis, according to recent estimates, has about 100,000 wandering dogs, many of them in packs. New York has half again as many as that. Two ownerless German shepherd dogs terrorized an entire neighborhood in the Queens Borough of New York City for several months recently. They attacked and bit people so often that mothers kept children off the street and adults took to carrying clubs and canes while taking sidewalk strolls. Anxious parents took to patrolling the streets while armed with axes and bats in hopes of finding and killing the dogs, which produced a litter of pups in a hidden den.

New Haven, Connecticut, experienced some serious problems with dog packs in 1973, when animals ranging through an inner-city housing project began to give chase to people. On one occasion, a pack of twenty dogs harried a group of students and adults on the streets near a school. Authorities said that the pack, composed of males, was agitated by a female in heat.

The presence of a female dog in' heat can draw dozens of individual males, which as they converge on the object of their affections, band together as a pack. Dogs in this state are highly stimulated and easily arroused into a frenzy.

A young woman in Paterson, New Jersey, had a harrowing experience a few years ago while trying to protect her own dog, a female in heat, from just such a pack outside her home. The woman had picked up her pet to get it away from the males, but they surrounded her. As the woman tried to shield her dog, the panting males lunged and leaped at her, tearing her clothes and bloodying her arms with their claws.

Terrified, the woman screamed, which alerted a man who lived nearby. He rushed from his house and into the pack, which turned upon him. Meanwhile the female dog had wriggled free of the woman's grasp, and darted for the open door of the house. The pack spied the female and gave chase.

"My baby's in the house," screamed the woman as her pet scurried through the door. Before the males entered the house, however, the female ran out again, giving the woman an opportunity to pick it up, run inside, and slam the door. The males, thwarted, sat down outside to wait. They remained for a half hour until the dog warden came to corral them.

Most of the dogs in the pack obviously were pets, for they were well groomed and wore collars and tags.

Even a small pack of dogs can be deadly once their killer instinct is aroused. Sad evidence of this occurred recently in Minooka, Illinois, where three dogs killed a five-year-old boy who was playing in his front yard. The dogs—two collies and a Labrador retriever—were passing by, and the boy ran over to pet them. For a moment the dogs seemed friendly; then, in a burst of fury they swarmed over the boy, snarling and biting as his mother watched horrified from a window. As she ran out the dogs fled but the youngster was so severely mauled that he died a short time later in the emergency room of a nearby hospital.

THE NEW PREDATORS

It is ironic that man has loosed packs of dangerous domestic canines on the very countryside from which, as we will discuss later, he has eliminated a much less dangerous wild dog, the timber wolf. Man's own animals have become the new predators. Dog packs in some areas are in fact the major predator of the deer herds once stalked by wolves. In one recent year dogs killed an estimated 5,000 deer in Georgia alone. Because the packs are not truly wild and not subject to all the natural checks and balances as wolves once were, however, it is probable that they do not contribute to nature's equilibrium like wild predators, but rather disrupt it further. After all, an animal that runs deer all night and returns home for breakfast can hardly be said to be part of the natural scheme of things—and this is what happens every day.

At least some of the kills of game animals and livestock blamed on coyotes are the work of dog packs, or of dog-coyote crosses which have appeared in recent years. The new crossbreed, called a "coydog," now ranges a wide area of the northeast, notably New York State and western New England. The coydog has the size and strength of a German shepherd and the native cunning of a coyote. Its effect upon wildlife, domestic stock and man remains to be seen.

The coydog is very much the result of man putting his finger into nature's pot. Scientists believe that coyotes have been able to extend their range from the west into the northeast because of the vacuum left by the disappearance of the timber wolf, exterminated by man from most of the country. Once established in the east the coyote has been able to mix with free-ranging dogs, which of course belong not to the world of nature but are man's pets running out of control.

The dogs that make up the packs either are or were pets, or else are the offspring of pets that have run wild. They are ranging the countryside because people have let them wander for the night, left them behind at the end of summer vacation, or dropped them by the highway because they messed on the rug. People are the one and only cause of dogs running in packs.

The crux of the problem is that proper care of the active, complex creature that is a dog demands considerable effort, more than many people want to exert, yet they get dogs anyway. Caught up in the pet craze that has swept America, they lose perspective, and fail to think whether or not the dog fits into their life-style, whether they can afford to feed it, and whether they can assume responsibility for its actions.

PETS IN PERSPECTIVE

The dog bite danger is but one of the many manifestations of the American preoccupation with pets, which has grown to the point where we have become a nation of compulsive animal keepers. America's pet population numbers in the hundreds of millions. It includes not only dogs, cats, canaries, and horses but millions of wild creatures, from tigers to horned toads. As will be shown in the next chapter many American homes have become mini-zoos.

The psychological drives behind the human urge to keep pets are as fascinating as they are deep-rooted. Obviously, some people identify with their pets, or compensate for feelings of inadequacy by parading about with showy or ferocious animals in tow. Psychologists are examining these and other reasons and their meaning in terms of the nation's pet population explosion.

A particularly interesting paper on the subject was presented at the Chicago conference on pet ecology by Dr. Boris M. Levinson, professor of psychology emeritus at Yeshiva University, New York City. Levinson's paper linked the American passion for pets to the increasing alienation of individuals from society: ". . . We cannot conceive of pet owner-ship and its psychological nuances in isolation from the problems of living in an alienating society where it is becoming increasingly difficult to get close to people and to establish friendships with them."

Lonely people, starved for human companionship, find solace in their pets, Levinson stressed. Children learn to identify with other living creatures from their pets, he added.

Levinson also pointed out a more elusive motivation for keeping pets, one that harks back to the darkness of human beginnings. For some people, he said, pets symbolize freedom from the fetters of conventional morality: "We wish that we, like our pets, had the unrestricted freedom to engage in pleasurable activities unhampered by religious, social or moral scruples."

Levinson's paper focused on a theme mentioned early in this book: that certain of man's attitudes and actions towards animals stem from his awe of natural powers symbolized by the beast, and that early man regarded the beast as existing on a higher plane than he.

"Man's first gods," said Levinson, "were animals which symbolized and represented the elemental forces of nature such as water, fire, earth, the stars and the moon."

Perhaps we no longer venerate animals, but pet owners in the United States certainly pamper their beasts royally.

The money we spend on our pets is astounding—about $5,000,-000,000, half of it on pet food. The pet-food industry is a major advertiser in print and on television and radio. Magazines directed at housewives, especially, are packed with pet food ads. The foods prepared for our pets are packaged at least as attractively as those sold for human consumption and, for that matter, much more tasty and nutritious than the food eaten by many of us or our fellow humans elsewhere in the world.

While a substantial portion of the world's human population starves, Americans stuff their pampered beasts with such delicacies as "beefy chunks in beef and gravy" and "burger . . . with real cheese flavor and protein-rich egg."

Secretary of Agriculture Earl Butz, not especially revered for his tact, drew yowls from the nation's animal lovers when he suggested not long ago that a decrease in our cat and dog population could make it possible to divert food to the starving millions of the world—many of whom doubtless would find the "real red meat" and "real tasty chicken" marked for our pets not only delectable but life sustaining.

Personally, I experience a twinge of conscience at times when feeding my dog, although I can find sufficient excuse for dog ownership to override such qualms. I also have stopped using any form of commercial dog food other than prepared chow or meal—the kind that comes in big sacks. To this I add suitable table scraps, which otherwise would be wasted. No dog of mine ever again will be fed opulently packaged dainties—meaty, beefy, juicy, or otherwise.

Granted that pets are fun, useful and even sometimes quite vital, but, as the nation's dog-bite crisis indicates, we have lost sight of the problems that our animals create. Dog bites are just part of the trouble, as anyone who has had to negotiate a sidewalk laden with droppings knows. America's dogs produce 4,000,000 tons of droppings and 42,000,000 quarts of urine each day, which makes them significant contributors to the waste-disposal problem. The Archives of Surgery editorial cited above called for a drastic reduction in the number of dogs in the United States as a solution to the problem. It pointed out that China has eliminated all four-legged pets as drains on society and beavers of disease.

Pets of one kind or another carry far more diseases than most people imagine, or fewer people would keep animals. A later chapter will explore this problem, and also the danger to the environment and even to human life, that is posed by the escape of the exotic pets that have poured into this country from all over the globe.

6. MAN, THE BEAST KEEPER

THE PARADOXICAL NATURE of human relationships with animals manifests itself clearly in the attitudes of Americans toward keeping pets. As a people we cannot even control our dogs enough to prevent millions of them from running wild, yet we seem to think we can make pets out of an improbable and often highly dangerous assortment of wild creatures. A rage to keep unusual wild animals as pets is sweeping the country. If you doubt it look in almost any pet shop. Giant serpents such as pythons and boa constrictors are run-of-the mill merchandise. Wolves, ocelots and, as noted previously, venomous snakes can be obtained from some of the more enterprising animal dealers, who sometimes are less than truthful about the hazards of keeping such beasts around the house.

As if that attack-trained Doberman down the street is not enough to worry about, a lion, tiger or leopard may lurk next door. At least 10,000 American households are believed to have these big cats as pets. Many more people keep smaller but equally fierce wild felines such as ocelots and jaguarundis. In their search for beastly novelty, Americans have filled their living rooms and backyards with creatures from virtually all over the globe.

The figures on the importation of wild animals from 1967 to 1972, the last available from the Interior Department, reflect the consumption of exotic wild animals by the American pet trade. In that period the number of live mammals, birds, reptiles, and amphibians imported rose from 820,324 to 3,890,374.

Some of these animals were imported for scientific purposes such as the testing of new drugs, but most were destined for captivity either as pets or in zoos. They were being exploited solely for the purpose of entertaining and comforting man, the only species that keeps other animals purely for pleasure.

As has been seen, the keeping of wild beasts in captivity is by no means new; it was practiced in prehistoric times, when it gave rise to domestication. Nor is the importation of vast numbers of wild animals peculiar to modern America. Many parallels have been drawn between the United States and ancient Rome, but one that has eluded many historians is that both siphoned off tremendous numbers of animals from other parts of the world. In the case of the Romans, described more fully in the next chapter, the pleasure provided by the captive beasts was in the degenerate spectacle of the arena. Moreover, not even the most unscrupulous animal collectors today can match the ruthless efficiency which which Roman beast catchers swept the landscape clear of large wild animals. At the same time, however, the trade in captive wild animals today is unlike anything before, because never before in history have even the most remote and forbidding regions, and their populations of animals, been so easily accessible to man. Animals can be in a distant jungle one day and flown halfway around the world on the next.

CAPTIVE KILLERS

Another chapter in this book will describe the ecological damage caused by the indiscriminate trade in wild animals, and later in this chapter the diseases and parasites that imported wild animals can bring with them from abroad will be discussed. For now, however, it is enough to consider how, just like the other forms of exploitation discussed so far, the act of keeping animals captive establishes the setting for violent confrontation between man and beast.

The heart of the problem already has been mentioned in connection with hunting. It is that man is in the greatest danger from wild animals when he does not permit them the luxury of flight. Man is the eternal

A young mountain lion is attractive but not suitable for a pet as it matures.

enemy of wild animals. In every wild animal there is a powerful instinct that tells it to avoid contact with man, to hide or flee. The drive for self-preservation also mandates that if the animal cannot get away, it probably will fight.

The likelihood that an animal will feel cornered when it desperately wants to flee is enormous in captivity, for man is omnipresent. The captive animal is surrounded by the world of man; indeed, in captivity, the animal is part of it, so there is no escape.

Once in captivity, a wild animal can be taught to associate man with good things such as food and shelter, rather than with fear. Little by little its urge to flee from human presence can be muted. In a word, it can be tamed.

Even when tame, however, a wild animal in captivity is subject to a host of unnatural pressures. There are times when the slightest additional stress—perhaps only a completely innocent human act that occupies just a second or so—can undo years of conditioning an animal to feel comfortable around man. Frightened, a seemingly tractable animal can strike out violently at anyone who happens to be near. Thus captivity can make an innocent animal a killer of man.

Animal exhibits in properly run zoos are designed to reduce—or at least counteract—the pressures on animals and to reduce the odds of dangerous confrontation. Zoo keepers are trained technicians who not only employ time-tested routines designed to keep them and their animals safe, but learn to know the pecularities of even individual animals.

Experienced zoo keepers know that when they work with large or venomous wild animals, only a slight lapse of judgment or casual oversight, even by someone else, can thrust them into mortal peril. It should be repeated, however, that in most such cases the attacks are not the work of animals which have been waiting for a chance to pounce upon their keepers. Rather, some kind of human action invites or even compels them to act aggressively.

Zoos are so constructed that their animals are kept from immediate contact with people as much as possible, except, of course, when proper care makes it necessary. A wild creature kept as a pet, however, lives intimately with people; we buy pets for the expressed purpose of having them around us. With man and beast in such proximity the opportunities for someone making the wrong move multiply tremendously, particularly since few pet owners have the expertise of zoo keepers. A wild animal pet may at almost any time experience human behavior that calls for an aggressive reply. Sometimes, after long captivity, the instinct to retaliate may be dulled, but it never completely fades. It is always there, ever capable of detonating a punishing response with fang or claw.

This is the sort of volcano that boils under anyone who keeps a wild beast for a pet, although most owners either are ignorant of the fact or convince themselves that it is otherwise.

LOVE DOES NOT CONQUER

No zoo keeper would ever knowingly cage himself with a dangerous wild animal, which in effect is what the owners of wild pets do. Strolling unarmed through a jungle teeming with wild beasts would be much safer. The risk taken by people who try to turn their homes into zoos is so great that it is incredible anyone chances it.

Only a lunatic, for example, would walk into the midst of a pride of lions, yet all over the United States there are people of supposedly sound mental state who have taken lions and other wild cats to their bosoms. Some of these people know the danger involved in their actions but just do not care, just as other people habitually drive while intoxicated. But I suspect that most owners of dangerous wild pets have persuaded themselves that love conquers all, that a little human tenderness can somehow charm the savagery out of even the most ferocious predators. What an overbearing presumption! It must take a colossal ego for someone to think that he can undo the millions of years of evolution that has patterned a beast's behavior.

Certainly, forced conditioning or the stagnation of captive life can blunt bestial instincts but, as circus animal trainers will tell you, savagery is part of a wild animal's nature and may surface at any time. It is right and proper for a lion, tiger, or leopard to be savage and fierce. That is precisely the way big cats should behave. The glory of these animals is that they are cunning, powerful predators. They are supposed to be killers, not friends of man.

Unfortunately, a blitz of sentimental nonsense on television and in films and books has convinced millions of people otherwise. The recent "Born Free" television series, fortunately short-lived, is a prime example of what I mean. Elsa, the lioness character in the series, was plugged as "a symbol of the love than can sometimes exist between man and other animals . . ." Elsa the television lioness may love people, all right, but real lions do not like us very much, except perhaps as occasional mealtime fare.

"THEY ONLY KILL TO EAT"

The unprincipled animal dealers who sell dangerous wild beasts to largely unsuspecting people capitalize on the belief that animals are just like people in furry suits.

"They kill only for something to eat," said a woman who answered my telephone call to a Florida dealer in wild pets. She implied that if I kept a lion or tiger well fed, I had nothing at all to fear. Two tigers recently sold to a Florida man, she explained, were regular members of the family. "They come right in the house and watch television," she said.

Noticing that a lion cub was offered for sale in the dealer's flyer, I asked about buying it. The cub already had been sold. What other cats were available? Several, although in the case of tigers and leopards federal laws governing interstate shipment of endangered species prevented her from sending them to me. She could, however, sell them in her own state, and she asserted that "the leopard makes a nice pet," and enthused that "the tiger makes a terrific pet."

She also could ship me a young cougar, for $750. The cougar was, she said, "super tame," broken to a leash, and eager to "ride in your car" and "sleep in bed with you." None of the big cats, the woman promised, would in any way endanger me or my family.

Since my conversation with the woman, Florida authorities have become so alarmed at the wild pet problem in their state that regulations have been put into effect making ownership of wild animals by private individuals a bit more difficult. Since October 1975, state permits have been required for people to own creatures such as gorillas, rhinos, elephants, lions, tigers, leopards, jaguars, baboons, cougars, ocelots, hyenas, African hunting dogs, and wolves. Those creatures deemed most dangerous, such as lions, tigers, and gorillas, but not cougars or clouded leopards, can be kept around the house only in "maximum-security facilities that are equal or superior in security to those required for the same species for public exhibition," according to the new law.

Cages and enclosures like those at zoos are expensive, sometimes costing several thousand dollars, but that it is not likely to discourage many wild pet owners, who habitually are big spenders when it comes to their beasts. In 1972, for example, a Clinton, Connecticut, man whose right to keep a pet lion was challenged by the town fathers offered to spend $4,000 to erect an enclosure for the beast. The town officials were not impressed by the offer and after five months of haggling forced the man to get rid of the animal. The lion, a cub of seven and a half months, was shipped to a man in Florida described as a "game breeder."

Admittedly, a lion cub or any other young cat is a cuddly, heart-warming little creature and in its first few months capable of little harm, except perhaps to household furnishings. But even before they reach adulthood, the young cats are dangerous. At less than a year of age a tiger or lion cub can flatten a man with a love tap intended as play, and can bite hard enough to cause serious injury. Television personality Jack Paar found this out while filming a television show at Jungle Habitat, a drive-through zoo in New Jersey. Paar, accompanied by John F. Kennedy, Jr., son of the late president, was playing with two tiger cubs for the cameras. When the filming ended and Paar ceased his play, one of the cubs bit him, opening a wound that required several stitches to close.

Sometimes in a zoo animals reject their young, which then must be reared by their keepers. I have known many big cats raised in this fashion, and most of them became unmanageable by six months of age. Some of these animals remembered their human foster parents long after maturing and even allowed themselves to be scratched through the bars of the cage. But even the people who had raised them would under no circumstances go into the cage with the animals.

PET PREDATORS AND THEIR VICTIMS

The practise of keeping wild cats as pets has spread terror, injury and death, not only to their owners but to innocent people as well. Here are some accounts gleaned from reports in journals and newspapers of the past few years:

—A leopard that had been left by its owner in the garage of a home near Clearwater, Florida, attacked and severely injured a woman who had agreed to care for it. The woman had brought a chicken to feed the 100-pound cat while its owner was away. After she opened the garage door the leopard attacked her, knocking her down. The leopard and the woman, fighting for her life, rolled out of the garage in full sight of several neighbors, who thought the two were playing. Suddenly the watchers realized that the fangs of the cat were in the woman's throat. They ran to her aid and one man, who had taken his shotgun with him, blasted the animal at point-blank range, killing it. The victim was rushed to a hospital where physicians managed to save her after performing an emergency tracheotomy.

Ocelots have seriously injured many people who have kept them as pets. Although gentle when young, they become vicious as they mature.

—Residents of a New Jersey community, alarmed over a lion kept as a pet by one of their neighbors, campaigned for its removal. They were unsuccessful, however, largely because other residents defended the owner's right to keep his beast. Shortly afterward, the lion killed the infant son of one of its defenders.

—A Houston family bought a lioness as a cub but when it reached 200 pounds decided to get rid of it. Awaiting shipment to a zoo, the lioness was sent to an animal shelter. While at the shelter the animal broke out of its cage and attacked a five-year-old girl who had come with her mother to look at puppies. As the lion loomed over the little girl, clawing her, the manager of the shelter ran over and wrestled the cat away from its victim, who was pulled to safety by her mother. A police officer who arrived moments later shot and killed the lioness.

—In Washington, D.C., a 220-pound lion displayed at a service station to attract attention created more of a stir than anticipated when it escaped, wandered about the street, and knocked down a passerby before it was rounded up.

—Despite orders from the Colorado Department of Health, the owner of a 200-pound lioness in Denver failed to get rid of the beast. Although confined behind a high fence and tethered on a chain fifteen feet long, the lioness nevertheless one day managed to leap the barrier and maul a three-year-old boy, who was standing nearby with his father. The tot's father beat off the cat with a broom handle, but not before his son had been severely bitten in the head and neck.

—Actor Steve Hawkes, who has played Tarzan in films, had to wrestle an animal for real when his pet tiger attacked a little boy in a park in Miami, Florida. The attack took place at an affair entitled the "Blessing of the Animals," sponsored by the Miami chapter of the Friends of Animals, a national organization whose avowed purpose is to preserve animals from persecution. Hawkes had brought his 200-pound cat to the park, where clergymen were invoking divine blessings upon pets assembled with their owners. As Hawkes held the tiger on a chain, a nine-year-old boy riding his bicycle bumped into the striped predator, which turned upon the youngster, mauling his face and legs. The animal lovers in the park watched in horror, as Hawkes tussled with his tiger and finally succeeded in yanking the animal off the boy. In the process, the movie Tarzan's pet bit him on the leg.

The bull elephant Ziggy ran amok at the Brookfield Zoo near Chicago in April 1941 and attacked his keeper. He managed to escape after the elephant's tusks jammed into the ground.

The incidents described above involve only larger wild felines but even smaller species can inflict harm, especially on children. Ocelots grow increasingly rambunctious as they mature, and when adult they are downright truculent. So is the margay, which like the ocelot is a spotted cat that ranges from the southwestern United States to southern South America.

The late Lee S. Crandall, general curator emeritus of the Bronx Zoo, often warned of the danger in keeping ocelots and other small- to medium-sized wild cats at home. He told me of a number of incidents in which people were injured by the creatures. In his classic book, *Management of Wild Mammals in Captivity,* Crandall left no doubt about how he felt on the subject. Commenting on ocelots and margays, he said, "Both animals are frequently taken when very young and reared by hand, so that they make tame and attractive pets. However, as they approach maturity, they are likely to become unpredictable, even dangerous, and serious accidents have occurred when such animals have been privately kept."

An accident of this sort occurred some years ago in California when a pet ocelot that had been given the run of a household attacked the family's three-year-old daughter and bit her viciously on the face, almost causing the loss of an eye.

The fact that such tragedies occur has done nothing to discourage the fad for wild pets; nor have repeated pleas from organizations concerned with protecting animals and wildlife. These groups fall into two camps, quite different in their approach to problems affecting wildlife. One is composed of organizations such as the various Audubon societies which are basically concerned with maintenance of all aspects of an ecologically sound environment, including wildlife. The other is made up of groups that can be loosely classified within the humane movement and which draw their support from the nation's animal lovers. Typified by groups such as the Fund for Animals and Friends of Animals, these organizations are chiefly concerned with animal welfare—preventing what they view as cruelty to animals as well as preserving rare species.

Some of the humane organizations have made a sincere effort to curb the craze for wild animal pets. Fund for Animals members have picketed pet shops with signs protesting the wild animal trade. The Humane Society of the United States works continually to make youngsters aware that keeping most wild creatures as pets is against the interests of both animals and people.

What the humane organizations fail to realize, however, is that because of their peculiar approach to the problem the attitudes they foster do not discourage people from keeping wild animals as pets but on the contrary encourage it. Their idealization of animals and naïve view of nature has filled the ranks of the humane movement with souls who think that the wild world belongs to Elsa and Bambi, that animals have the same hopes and fears as people, and therefore the same rights. Theirs is a distorted biology warped by anthropomorphism, and as their general opposition to sensible wildlife management testifies, based more on emotion than hard ecological fact.

Underlying the philosophy of the humane movement is the notion that the beasts of the wild are man's furry, feathered, and scaly brothers. If this is true, then why not invite brother beast to join the family circle as a pet? Together with nonsensical television programs, the humane movement has convinced masses of Americans that animals are really just like people, at least under the skin. No wonder that people let tigers watch television with them, and that a Florida woman testifying at a public hearing on her state's new pet regulations could say in all sincerity that her pet cougar "seems more like a part of the family than an animal."

Moreover, in preaching the need for kindness to animals, humane organizations have failed to make their adherents realize that wild creatures seldom return human benevolence. Unwittingly, the people who speak for the nation's animal lovers have played right into the hands of pet dealers who would have us believe that lions and tigers "kill only for something to eat."

Americans have such an attraction for wild pets that it takes only a whisper of encouragement to send them scurrying to the pet shop in search of the exotic. Because of this, people identified by their fellow citizens with wildlife conservation must be exceptionally circumspect when it comes to dealing with captive wild animals, and aware that the best-intended acts can backfire.

Personally, when I bring wild animals from a zoo or nature center on television or into a school to promote wildlife conservation, I often wonder whether I am doing more harm than good. Do the audiences remember my reminder that the animals are not pets but from an institution, or do they just remember how appealing the animals are?

MISS KITTY AND HER CATS

Anyone who works with wild animals in behalf of conservation must constantly bear in mind that even a positive act can set a bad example for people who find wild pets appealing. A case in point occurred recently when actress Amanda Blake, known for her portrayal of Miss Kitty, the saloon keeper in the "Gunsmoke" television series, purchased and successfully bred rare African cheetahs—an accomplishment that drew accolades from zoologists.

Miss Blake has been extremely active in the Humane Society of the United States and the Fund for Animals, and has made many public appearances in behalf of wildlife conservation. Humane organizations, in fact, have drawn considerable support from show business personalities, particularly such actresses as Mary Tyler Moore, Jayne Meadows, and Angie Dickinson.

Obtained from an animal dealer in Los Angeles, Miss Blake's cheetahs reproduced while living in a compound where she had caged them near Phoenix, Arizona. Her accomplishment as a breeder of rare animals was noted with some fanfare in the press. Zoos have been trying to breed cheetahs in captivity for years, and to date only a few institutions have succeeded as well as Miss Blake. The five cubs born at Miss Blake's compound were shown in a photograph in *The New York Times.* Mewing and cuddled together in a wicker basket, they looked absolutely irresistible. It was the kind of picture that makes people want to own cheetahs, just like Miss Blake.

Granted that Miss Blake bred a rare species and thus helped add to its numbers, albeit in captivity. But particularly in the light of the publicity she received and her reputation as a conservationist, her ownership of the big cats raises a knotty question: if Miss Blake can keep cheetahs in a compound, why can't anyone else with a couple of acres of land to spare?

Miss Blake, according to the *Times,* also had a leopard around the premises. Any wild pet owner would be justified in asking, "If she can, why can't I?" And indeed, at least one protest of this type was filed with the Arizona Game and Fish Commission. A man complained in behalf of a boy whose pet quail, raised from an egg, had been seized by the game and fish agency.

Of course, the successful reproduction could well be used as justification for Miss Blake's keeping the cheetahs, but many other wild pet owners claim that like Miss Blake their purpose in having wild beasts is somehow to further wildlife conservation—just as many of the disturbed people who keep venomous snakes around the house claim they do it for "scientific study," despite lack of affiliation with any recognizable scientific institution.

"ONE OF MY FAVORITES"

Like Amanda Blake, Cleveland Amory, author of *Man Kind? Our Incredible War on Wildlife*, is a darling of the nation's animal lovers. His book not only rails away at hunters but verbally scourges the National Audubon Society, New York Zoological Society, Sierra Club and similar groups which have led the fight to conserve wildlife because they merely tolerate legitimate sport hunting.

The book also contains a series of photographs which seem rather unusual for an author whose organization, the Fund for Animals, has criticized the keeping of wild pets. The photographs are just the kind to make people want to own wild animals. There for Amory's readers to see are humans of assorted ages and both sexes nuzzling, holding and otherwise fondling a variety of predatory mammals. We have, for example, television personalities Jim Fowler with "Arthur" the cheetah sitting on his lap, and Jack Paar embracing a lion. The message the pictures transmit is that man and beast can cuddle safely; all it takes is love.

One of the photographs shows an otter held up in a human hand, obviously Amory's, with a caption reading, "Here I hold one of my favorites—the otter."

The otter is also the favorite of a former zoo colleague of mine, Joseph Davis, who now is on the staff of North Carolina's state zoo. Davis's research on otters has gained him an international reputation and not long ago it was enhanced by his breeding of the African spot-necked otter *(Lutra maculicollis)* for the first time in captivity outside of its native continent.

Davis knows that otters can be among the most captivating and amusing of wild creatures. He also knows that they are capable of inflicting grievous injury on a human. After his spot-necked otters had

A bull moose in rut, like this one at the Milwaukee Zoo, can be one of the most dangerous animals for zoo keepers to handle.

their young, Davis and his wife Dorothy maintained constant watch on the animals in their home, for captive wild creatures do not always make the most stable parents.

When the female otter suddenly killed one of her cubs, Davis decided to remove the remaining youngster from its parents and rear it himself. The decision required some rearranging of the adults in their pens. As Dorothy was accomplishing the transition, the male otter turned on her and ripped at her leg with its needle-sharp teeth. The bite, accomplished in a moment, leave a wound that required thirty-five stitches.

WOLVES AND KIDS DON'T MIX

If you believe other photographs in Amory's work, it would seem that wolves and people—especially children—get along just fine. One picture shows a big, black wolf and a slim blonde beauty sitting side by side. "A wolf and her person—'Cadillac,' a black timberwolf at Mountain Place Sanctuary California," declares the caption. The cover shows Amory himself hugging a wolf and two other photos have wolves snout to cheek with young children.

Both of the wolves shown with youngsters were animals belonging to Californian John Harris. He regularly tours the nation with "tame" wolves to promote public sympathy for preserving wolves which, like most of the world's large carnivores, are in real danger of extinction.

Public appearances by Harris and his animals have done much to erase the evil image of the wolf, which needs all the help it can get to survive as a species. His wolves are so attractive and calm that they dispel all fears. I know this for a fact because, I confess, my own children have been among the thousands of youngsters whose parents have allowed them to pet Harris's animals. It is very easy to think of them as big, lovable pets, and that is just the trouble. Wolves are not supposed to be lovable. Worthy of respect and even awe, yes, but not lovable. Wolves belong out there on the tundra or in the forest coursing after and killing prey. Wolves are predators—a fancy word for killers and, while this can in no way be construed to mean that they are evil, wolves should not mingle with people.

This fact of life was unpleasantly demonstrated by one of Harris's own wolves which injured an infant in July 1975. The incident demonstrated once again that even if a captive wild animal has been as friendly as a lap dog, it should not be taken for granted, especially around children.

The wolf, named "Rocky," was one of two brought by Harris to a softball game staged in Teaneck, New Jersey, by WCBS-TV of New York City and *The Record,* a New Jersey newspaper, for the benefit of Cleveland Amory's Fund for Animals. (Coincidentally, I have been associated with both of the sponsors for I was a reporter for *The Record* and have appeared as a member of the cast of a WCBS-TV children's program.) A spectator brought his year-old daughter close to Rocky so he could take a photograph of the child with the wolf. Contact between youngsters and wolves has been encouraged at Harris's appearances. As the child neared the wolf, the animal turned suddenly and slashed the infant's face with its teeth. The wound required hospitalization.

The attack sparked a mild controversy. New Jersey fish and game officials, obviously relishing the embarassment the incident had caused for the antihunting Fund for Animals, declared that Harris had brought the wolves into the state illegally, without the required permit. Harris, meanwhile, took his wolves and left New Jersey for other parts.

Newspaper accounts of the attack differed as to what had happened. *The Record* quoted a representative of the Fund for Animals as explaining that the wolf was merely showing affection for the child, accepting it into the pack, as it were. Howard Brant, hunting and fishing columnist for the Newark, New Jersey, *Star-Ledger,* described the wolf's act as an unprovoked attack. An account in the New York *Daily News* said the wolf merely had tried to grab the baby's bottle and missed.

While bites by captive wolves certainly do not occur every day, every so often a wolf which someone or other is trying to make into a house pet serves painful notice that once a wild animal, always a wild animal. Recently, for instance, a wolf kept by a Maryland man in his basement savagely bit and clawed his two-year-old son, while another wolf belonging to a New York City resident bit a woman who failed to respect that although tame it was after all still a wild animal.

A QUESTION OF RESPECT

There is a world of difference between an animal whose kind has been domesticated for thousands of years and a wild animal in captivity, even after several generations of captive existence. By and large, domestic animals have been bred to get along with people, or at least to serve them. Even an aggressive guard dog responds to some master. Domestication implies than an animal has been tailored by man to act in prescribed ways, beneficial to man. This is not the case with wild animals.

Their instincts have not been modified for the world of man, but rather for survival in nature. Captive life may condition an animal to respond to human affection, but this is entirely unnatural and at any time the creature may revert to more normal behavior, either recoiling from man or striking out against him.

This sort of behavior by wild animals often is labeled unpredictable. It is not. Wild animals act in ways that are entirely predictable; their instincts permit them little choice. Our ignorance of animal behavior may make an animal's act unexpected, but if we knew more, it would be entirely predictable.

It should be anticipated, for instance, that a baby raccoon which is affectionate to people in the spring will be snappy and untrusthworthy by the fall, especially if it is a male. Racoons grow to almost full size in their first summer and in the wild, part from their mother in the fall. By then they must be tough enough to take care of themselves and hold a piece of territory for their own. Aggressiveness in this situation is an advantage, but if the raccoon happens to be someone's pet, it means trouble for all concerned.

SMALL ANIMALS, SHARP TEETH

Racoons *(Procyon lotor)* are among the most common wild animal pets. Their handlike paws, remarkable intelligence, and comical antics make it almost impossible not to regard like them and regard them in an anthropomorphic vein. They relate exceptionally well to humans, particularly when the raccoons are young and although mortal enemies of dogs in the wild even can learn to get along with the family dog.

Raccoons also have some of the sharpest teeth in the animal kingdom and when adult use them readily to make their feelings known. Pet raccoons given the run of a home may attempt to establish a pecking order among the youngsters of the family, bullying, chasing, and even biting smaller children to make it known who is the boss. Many people who have kept raccoons have been bitten by animals that they assumed would never turn on them.

While the disadvantages of having a lion or tiger around the house are rather obvious, it is much more difficult to convince people that raccoons and other small wild mammals belong in nature, not the living room. It is hard to think of an animal as cute as a raccoon as a threat, but with one bite a coon can remove part of a child's face, or a substantial hunk of finger. I nearly lost the top of an index finger to the lightning bite of a cousin of the raccoon, the coatimundi *(Nasua nasua),* because I mistook bright eyes and an appealing manner for tameness. Because the animal seemed friendly I did not use gloves while rehearsing with it for a television show. It suddenly turned on me and with a lightning bite almost took off the top of the finger. I rushed to a hospital, had my finger bandaged, and taped the show with my hand behind me. Later in this chapter I will tell how a coatimundi in a zoo almost killed a keeper, although the animal is only about as large as a big housecat, and also is a popular pet.

Among other small mammals that people sometimes keep as pets is the ferret, which is the domesticated version of the European polecat *(Mustela putorius)*. Ferrets still retain many of the characteristics of their wild relatives, although they normally can be handled with ease. Because of the damage they could do small game, however, many states forbid people to keep ferrets, but in the past they were used extensively to hunt rabbits and rats. Even in places where possession of ferrets is permitted, it is not at all wise to allow them the run of the house, as some people do. The late Lee S. Crandall of the Bronx Zoo once told me that a bite by a pet ferret was one of the worst animal bites he had ever seen. The ferret, he said, was owned by a family which had a small child. One day while the child was sleeping, the ferret slipped into the youngster's room, and tore off much of the child's face.

This is not to say that when under the strictest supervision children should not be allowed to touch ferrets. Indeed, they make excellent demonstration animals for lessons on natural history. But, after all, the ferret is a weasel with all the savagery of that tribe of animals, and even in domestication has functioned primarily as a killer of other creatures.

MONKEYS AS A MENACE

The monkeys are another group of animals which are considerably more dangerous pets than most people imagine. Why anyone would want to keep a monkey is beyond me. It is like sharing one's home with an incorrigibly dirty, nasty, and thoroughly uncontrollable human being. Monkeys get into everything. They cannot be toilet trained and throw garbage about with abandon. Moreover, when separated from social contact with other monkeys, these creatures become as psychologically unbalanced as a human would be isolated from his fellow men in a society of monkeys.

What many people do not realize about monkeys is that even small ones can bite viciously and the larger species can kill a man. The Bigger monkeys are immensely powerful and have huge, curving fangs. In the wild baboons and other big monkeys occasionally kill small and young animals and eat them.

Hunger was one of the motives which was considered in the killing of a Jersey City, New Jersey, infant by his father's pet monkey in July 1975, although based on a description of the attack it is difficult to say for certain. The monkey, identified as a macaque—a large animal that can reach about thirty pounds in weight—was kept tied on the vacant second floor of a two-family house. On the day the attack occurred the animal broke free, jumped out of a second-floor window, and entered another window on the level below, where the family lived.

There it encountered its master's wife and four-month-old son, who was lying on a couch. When the monkey attacked the infant, the mother attempted to drive it off with a broomhandle, but the powerful creature took it away from the woman and chased her from the house.

People gathered outside the home, trying to lure the monkey outside with an offer of cherries, but the beast remained inside with the child. An unidentified man who arrived on the scene tried to shoot the monkey with a pistol, but missed. Finally the infant's father arrived and got the monkey out where police managed to shove the killer animal into a garbage can. It was too late, however, to save the baby, who was found lying on the floor in a pool of blood. Savaged by repeated bites, it was pronounced dead by doctors at a Jersey City hospital. The monkey was taken to an animal center and later was killed. Interestingly, large monkeys in the wild have been known to steal babies and kill them.

Most incidents in which pet monkeys escape do not end so tragically but nevertheless create considerable turmoil. A pet monkey in Rockville, Maryland, for instance, bit a youngster after escaping from its cage and led police on a hectic chase through the community. The animal could not be captured and had to be shot from ambush.

Hopefully, the availability of monkeys as pets will soon decrease because of new quarantine regulations imposed in October 1975 by the Department of Health, Education and Welfare. The regulations authorized the Public Health Service to ban importation of monkeys and all other nonhuman primates except for exhibition, educational purposes, or scientific research.

As justification for the new rules H.E.W. cited the danger of disease spreading to humans from monkeys and apes which are not kept under exceedingly strict hygienic conditions. This is a very real threat, as will be seen in a later chapter, but perhaps not the only motivation behind the H.E.W. action.

Biomedical research institutions, including some of those operated by H.E.W., import vast numbers of monkeys and apes for use in the laboratory. Together, research institutions, zoos and the pet trade account for almost all of the almost 100,000 primates brought into the nation yearly. Some conservationists fear that the great demand for monkeys and apes is draining too many animals from wild populations and have urged that the importation of these animals be sharply curtailed.

The agency responsible for regulating the importation of animals—in most matters except health—is the Department of the Interior, which has been under some pressure to do something about the primate situation. There is reason to believe that the action by H.E.W. was taken at least in part to head off the threat of considerably more severe curbs by Interior.

Whether the new regulations will completely shut off the supply of pet monkeys remains to be seen. There is nothing in the rules covering the domestic sale and possession of monkeys. This means that a monkey born in captivity within the United States could be placed in the pet trade without violating the law. It also is unclear how strictly the Public Health Service will define the "scientific, educational, or exhibition purposes" for which monkeys may be imported. At the very least, however, it is going to be much more difficult for people to find monkeys to keep as house pets.

A number of other federal and state regulations have made it slightly more difficult to own dangerous wild animals. Protection given to endangered species by federal laws administered by the Interior Department, for example, has curbed the trade in species such as the tiger, which can be shipped in interstate commerce only after Interior is satisfied the transaction is not against the interests of wildlife conservation. Many states require permits for private ownership of wild animals, which at least enables state conservation agencies to know what kinds of wild beasts are being kept by various citizens.

None of these acts, however, has really been more than an inconvenience to people who want wild animals as pets, and the traffic in beasts still flourishes. The one measure that could stop it has been bottled up in the Interior Department, where it is the victim of an increasingly visible feud between bureaucrats who have a protectionist viewpoint on one hand, and those who tend to favor flexible management on the other. The proposal that is the focus of the controversy is a proposed change in the provisions of the Lacey Act, the law which gives Interior authority over import and interstate commerce in wild animals. The revision would permit the department to ban the importation of virtually all noxious and dangerous wild animals for the pet trade, while continuing importation for zoos and scientific institutions, although under more rigorous supervision.

PETS, PEOPLE, AND DISEASE

Strict federal regulation of the exotic pet trade can be justified solely on the basis of the threat of disease that many wild pets carry with them. One of the most underrated hazards in keeping and living close to pets, domestic as well as wild, is the unpleasant assortment of diseases they can transmit to man. Unknown to most of their owners, the animals commonly kept as pets in this country can infect people with at least 100 different diseases; dogs and cats alone carry 65 maladies ranging in severity from ringworm to rabies.

Monkeys and apes present the worst danger because as close relatives of man they share with him a common susceptibility to many serious diseases. Not only can monkeys and apes transmit illness to man but they also can catch them from one person and carry them to someone else. Among the diseases nonhuman primates can give to man are:

—Tuberculosis, a common ailment of monkeys and apes;

—Shigellosis, a form of dysentery which can be fatal;

—Hepatitis, which often is carried by chimpanzees.

An example of how tuberculosis can jump from man to monkey to man occurred in 1972 on the West Coast. A California man who had tuberculosis owned two monkeys, one of which he unknowingly infected with the disease. The sick monkey transmitted the illness to its cage mate, which later was sold to a family in Seattle, Washington. Once in the possession of the family, the monkey began to cough persistently and when a veterinarian examined it, he discovered the presence of the disease. Two months later, two of the children in the family reacted positively to a tuberculin skin test, and had to be put on drug therapy to combat the illness.

The Public Health Service estimates that thousands of the monkeys and apes which have been imported into the United States in recent years may have tuberculosis, and thus are capable of spreading the disease among the nation's human population. The threat posed by such diseased animals once they enter the pet trade had much to do with prompting the new federal regulations controlling the importation of nonhuman primates.

Shigellosis, which causes severe gastric distress, is even more common than tuberculosis among imported primates. Usually the victims of the disease recover after a distressing siege of a week or two. An Air Force sergeant and his son in Texas, who contracted shigellosis from a woolly monkey *(Lagothrix lagothricha)* bought from a dealer in Florida were well again after ten days. For some people, however, the sickness can be fatal, as it was for a seventy-five-year-old woman whose son bought her a spider monkey *(Ateles geoffroyi)* from a pet shop in New Hampshire. She was found lying semicomatose in her hotel room. Two days later, despite intensive hospital care, she died. Examination showed that both she and the monkey were infected with the same type of Shigella germ.

Chimpanzees have been the origin of several outbreaks of hepatitis in recent years. One chimpanzee imported from Africa infected the animal dealer in Florida who received it, and then three keepers at a zoo in Houston, Texas, which purchased it. Another chimpanzee in Houston passed on the disease to the man who owned it as a pet, and also to his nephew and niece, who had visited and played with the ape. A zoo man I know once developed a special affection for a chimp in his care, and often allowed the animal to nuzzle him. He ended up in the hospital with a severe case of hepatitis. In California, more than a score of people all contracted the illness from a single chimpanzee, the pet of one of their friends. The animal had been popular among the victims, all of whom had close contact with it before becoming sick.

The danger of exposure to illness is not restricted to people who keep exotic creatures, such as chimpanzees, but also to the owners of the more usual, run-of-the-mill pets. As mentioned, cats and dogs can give people scores of diseases, some spread by germs, some by parasites. In 1975, for example, the American Medical Association warned that healthy dogs and cats which scratch or nip people can give them a bacterial infection caused by the microbe *Pastuerella multicoda*. The germ may be found in half of the nation's dogs and almost three-quarters of its cats, according to the A.M.A. The infection is not serious if it is treated with antibiotics, but it is not readily recognized by physicians.

Several parasitic worms can be transmitted by dogs and cats to people. These nasty parasites get at people who come on contact with the feces of the animals, so good pet sanitation can virtually eliminate the risk of infection.

The trade in pet baby turtles was permanently banned in 1975 by the Food and Drug Administration, because many of the turtles carried Salmonella bacteria. These bacteria cause severe cramps, nausea, fever, and diarrhea, especially in youngsters. Before the ban, each year 280,000 Americans caught the disease from turtles.

The possibility that another small pet kept by millions of people can be the source of illness arose in 1975 when scientists linked the spread of a flulike sickness called lymphocytic choriomengitis (LCM) to hamsters. An outbreak of LCM occurred in New York State among fifty-seven people who all had contact with pet hamsters from the same distributor in Florida. The malady, which is normally not severe, is caused by a virus, which people can pick up from the air. It can be contracted merely by passing close to a cage of hamsters. Workers in laboratories where hamsters are used in medical research, it turns out, often are in danger of catching LCM.

RABIES

The most dangerous disease people can get from their pets is rabies, but although people often associate it with dogs, they no longer are the most common carriers of the disease. Only 180 cases of rabid dogs were reported to the United States Public Health Service in 1973, the last year for which figures were available.

As late as the 1950s, however, canine rabies cases numbered in the thousands each year. The decrease is due to the success of programs to immunize dogs to rabies with vaccine, which has made most dogs in America resistant to the disease.

Rabies is caused by a virus in the saliva of the infected animal. Once the virus is transmitted, the disease will break out after an incubation period that averages about two months, unless the victim has received vaccine. The virus attacks the nervous system and virtually always causes death within two weeks after the onset of the first symptoms.

Cattle, horses, cats, and other domestic animals in addition to dogs can carry rabies, but today in the United States it is most prevalent in wild animals. Foxes, skunks, raccoons, and bats are among the wild animals that most commonly carry rabies. In 1973 the disease was found in 1,851 skunks, 474 foxes, 114 raccoons and 432 bats.

Bats have replaced dogs as the main source of rabies infection in humans, and since 1951 nine people have died after being bitten by bats infected with the disease. The most recent death was in 1973. The victim was a twenty-six-year-old Kentucky man bitten on the ear by a bat that entered his home while he slept. The man did not seek treatment for the bite, which seemed minor, and a month later he suddenly sickened. He died two weeks afterward.

Bat rabies occurs in almost all states, but the incidence of the disease in other animals is not as widespread, and is concentrated only in certain areas. The highest concentration of rabies in skunks is in the plains states, the Mississippi and Ohio valleys, and northern California. Rabies in raccoons is very restricted and occurs mostly in Georgia and Florida, while rabid foxes turn up most often in Tennessee, Kentucky, and areas immediately adjacent to those states.

The reservoirs of rabies in wild animals represent a constant source of infection that can spread to domestic animals and people. Except for bats, however, most of the small wild mammals that carry the disease do not travel very far and so barring major epidemics, rabies in various species will continue to be concentrated in some regions, and absent from others. Rabid raccoons and skunks could be dispersed, however, by the pet trade. Because rabies can have as long an incubation period as two years, wild animals which carry the disease could be trapped and shipped to areas where the disease has not been a problem. Should but one such infected creature escape into the environment, rabies could become established in an area previously free of it. This seems to be sufficient reason for a federal ban on the interstate trade in live wild mammals, similar to that restricting commerce in pet turtles.

DEATH FOR SALE

Nothing illustrates the need for tighter controls on the pet trade more than the commerce in venomous serpents that goes on in the country today. The Pennsylvania youth mentioned in Chapter 2 who was bitten by his pet cobra purchased the snake for $45 from a reptile dealer in Florida. It is illegal to send venomous snakes through the mail, but that prohibition did not stop the teenager from getting the deadly reptile, which was shipped to him by truck. On occasion people even violate the mail ban. Not so long ago postal workers in New York City opened up one package and discovered it held four cobras and a couple of coral snakes.

Anyone foolish enough to want to share his home with a venomous snake can find a wide assortment of these creatures advertised in flyers distributed by reptile dealers in different parts of the country. Many of these dealers supply animals to zoos but also will provide their deadly merchandise to anyone with the money or credit to pay for it.

Among the dangerous snakes listed in the flyer of a California dealer are cobras, green mambas, tiger snakes, and fer de lances, which the price list states can be purchased on credit with a Bankamericard.

All it takes is a telephone call to "reserve any specimen until payment or confirmation can be sent." Once purchased, "All venomous reptiles will be shipped by the Federal Express Company." And that's how easy it is to buy a serpent capable of dealing death.

PETS AND COMMON SENSE

The irony of keeping venomous snakes as pets is that some of the harmless snakes—such as king snakes and corn snakes—are among the few wild creatures that really do make good pets if their needs are met. Thus far I have stressed the harm that wild animals cause as pets. However, common sense says that some small wild animals can be kept in the home without any fear they will injure or kill anyone. Deer mice, crickets, the snakes just mentioned, pollywogs, and salamanders are fine pets, and these animals can teach youngsters a lot about the natural world. Certainly, too, there is nothing wrong with keeping certain cage birds, or tropical fish, provided, however, the birds belong to species that are neither endangered or potential pests if released, and the fish are harmless sorts.

At the same time, even small creatures such as frogs, toads and salamanders require considerable care, and unless you are prepared to give it, the animals have no business in your home. This is the other side of the pet problem. Animals also have suffered as a result of the fad for wild pets. Although this aspect of the situation will be mentioned only briefly here, because it is outside the scope of this book, it deserves serious attention.

Thousands of wild animals die in transit to pet owners. Thousands more die after they are taken home; in fact, few wild animal pets live more than a few months in captivity. Countless other creatures languish because their owners do not know how to maintain them, or have grown tired of them and just don't care. Very often it is a case of the pet owner getting much more than he bargained for, because few people realize the great amount of attention and expense that wild pets require.

People are astonished. Their boa constrictor will not eat. Their ocelot rips up the furniture. Their raccoon bites. Their monkey smells up the house. What can they do?

For many pet owners, the answer is simply dump their burden at the roadside. All over the country wild pets have been set loose without any thought to whether they can cope with a new environment, and without regard to the way they can upset the balance of nature and even endanger the public health (a subject to be discussed in Chapter 8). Other pets have simply been left to die. During the summer of 1974, for example, officials of the Humane Society of the United States discovered a lioness locked in a shed in Providence, Rhode Island. The creature had been left there without food or water. It was given a home in a zoo at nearby Pawtucket. Similarly, in the spring of 1975, Leo, a 4-month-old lion cub, was found in an abandoned house in Staten Island. He was taken to the Staten Island Zoo, where he's quite comfortable.

The lioness was lucky because there are simply too many unwanted wild pets for zoos to handle. Sometimes, however, zoo employees will accept the leavings of disenchanted pet owners and take the animals to their own homes. People who work for zoos and nature centers often become known in their neighborhoods as soft touches for cast-off creatures. It has happened to me time and time again and at one point a few years ago so many animals were finding their way to my home that *The New York Times* called it an "animal halfway house."

By accepting wild animals, I may seem to fall into the same trap as the pet owners I have been discussing, but there is a difference. I have been associated with zoos, aquariums and nature centers, either as a member of the staff or consultant. Therefore, the resources available to me are immeasurably greater than those upon which most pet owners can draw. I can obtain food, cages, and professional advice on care in cases where my own knowledge is insufficient. Even so, however, I have never brought home large cats, venomous snakes, or other animals that are extremely dangerous. Moreover, very often I hold the animals only until I can find a zoo or nature center that will accept them.

And, I must add, it never has been easy for me or my family, particularly when the animals have been young. An infant raccoon or opossum can be fun, but it also can require considerably more attention than a human baby. We have had furniture wrecked and have experienced the heartbreak of caring for animals for weeks only to have them suddenly die. We have been faced with the problem of what to do with a caiman—an aggressive relative of the alligator—which has appropriated the bathtub, and where to place a boa constrictor, raccoon, and spiny-tailed lizard while we go on vacation.

We never have had to rear a young leopard, lion, tiger, or macaque, but colleagues of mine have had to undertake such tasks while working for zoos. Undeniably, for a person who likes animals it is exciting, but it also is very nearly a full-time job. Fortunately for the people of whom I speak, it was part of their professional duties and some of them actually lived on the grounds of the zoos where they worked, which made life much easier.

ON THE JOB WITH WILD BEASTS

Zoo people, who spend most of their working lives in close contact with captive wild animals, are among the most vocal critics of the fad for wild pets. No big-game hunter, field biologist or animal collector lives as closely with the perils of the animal kingdom as the zoo keeper, whose daily routine brings him within striking distance of creatures that can bite, claw, peck, envenomate, smash, stomp, and gore him.

However, although most zoo keepers have been bitten or scratched a few times during their careers, relatively few seasoned zoo people are seriously injured, and fewer still are killed, on the job. Veteran zoo men respect the dangerous capabilities of wild animals and know not to take even the tamest or seemingly innocuous creatures for granted. The only keeper ever to die at the Bronx Zoo was the victim of a zebra bite early in this century. He died of gangrene after a stallion had removed a large chunk of flesh from his arm.

THE MOST DANGEROUS ZOO ANIMAL?

People often are surprised to learn that zoo keepers consider elephants among the most dangerous animals to handle. The elephant—both the African species *(Loxodonta africana)* and the Asiatic—can be a real Jekyll and Hyde. Zoo visitors usually see the animal's affable side as it gently receives peanuts from the hands of little children. When my own youngsters were quite young they regularly visited two Asiatic elephants in their stall at the Beardsley Zoo in Bridgeport, Connecticut. As the huge beasts took greens and bread from my daughters' hands the creatures moved ever so cautiously, avoiding the slightest contact with the little girls who stood among them. At Lion Country Safari in California, I walked through a herd of African elephants with their young keeper, who had even trained a nearly adult bull to respond affectionately to him. Another zoo man showed me how one of his elephants would perform an animated jig to avoid stepping on his foot, even when he thrust it in the animal's way.

As stated, much of the time the zoo elephant is a gentle giant, but there is another aspect to the creature as well. Elephants probably kill and seriously injure more zoo men than any other animals.

Thomas Livers, director of the zoo in Oakland, California, was an elephant handler for several years. "I consider elephants the most dangerous animals in the zoo with which to work," says Livers, who nevertheless is very fond of pacyhderms. The secret of handling elephants according to Livers is to do just that—to constantly maintain tactile contact with them, either by hand or with an elephant hook. Livers has been assaulted by an elephant one time, while unchaining the animal's foot. The elephant flipped Livers over bodily with its tusks, sending him sprawling on his back, but then left him alone.

Keepers in Japan and Germany have been killed in recent years by elephants. An elephant in an Italian circus trampled an attendant to death in July 1975 and another in January 1976. In June 1973, before the eyes of a horrified crowd, a female Asiatic elephant wrapped its trunk around the middle of a forty-six-year-old laborer at the Clyde Beatty Circus, lifted the man in the air, then put him down, kicked him and stepped on him. By the time another circus employee drove the elephant off with a stick, the laborer was dead. He was later identified as Alvin Kelly, the son of Shipwreck Kelly, a famed flagpole sitter of the 1920s and 1930s.

Mandarin, a notorious elephant of the old Barnum & Bailey Circus, killed three men earlier in this century. One was a drunk who committed the mistake of teasing the beast. Another was a trainer, and the other was a stable boy, who was crushed when Mandarin suddenly knelt upon him while he was at work. For these transgressions Mandarin was hanged from a ship's winch until dead.

THE LIBERATION OF ZIGGY

The world's most famous living captive elephant, a veteran of both the circus and the zoo, also has a reputation as a killer. The animal is Ziggy, an Asiatic bull at the Brookfield Zoo near Chicago. Whether or not Ziggy actually is a mankiller has been disputed, but for almost three decades the zoo took no chances and kept the elephant chained within the confines of a single stall. In 1970, however, Ziggy was released in an outdoor exercise yard, fortified to resist the tremendous power of the

13,000-pound creature. Ziggy's emergence into the light of day was accompanied by considerable fanfare, because few zoo animals have had such a colorful history as the Brookfield Zoo's pachyderm.

Ziggy derived his name from the fact that, as a two-year-old calf, he was purchased from John Ringling by showman Florenz Ziegfeld, who presented the elephant to his daughter as a pet. Ziggy's life as a pet was short, however, and he was sold first to the Ringling Bros. Circus, and then to the Singer's Midgets Circus, in which he performed a dance called the "lurch." Once, while the circus toured Spain, Ziggy danced so vigorously that the stage collapsed.

According to stories that have been around for many years, Ziggy killed a man while on European tour, and another when the animal was exhibited in 1936 at the San Diego Exposition. Neither case ever has been documented, but while at the exposition Ziggy did break free and wander the grounds for a while, and after that the circus sold the bull.

The buyer was the Brookfield Zoo, which paid $800 for the elephant that was to become one of the zoo's star attractions. Officials at the zoo say that Ziggy did not deserve the unsavory reputation he had gained by the time the circus sold him. A zoo publication about the elephant asserts:

"Records have been discovered of at least three deaths caused by bull elephants about that time (1936)—all in the western U.S.—and it is possible that one of these deaths has been unjustly attributed to Ziggy."

If Ziggy was blameless before the zoo bought him, however, he changed things within a few years after his arrival. In 1941 Ziggy suddenly turned on his keeper, George Lewis, the only man whose commands the elephant normally obeyed. Picking up Lewis in his trunk, Ziggy slammed him across the outdoor elephant yard, then charged the keeper, trying to gore him with his tusks.

Three times Lewis evaded the elephant's fearful rushes, but on the fourth charge he was caught between the elephant's tusks and pinned to the ground. Kneeling, the berserk bull shoved his weight against the keeper, who struggled frantically for his life. It seemed as though Lewis would be squashed, but although the elephant tried, he could not crush the helpless man. Lewis was saved by the extreme length of the tusks that had imprisoned the keeper. The tusks were so long that with their points buried in the ground they prevented Ziggy from bringing his weight to bear upon his victim, who managed to squirm about enough to suddenly punch the elephant in the eye.

Startled by the blow, Ziggy drew back for a moment, which was all the time Lewis needed to scramble to safety. The damage was done, however, as far as Ziggy's future was concerned. Zoo officials decided it would be dangerous to keep Ziggy in the yard, and the animal's long confinement began.

Lewis eventually left the zoo and moved to Seattle, Washington, but his association with Ziggy was not over. When the zoo decided to test Ziggy's reaction to freedom in 1970, Lewis was summoned to handle the elephant. As newsmen watched the doors to Ziggy's stall were opened. For almost an hour, Ziggy remained inside, but then, responding to the calls of the keeper he once had tried to crush, the bull eased his ponderous bulk into the yard, and for the first time in twenty-nine years stood under the sky.

A TALE OF SOME ELEPHANTS

During its early years, the Bronx Zoo had several elephants of somewhat volatile temperament. One of the zoo's first elephants was a female Asiatic named Luna, because she had been obtained in 1908 from the Luna Park amusement center at Coney Island. Luna was not aggressive, but was easily panicked, which gave zoo keepers problems shortly after her arrival in the Bronx.

Nervous in unfamiliar surroundings, Luna bolted from her new keepers and lumbered across the zoo's grounds into the open door of the reptile house. Luna was not a huge elephant—merely about seven feet high—but the sight of her was enough to trigger a mass exodus of visitors from the reptile building. One woman visitor fainted from fright and hit her head upon a guard rail.

After some time Luna's keepers managed to lead her out of the reptile house but then she bolted again. This time she somehow managed to squirm through a small door into a building housing giant tortoises, where she remained for several minutes, trembling in fright.

Before keepers could tether her, Luna lurched out of the tortoise house and with the keepers after her set off about the zoo. Twice more she entered the reptile building. The second time, keepers caught and chained her. She was left there for the night.

The next morning, as keepers loosed her chains, Luna panicked again, wrecking several reptile cages in the process. She was finally shackled outside the building, where her old keeper from Coney Island arrived and calmed her. Then, with the help of another elephant, keepers led Luna to a stall, ending the incident.

The elephant used to lead Luna was an African bull named Khartoum, which grew into one of the largest elephants in captivity, eleven feet high at the shoulder. Khartoum was not a vicious animal, but had a penchant for smashing steel bars and tossing pieces of his corral fence about. In 1922 he broke off a ninety-pound chunk of iron from the fence and tossed it into a crowd of visitors, injuring one woman. Such actions, however, did not appear malicious, but merely playful.

Gunda, an Asiatic bull which arrived at the Bronx Zoo in 1904, was anything but playful. One day in 1913, as his keeper entered his stall, Gunda slammed the man into a corner with a blow of his trunk. As the man crouched in the corner Gunda tried viciously to get at him, attempting to kneel on his victim, smash him underfoot, and gore him with three-foot tusks. One tusk shattered as it hit the wall, which was sheathed in steel, but the other lanced into the keeper's thigh. Meanwhile, however, another keeper arrived and jabbed a pitchfork into Gunda's flank, driving the beast away from the injured man, who was hospitalized for three months as a result of his wound.

It can be seen that just because the elephant is not a meat eater like a lion or a tiger, it still can be extremely dangerous for a zoo keeper to handle. The same is true of several other herbivorous creatures.

HORNS AND ANTLERS IN THE ZOO

Obviously, the big species of wild cattle that pose a danger in the field can be ticklish to manage in zoos. I have already described in a previous chapter how bison will try to maneuver people who enter zoo enclosures into compromising positions. In 1974 an employee of the Lion Country Safari in West Palm Beach, Florida, was trampled to death by an African buffalo. Even deer and antelope, which in the wild are skittish, can be rough customers in a zoo enclosure. Recently an eland, a cow-sized antelope, fatally gored a keeper at a safari park in England. Bull elk and moose become real terrors when in rut and not only charge zoo keepers during this period, but even go so far as to stalk them. I have seen a rutting moose, with huge rack of antlers lowered and head shaking slowly side to side, prowl around the perimeter of its pen with its little red eyes following the movements of people on the other side of the fence. Several times I have watched bull elk in rut charge the fences of their enclosures, trying to gore keepers on the other side. Even smaller deer can be a menace when in rut, as a photograph in a New York Zoological Society publication of several decades ago shows. The photo is of a battered iron pail with a large hole pierced in its side. The bucket had been full of oats, in the hand of a zoo keeper when a black-tailed mule deer *(Odocoileus hemionus)* suddenly lowered its head and charged. The keeper shielded his body with the pail, which took the impact of the deer's rush. One tine of the animal's antlers jabbed right through the iron.

TUSSLE WITH A TAPIR

The fact that virtually any animal in a zoo merits watchfulness is demonstrated by the harrowing ordeal of a friend of mine a few years ago. Richard Sweeney, now director of the Beardsley Zoo in Bridgeport, Connecticut, once was almost killed by a tapir, a creature reputed to be totally harmless.

Tapirs are primitive relatives of the horse and rhinceros which live in southeast Asia and in the American tropics. The species in this case was Baird's tapir *(Tapirus bairdi),* a pony-sized creature that ranges from southern Mexico to northern South America. It is a rather primitive, dull creature that is a staple item on the menu of the jaguar. When it senses man in the wild, its reaction is to crash off through the brush and forest as fast as it can.

In the zoo, however, tapirs become tolerant of man and show no fear when someone approaches their enclosure. They often stand on their hind legs with front hooves resting on the barrier of their enclosure.

Sweeney's encounter with the tapir took place at the San Diego Zoo,

Tapirs are generally considered gentle creatures but on occasion pose a danger to zoo keepers.

where he was a keeper of mammals for many years. With the mammal curator, Clyde A. Hill, Sweeney was escorting a young couple who were conducting research on tapirs to the zoo's tapir exhibit.

When the party arrived at the enclosure, the tapir, a male, galloped up to the low fence that served as a barrier, and stood up on it. Surprisingly for someone experienced in the ways of wild animals, the woman visitor reached out to pat the tapir on its snout, whereupon the animal promptly clamped its jaws over her fingers and held on as she screamed in pain.

Sweeney, hoping to distract the tapir, vaulted the fence into the enclosure. The ploy worked, but in an unexpected manner, for the beast, which weighed about 600 pounds, charged the zoo man, knocked him down, and savagely tried to rip out his throat. When Sweeney threw his right arm across his face to protect it, the tapir began to gnaw on his arm; then, as Sweeney struggled, it bit his leg.

Seeing that Sweeney was in danger of being killed, Hill went over the fence, picked up a rock the size of a baseball, and bashed the tapir on the head with it. Hardly seeming to notice the blow, the beast left Sweeney on the ground and charged Hill, who managed to grab the tapir around its neck.

Gasping and battered, Sweeney was hauled over the fence by zoo visitors who had rushed to the scene, while Hill desperately wrestled with the tapir. The animal's hide was so oily that the curator quickly lost his lock on its neck, and his hands slid into the animal's mouth.

Even though the tapir was chewing away at his hands Hill managed to hang on and maneuver near the barrier until two spectators were able to reach over, grab his belt, and lift him to safety. All three of the tapir's victims were taken to the hospital, where they remained for six days. Hill had lost a piece of his left index finger, and his right fingers were mutilated so badly that even the bone had been chewed. He later told of feeling no pain as he fought the beast and heard the sounds of the tapir's teeth crushing his fingers. The woman whose action triggered the mishap suffered a mangled finger and Sweeney had severe wounds from the bites. He still carries the scars several years later.

Sweeney believes that the tapir turned on him because he entered the enclosure in an unorthodox manner, by vaulting suddenly over the barrier. "I had been in the exhibit thousands of times before," he says, "but always by way of the gate. The tapir never gave me any problems. When I jumped the barrier, it frightened him; perhaps he had to defend his territory."

BEARS AND BIG CATS

While keepers can get away with a mistake or two when they work with some of the herbivorous animals, they can take absolutely no chances with the larger predators, such as the bears and big cats. I know of several cases over the years in which a single slip-up with bears has cost a life or serious injury. A keeper at the Denver Zoo in the late 1920s was killed because he acted too casually with a pair of grizzly bears he had reared from cubs. The present director of the zoo, Clayton Freiheit, described what happened: "At one time it was fairly common practice for keepers in many zoos to enter bear exhibits without transferring them. Wyman [the keeper who died] had reared the grizzlies from cubhood and had been on good terms with them for years. Both animals had to be shot to recover his mauled body."

Today most conventional zoo exhibits for very dangerous animals are designed so keepers can feed the animals and clean up while the animals are held in auxilliary cages. However, sometimes even entering a cage with small creatures can be very risky. A keeper at one eastern zoo narrowly escaped a severe, possibly fatal brain injury when he opened the door to a cage housing coatimundis and leaned in to leave food there. One of the coatis that had been overhead on some branches leaped on his head and sank its teeth into his skull. If the animal's fangs had penetrated a quarter of an inch more, physicians said, they might have entered the man's brain.

At the large drive-through zoos that have been built in recent years —Jungle Habitat and Lion Country Safari are examples—keepers continue to work within the same enclosures as lions and other potential mankillers. Usually the keepers are in vehicles, but sometimes they must dismount to perform various tasks. However, the compounds at such zoos are usually several acres in size, which means that man and beast need not be close to one another.

More recently, a keeper at the Milwaukee Zoo who disobeyed orders to stay away from grizzly bears in a maternity enclosure lost an arm to one of the animals. According to George Speidel, director of the zoo, the man attempted to hand the bears a morsel of food through fencing in the rear of the enclosure. "Eventually, as bears will do," Speidel says, "one of them got a hold of the keeper and he lost his arm. . . . Fortunately with bears we always keep two men on duty and the other one was there to help the man who was attacked. We were able to get him to the hospital in about ten minutes."

Elwin R. Sanborn, the first staff photographer at the Bronx Zoo, once saved a keeper from an attack by a bear. Sanborn, who had a colorful reputation, entered the zoo's bear dens one day to photograph a Russian brown bear and her cubs. He took several photos, including one of the bear, a relative of the grizzly, nuzzling her keeper.

At this point, however, the bear's mood abruptly changed, and it suddenly knocked the keeper down, then seized his arm in her jaws and began to drag the horrified man to her den. Sanborn dropped his camera, seized a club—bear keepers often were armed with clubs in the old days of American zoos—and beat the bear until she dropped the keeper. The man's arm was bitten so savagely that two main arteries were severed. In the melee, Sanborn's camera was rescued as well, by an attendant at a nearby refreshment stand who bravely ran into the fray.

Oddly enough, big cats account for relatively few of the attacks by zoo animals on keepers. I believe this is because people naturally are on guard around these animals and while even an experienced zoo man might be tempted to be overly friendly with a bear, it is hard to conceive of anyone handing tidbits to a lion or tiger.

Once in a great while, however, a cat manages to kill or injure one of its handlers. I know of one case a few years ago where a keeper in a California safari park let down his guard around a lion and was so badly mauled that literally hundreds of stitches were needed to close his wounds. At a drive-through zoo in England, a keeper was almost killed when a tiger jumped him. He was saved when two other keepers attacked the tiger with heavy staves, and drove it from its victim.

Not long ago one of the most bizarre cases in zoo annals occurred at the zoo in Fréjus, France. The director of the zoo customarily drove to work each morning with one of his assistants. One Sunday morning, for reasons that will remain unknown, the two men left the car and walked through the zoo's lion enclosure. Lions attacked and killed the men, then began to devour their mangled bodies.

When the gruesome event was discovered, the lions were shot and killed. The summary executions of the lions provoked a nationwide protest by French veterinarians, who blamed the zoo director for his own death. The director, who had been a hairdresser, had no previous experience, the veterinarians claimed, and his death was caused only by his own blunder.

SNAKE MEN

Zoo keepers in charge of venomous reptiles tend to be the most circumspect of all in dealing with their animals, not surprisingly, for no other creatures in the zoo can kill with just one bite on almost any portion of the human anatomy. I know many reptile keepers, but only a few who have been bitten. One man I have known for several years escaped by literally a fraction of an inch when the fangs of a serpent bracketed one of his fingers without striking flesh. An inexperienced young keeper in the Nairobi, Kenya, Snake Park was not so lucky in 1972 when he picked up a cobra on a snake stick prior to cleaning its cage and allowed the animal to get too close. He was bitten on the finger, but fortunately prompt administration of antivenin took him out of danger.

Years of experience handling venomous snakes in captivity failed to save the director of the Hogle Zoo of Salt Lake City, who as mentioned in Chapter 2 died in 1964 after a puff adder bit him. The zoo director, Gerald de Bary, was especially fond of snakes and often cared for them himself, rather than entrust them to keepers. His death resulted not from an error on his part but from an awful piece of bad luck.

One evening while recovering from a bad cold, de Bary decided to feed his snakes. As he opened the door to the puff adder's exhibit, he suffered a sudden spell of dizziness, and reached out with his hands to steady himself. Tragically, his arms went through the open door of the cage and the snake struck him. For almost two days physicians tried to save him but despite their efforts he died. The doctors who treated him said de Bary was cheerful and showed great courage throughout his ordeal. As de Bary died, a second batch of puff adder serum was on its way to Salt Lake City from Africa, but it did not arrive in time, and even if it did, it is not certain that it would have saved him, since he already had not responded to serum.

Serums are routinely used to treat venomous snakebite in this country today. Most zoos stock antivenin serums effective against a variety

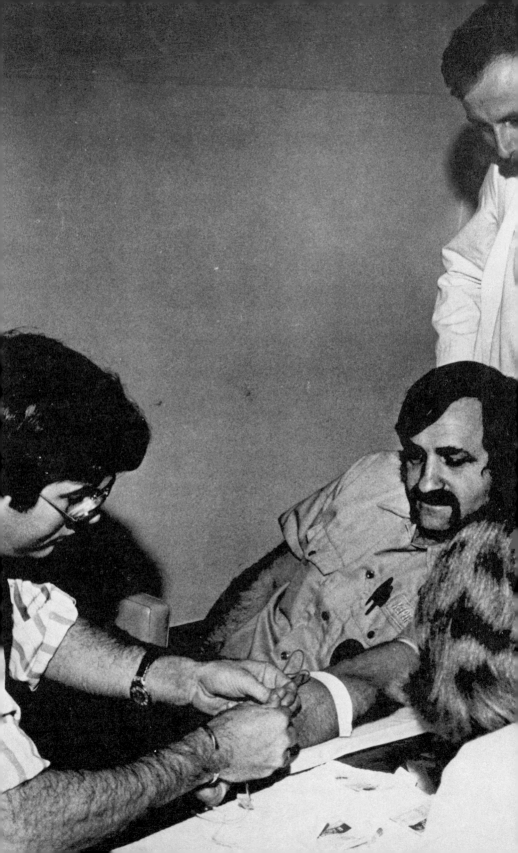

of serpents. The Bronx Zoo, for example, keeps in its reptile department 15 different serums, sufficient to cover the bites of the 30 venomous species in its collection and of several others from all over the world. This was not the case many years ago, however, for in the early 1900s the only serum available in the United States was to combat the bites of cobras and their relatives.

Thus, when on January 27, 1916, keeper John Toomey was bitten by a western diamondback rattlesnake at the Bronx Zoo, his future did not look very promising. However, an unusual coincidence not only turned his case into a medical milestone, but probably was what tipped the balance in favor of his survival.

Toomey was bitten as he made the morning rounds of the reptile house. One cage, which needed cleaning, housed several rattlesnakes that just had arrived from Texas. Toomey opened the door just a bit, and with a long-handled shovel held on one hand, reached in to remove some waste.

On the opposite side of the cage lay coiled a very large rattler, of about ten pounds. As Toomey reached in, the serpent launched itself fully across the cage and drove its fangs into the keeper's left arm.

Coworkers immediately placed ligatures above and below the site of the bite and both the park veterinarian and a physician were called. The physician administered some of the zoo's cobra serum, but it appeared to do little to thwart the effects of the rattler's poison.

By afternoon Toomey's hand and arm had ballooned with swelling, and he was vomiting, so he was hospitalized. Before long he sank into a coma and the swelling spread to the left side of his trunk. When Toomey's future looked most bleak, his physician discovered that a scientist from Brazilian who had just developed a serum for pit vipers was attending a meeting in New York City—and, moreover, he had brought samples of the new serum with him.

The Brazilian was contacted, Toomey was treated with the new serum, and improved so quickly he was discharged three weeks later. The case marked the first use of the serum in the United States.

As part of their snakebite prevention and treatment program, keepers in the Bronx Zoo's reptile house are trained to give intravenous injections of antivenins to one another in case of emergency. Here training goes on under supervision of physicians.

It is interesting to compare Toomey's case with a more recent case of snakebite in a zoo. The victim was Gary K. Clarke, now director of the Topeka Kansas, Zoo, who described his travail in the scientific journal, *Copeia.*

Clark was bitten in 1959, while he was working at the San Diego Zoo. He was twenty years old at the time. The snake that bit him was a red diamond rattlesnake *(C. ruber),* a species that ranges from the southern border of California south through Baja California. An expert snake handler, Clarke had placed the serpent in a cloth sack, in order to weigh it; he needed the weight of the creature for a study he was doing on the metabolism of serpents. The snake had fought determinedly against being put in the sack, so by the time Clarke managed to get the creature inside and knot the top of the bag, the snake was thoroughly aroused.

Clarke had set the sack on the floor and as he prepared to lift it again the snake lunged within the sack and managed to strike Clarke's leg—through the cloth of both the sack and his trousers.

"The snake actually hung from my leg attempting to close his lower jaw in spite of the double thickness of cloth," Clarke later wrote.

The fangs of the snake were dislodged only after Clarke pulled the sack away from his leg. As the fangs left Clarke's flesh, the snake released a large amount of venom on the floor, the sack and Clarke's trousers. The snake sprayed so much venom about, in fact, that despite the burning pain in his leg Clarke believed he had received only a small dose, and even thought about resuming his work.

After returning the serpent to its cage, however, he began to treat himself with a snakebite kit, and summoned help. Then he was taken to a hospital where physicians began to administer antivenin and drugs.

Clarke remained in the hospital for a week under treatment. During that time he kept a diary of what turned out to be an excruciating ordeal. His leg swelled hugely and pulsated with searing pain; so sensitive was the limb that even the breath of a physician who was examining it and the heat from a flash bulb used by a photographer who took a photograph of it caused great agony.

After a week of treatment, however, Clarke was discharged and within a few days after leaving the hospital he could walk without too much discomfort. Clarke believes that the snake was so thoroughly angered it had emptied its venom glands, which is why the consequences of the bite were so horrendous even though much of the poison had spilled on the floor. Normally a snake does not expend all its venom in one bite, and the species which bit Clarke has relatively weak venom, and is rather mild mannered.

GIANT SNAKES IN THE ZOO

Some of the large nonvenomous snakes also have given zoo keepers trouble on occasion, although the so-called "giant snakes"—boas, anacondas, and pythons—are not nearly as dangerous as commonly believed.

Pythons and boas (the anaconda is really a very large boa) belong to the same family of snakes, all of which kill prey by constriction. Contrary to what many people think, the constrictors do not crush the victim entwined in their coils but rather squeeze until their prey suffocates. Their powerful loops compress the chest cavity until the prey can no longer inhale; the snakes also can strangle their victims by tossing coils around its neck.

Both the size and the strength of the big constrictors are vastly overestimated, although unquestionably the biggest of these serpents weigh as much and are as strong as several men. For the record, the largest of the giant snakes are the anaconda *(Eunectes murinus)* of South America, and the reticulated python *(Python reticulatus)* of southeast Asia. Both are believed to reach a length of more than thirty feet, although no one ever has claimed the Bronx Zoo's standing reward of $5,000 for the person who first brings back a live snake of that length.

Several other pythons attain a length of twenty feet or more, and the boa constrictor *(Constrictor constrictor)* has been known to reach eighteen feet, although most boa constrictors are less than half that length.

A healthy man probably is strong enough to fight off all but the biggest of boa constrictors and pythons and anacondas up to a length of about ten feet. Especially if he tangled with the last-mentioned two varieties, however, he would know that he had been in a battle. The loops of a ten-foot anaconda, for example, feel like flexible bands of steel. I have found that the pressure that an anaconda of this size exerts is much greater than that applied by a boa constrictor of equal size.

The danger of wrestling with a giant snake—a task which zoo keepers sometimes must perform—is that the animal will be able to toss loops about your head and neck, or anchor its tail on something solid. Keepers generally work in twos with the larger constrictors so one can unravel the other if he gets entwined.

The major hazard posed by the giant snakes is their bite—it is not venomous, of course, but nevertheless extremely damaging. The teeth of these snakes, which fill their jaws, are needle sharp and recurved so that once they are embedded in the flesh of a victim it can pull away only at the expense of severe lacerations.

My own boa constrictor, a six-foot reject of a former wild pet owner, once bit a zoo keeper badly enough on the hand that he received five stitches. I had loaned the snake to a zoo, where it was placed in a large cage. After exploring the cage it crept into a crevice around a lighting fixture. The keeper, not experienced with such snakes, tried to pull it from its haven, and was bitten.

Jackson Iha, curator of the Nairobi, Kenya, snake park, shows how to handle a forest cobra. The snake is extremely deadly.

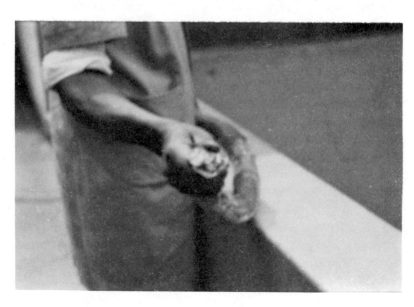

In June 1975 Jack Hanna, the director of the Central Florida Zoo in Sanford, Florida, almost lost his finger to a fourteen-foot anaconda that he and two assistants were attempting to bathe in the waters of a pond near the zoo. As the three men and the one-hundred-twenty-pound reptile sloshed around in the water the snake clamped its jaws around the ring finger of Hanna's right hand. Several of the teeth went through the finger—there were about two dozen punctures in all—and it took Hanna's companions five minutes to work his hand free from the snake's grasp.

Wrestling with an anaconda is dangerous under any conditions, but doubly so in the water, because the species spends most of its time in lakes and streams, and is very much at home in the water.

VISITORS IN THE ZOO

Carelessness, unforseen mishaps and just plain bad luck are what get zoo keepers into trouble with animals. Only rarely, as in the case at the Milwaukee Zoo where the keeper disregarded orders to stay away from bears, are keepers injured because they deliberately violate the rules. When a zoo visitor is injured, on the other hand, it is almost always because the agrieved person has broken zoo regulations, which are usually posted in the most obvious places.

People seem to be afflicted with a sudden reading disability once they enter the zoo. Signs warning not to feed or touch the animals are disregarded. In their desperation, zoos have tried all types of approaches to dissuade visitors from getting too close to the animals. Some zoos use the tough approach and warn of arrest. Others try humor. "Trespassers will be eaten," read signs at Lion Country Safari. "These cute little beggars can hurt you," warns a sign in the baboon compound of Jungle Habitat, a drive-through zoo in New Jersey.

After several years working in and visiting zoos, I can say that none of the approaches work. People insist on opening car windows and tossing tidbits to the bears, shoving their hands into cages to pet ocelots, and letting their children climb over barriers designed to keep them out of the reach of dangerous animals. Time and time again I have seen people shove their youngster close to animals to let the children have a better look or feed the captive beasts.

The parents who do this expose their youngsters to grave danger. An example of what can happen was provided for my by Clayton Freiheit of the Denver Zoo. "In this instance," Freiheit wrote to me, "the parents apparently lifted the girl over the guard barrier and down into the moat so she could feed the zebra. She did." The zebra, Freiheit explained, bit off one of the child's fingers.

Parents who fail to keep a close eye on young children around zoo animals also are playing with fire. Little children can squeeze through railings and bars that are designed to separate visitors from dangerous contact with animals. An example of this occurred late in 1975 at the Beardsley Zoo in Bridgeport, Connecticut. A two-year-old boy who had wandered several feet away from his father squirmed through a space of less than eight inches beneath a guard rail around a leopard cage and toddled up right next to the bars. One of the two leopards in the cage reached a paw through the bars and clawed the youngster's face. In 1976, at the same zoo, a man who shoved his hand into a tiger's cage lost a finger and several inches of tendon which came off with the digit. The tiger then spat out the finger, with the tendon still attached. At a zoo in Idaho, a little girl walked up to a cage housing a wolf and reached through the bars. Her arm was bitten so badly that it had to be amputated.

DRIVE-THROUGH DANGER

The temptation to touch the animals is very strong at drive-through zoos where visitors in their cars are surrounded by all sorts of wild creatures, some of which have learned to beg for food. Despite signs pleading with people to keep car windows up and not to leave their vehicles even in the case of breakdown, people do not listen. At one safari park I watched a man change a flat tire only a few yards from a herd of white rhinos, and not very far from a big Cape buffalo. When a keeper drove up and asked the tire changer to get back in his car, the man became irate. He had no idea of the danger than surrounded him.

Some other recent incidents at drive-through zoos speak for themselves:

> Visitors and animals often come close together at safari parks. It is safe enough, as long as the rules are obeyed, but visitors often disregard them and try to touch animals.

—A little girl, two years old, visited a drive-through zoo with her parents, who left a window of the car open. The opening was wide enough for a lion to reach its paw through and claw the youngster so severely it took more than 100 stitches to close her wounds.

—At another safari park a woman was nearly dragged through the open window of her car by a lion which reached in and grabbed her.

—In December 1975 a woman who was in the habit of bringing a trunkful of meat to a lioness, named Elsa, in a Florida safari park was attacked by another lion when she got out of her car to feed Elsa. An employee of the park drove the attacker off with a rake. The woman suffered a broken jaw and severe cuts.

—Not content to view lions from a distance, a man opened the window of his car, leaned out and called to the cats. One of them sauntered over, and mauled the man.

—A tourist who was riding through a lion compound in a car with its window open was clawed on the head, arm, and shoulder by a lion which ceased its mauling only when a keeper drove into it with his vehicle.

—A family riding through an animal park in their motor home left a window open wide enough to admit a cougar, which began to maul their eighteen-month-old baby. The infant's grandmother saved him from death, but not from serious injury, by killing the cat with a butcher knife.

Why do people leave their senses behind when they enter the zoo? For the same reasons they keep wild animal pets. By petting and touching an animal, they show that they are its masters. They are convinced that captivity somehow makes an animal a friend of man. They have been conditioned by Elsa and Bambi to think that animals can love and reason. They misinterpret the sleepiness of a leopard in a cage for docility, and think that zebras are just like domestic horses. Most of all, they do not realize that when faced with human intrusion upon the enclosures they regard as their domain, the most innocuous zoo animals can become furious beasts.

Polar bears attacked and killed a young man who jumped into their exhibit at the zoo in Perth, Australia, in 1972. By the time the bears were driven off, he was dead.

A QUESTION OF TERRITORY

To many people, a captive animal takes on the status of a pet. Pets exist to be petted, so people cross guard rails and other barriers without regard to the animal's territorial sensibilities. Clayton F. Freiheit, director of the Denver Zoo, once remarked to me that if the visitor and animal are where they belong, the chances of either being hurt are virtually nonexistent.

Warren J. Illiff, assistant director of the National Zoo, has been particularly concerned with trying to stop harmful interactions between visitors and zoo animals:

I really wish that we could do more in explaining to the public why they shouldn't cross barriers. An animal's enclosure becomes its territory, and protecting it from intrusion is as important to it as its food and water. A visitor who comes to or sticks something into this territory leaves the animal no choice but to strike out in self-defense and often in terror.

For those animals which are nomadic and have no fixed territory or which have territory that shifts with them as they move in search of grass or browse, the key to their well-being is the flight distance. This distance between a potential enemy and the animal must be maintained in a zoo situation. It is the distance between the visitor railing or walkway and the boundaries of the enclosure. When a visitor places himself inside this barrier the animal panics, often crashing into the far fence. Even when this doesn't occur, the trauma that the animal suffers is the worst kind of torture imaginable.

The people who violate the territories of zoo animals also are running a very serious risk of trauma. A much-publicized case occurred in 1971 when a polar bear at the Central Park Zoo in New York City savagely bit a man who had shoved his arm into its cage. The bear held on with grim tenacity, and the man was able to get away only after a policeman shot the bear to death.

Wolves in zoos are extremely protective of their territory and several people have been chewed up because they ventured into exhibits housing these powerful wild dogs. While I was a curator for the New York Zoological Society I witnessed the damage that wolves can inflict on a human trespasser when a twelve-year-old boy climbed into Wolf Wood at the Bronx Zoo. The youngster had scaled a high chain-link fence on the side of the exhibit in order to pet the wolves, which he believed were German shepherd dogs.

The moment the youngster dropped into the compound, which was a large, wooded area housing a male and two females, the male wolf raced over to him and attacked. The females joined in on the assault moments later, ripping at the boy's clothing and flesh with their fangs. Instinctively, the youngster doubled up into a ball, protecting his head, chest, and belly, and with the wolves chewing on his back and legs, managed to crawl into the moat in front of the exhibit.

The moment he reached the water, the wolves ceased their attack. In terms of their own behavior, they had driven the intruder beyond the boundary of their territory. Stunned and in shock, the boy climbed the wall at the far edge of the moat and collapsed. I was one of the first zoo personnel on the scene and remember being amazed that the boy was alive. The bites were severe, but the youngster recovered after hospitalization.

Similar mishaps have occurred three times at the San Diego Zoo, which like the Bronx has a large wolf compound. The first incident took place in 1971 a few weeks after the exhibit was opened. A fifteen-year-old boy climbed the fence and tried to take a shortcut across the exhibit. His mother later said he did not see the wolves and thought no animals were in the enclosure. As his feet touched the ground, however, he saw the wolves and tried to run away from them, but the animals quickly caught up with him and five of them attacked.

When the wolves seemed to be trying to drag him off by the leg, the boy wrapped his arms around a tree in the enclosure and held tight. Meanwhile two bystanders courageously jumped into the enclosure to help him. The two men, a teacher and a technician, armed themselves with tree limbs and pounded the wolves, which astonishingly did not attempt to bite their assailants, but continued to maul the boy. Dragging the boy and swinging their clubs at the same time, the two rescuers finally got the teen-ager to a wall at the front of the enclosure, where he was lifted to safety. All of the wolves in the exhibit were young animals. Had they been mature, they might have killed the boy before he was rescued.

A few months after that, a twenty-year-old man scaled the fence and dangled his arms over to attract the attention of the wolves. The beasts responded, streaking over to the man and biting his arms deeply.

Two years later another boy tried to cut across the compound. The youngster, an eleven-year-old, also was immediately attacked. This time a security guard shot and killed one of the wolves, and the others fled as the boy was pulled to safety. His arm, however, was badly bitten.

Wolves may react viciously to even a slight infringement on their territory. In 1975 three wolves at a small zoo in Worcester, Massachusetts, savagely bit a two-year-old boy whose leg had slipped through an opening three inches wide between the ground and the bottom of an eight-foot fence around the exhibit housing the animals.

The wolves tore at the boy while his mother and two men who had witnessed the attack tried to pull him free. So savage was the attack of the wolves that they did not stop ripping at the boy until one of the men heaved a railroad tie, from the zoo's miniature railway, over the fence into the midst of the animals.

The initial response of the wolves to attack the youngster probably was one of territorial defense, but the tenacity of the attack might have been due to another reason. The wolves customarily were fed through the opening, which was later closed to only one inch.

Another attack by a wild animal occurred in Perth in 1973 when a tiger in a circus parade pounced on and mauled a fourteen-year-old boy who was watching the show. Circus men managed to pull the beast off the wounded youngster.

BOTH SIDES OF THE FENCE

The killers at zoos are not all within the cages. In addition to people who cannot resist the urge to try and touch animals, zoos attract deranged individuals who make the animals the focus of their abnormal behavior. Some of these sick people place themselves in grave danger. Keepers at the Bronx Zoo once found a man standing in the moat of a lion exhibit declaring in a loud voice that he knew "the lions of Judah" and the zoo cats would not hurt him. One of the keepers replied that the lions in the exhibit were not of Judah but of the Bronx, and that he was in danger. They managed to talk him out of the moat before he was attacked.

During World War II a woman mental patient killed herself at the Zurich, Switzerland, Zoo in a most gruesome fashion. During the night she crept into a stall with a bull Asiatic elephant, who dismembered and then trampled her. Later that same elephant attacked several keepers, killing one of them.

The worst of the cranks who appear at zoos, however, are people who are sadists towards animals. Any zoo man can recite a list of horrors perpetrated by these human beasts: lye tossed into the mouth of a hippo, birds stoned to death, big cats poked with sharp sticks, small mammals knifed, animals fed poison, broken glass, pins, and hooks.

Perhaps this vicious behavior represents the darker side of man's compulsion to demonstrate his mastery over the beasts. Perchance, in fact, all of the fascination we have with captive animals arises from this urge. I think that it is what underlies the way zoo visitors are spellbound by the sight of keepers feeding big cats, why in fact people who go to zoos will pay for the privilege of throwing fish to sea lions and peanuts to elephants, and especially, why today as in the distant past spectacles which pit man against beast are among the most popular of all entertainments, a subject that is the focus of the following chapter.

In earlier days bullfights often took place on the streets of Spanish villages. The tradition is carried on today in the city of Pamplona, where bulls are loosed in the streets.

Fighting bulls are bred on vast ranches in Spain. Only the bravest are brought to the arena.

7. MAN VERSUS BEAST

A FEW YEARS ago a man made the rounds of country fairs in the southeastern United States with a muzzled orangutan, which was shoved into a boxing ring to fight all comers. The prize to anyone who could last three rounds with the ape, whose hands were cushioned with boxing gloves, was $50, so a friend of mine who at the time was a student in need of cash, took up the challenge. He won easily for he also was an accomplished boxer who had no trouble keeping away from the ape for the prescribed period of time.

I suspect the orangutan was either very young or old and feeble, because even with its jaws fettered and its hands encumbered a healthy adult orangutan would be more than a match for a man. Eventually, I am told, a U.S. Marine less merciful than my friend, beat the animal to death.

The story just related is not pretty nor complimentary to human nature but it reveals that even in a supposedly civilized nation people can make a living by staging combats between man and beast. Deep within man lives a primitive chord that responds to the sight of a man challenging the beast. Hopefully, most Americans would find the sight of a man punching an ape to death disgusting, but we demonstrate our enthrallment with man versus animals in many other ways.

It is manifested by the crowds who turn out for rattlesnake roundups, and by the popularity of rodeos. It is the reason why lion and tiger acts are the most featured performances in circuses, and, I suspect, why some of the monster movies which abound on television have such broad appeal.

The sustained appeal of the character Tarzan for at least three generations of Americans is a prime example of what I mean. Tarzan epitomizes the primal man in his struggle against the animal kingdom as he takes on beast after beast in an endless round of film battles.

King Kong, Godzilla, and the other beastly monstrosities of the movies which war against humanity, on the other hand, represent the challenge of nature. Towering atop a skyscraper, Kong might well symbolize the ancient fear of the brute that still looms in man's subconscious. Is the giant ape toppled from his perch a modern substitute for the cave bear ritualistically killed by Neanderthal man?

Not all ritual fights to the death between man and beast have been relegated only to film, however, and one has to go no farther than just across the Mexican border to see the real thing. The combat, of course, is the bullfight, part of the heritage of Spain, to be sure, but also a legacy of other, much more ancient cultures as well.

FACING THE BULL

Man has seen the awesome forces of creation reflected in many animals, including the great bear of prehistory, the lion and the stallion, but no creature so symbolizes the potency and vigor of nature as the bull. Perhaps this is why in almost every age since the birth of civilization, man and bull have been matched in combat.

Archaeologists have found depictions of man fighting bulls in the ruins of ancient Sumerian cities. Prehistoric Egyptians tossed prisoners to wild bulls. King Narmer, who unified Egypt at the dawn of history more than 5,000 years ago, is shown on a palette in the form of a bull trampling one of his foes.

Almost 4,000 years ago, on the Mediterranean island of Crete, bulls were the center of one of the most mysterious and intriguing spectacles of ancient times. Young men and women were pitted in small arenas, or courts, against huge great-horned bulls in contests whose meaning still eludes scholars.

Were the bull pageants of Crete religious rites, sporting events, or perhaps both? Scholars have taken various positions on the question, but all remain pure speculation. We do know, however, what the bull games looked like. Wall paintings and other art works found in the crumbling palaces of the ancient Cretan sea kings depict the events in the bull court with stunning artistry and vivid clarity. From these works of art we can reconstruct the following scene.

Agile, wasp-waisted youths and maidens, nearly naked in the warm Mediterranean sun, dance with graceful assurance about the snorting bull. Slim, but with the firm bodies of acrobats, the young men and women move fluidly, evading the bull's charges with little apparent effort. Suddenly, one of the bull dancers darts forward, towards the beast. Incredibly, the dancer seizes the bull by the horns, vaults on to its back, and with a high, arching sommersault flips up in the air and down into the waiting arms of another dancer.

This is the performance preserved for us in the so-called toreador frescoes, wall paintings discovered in a Cretan palace many years ago by Sir Arthur Evans, the British scholar who unearthed the ruins of ancient Crete. The frescoes depict the bull games as they were about 3,500 years ago, before earthquakes and, it is believed, raiders from the Greek mainland destroyed the Cretan civilization.

Evans pondered the purpose of the bull games and suggested that the bull dancers were the flower of their people—young nobles who matched their speed and agility against the bulls for religious motives, or perhaps just to demonstrate their bravery. Possibly, as time passed the games in the bull court lost their real meaning, and professional athletes replaced the princely dancers. Much the same change occurred in Spain, where once only aristocrats matched themselves against the fighting bulls.

Perhaps the Cretan bulls were sacrificed at the climax of the games. A hint that this might be true is contained in a Cretan seal that shows a man standing next to a bull and stabbing it with a dagger in the neck (rather than between the shoulder blades in the style of the Spanish matador).

On the other hand, it just might be possible that the bull dancers were themselves ritual sacrifices, at least in the beginning. The preclassical civilizations of the Aegean practiced human sacrifice more often than commonly known. As the civilization of Crete mellowed with time, perhaps the bull dance became a bloodless reenactment of the earlier sacrifice.

Author Mary Renault, in her novel *The King Must Die,* made a strong case for linking the games in the bull court to one of the best-known of all the legends that have come down from Bronze Age Greece, the story of Theseus and the Minotaur. Theseus, according to the legend, was an Athenian prince. Chief among his many exploits was the slaying

A fighting bull, shown with a herder on a Spanish ranch, closely resembles the extinct wild ox, the aurochs.

of the Minotaur, the half-bull, half-human offspring of the queen of Crete.

From its beginnings the ruling house of Crete was associated with the bull. Legend has it that Minos, the first king of Crete, was the son of a Middle Eastern princess called Europa and Zeus, who kidnapped her in the shape of a bull and took her to Crete.

Crete was a sea-going nation, and as its ruler, Minos was beholden to the sea god Poseidon, who demanded bulls as sacrifice. When Minos decided to keep one of Poseidon's bulls for himself, the god let the punishment fit the crime. He saw to it that Minos's queen developed an unnatural passion for the bull and coupled with it. She gave birth to the Minotaur, a monster with the head of a bull and body of a man, who Minos had confined in a maze called the Labyrinth.

The Minotaur lusted after human victims, so Minos demanded that Athens, a tributary state, provide young men and maidens to sate the appetite of the monster. According to the legend, Theseus volunteered to go as part of the human tribute, and when he and the Minotaur finally met, it was the bull-man, not the prince, who perished.

In *The King Must Die,* Renault speculates that the young Athenians were brought to Crete not to feed a monster, but to perform in the bull court. She suggests that the dancers were carefully trained before they were risked against the bulls. The Minotaur slain by Theseus is not a monster but the king, who dons a sacred bull mask before doing battle with the Athenian hero.

Whatever the significance of the contest in the bull courts, the games represent the elemental conflict between man and beast or, more accurately, man against nature.

Naked, or nearly so, the bull dancers faced the fearsome strength and dangerous horns of the bull with no more weapons than the half-ape ancestors of man had when they first ventured down from the trees to face the beasts of the open plains.

The bull was, of course, the symbol of fertility in many ancient religions. The worship of the golden calf by the Israelites, for example, was nothing more than their reversion to the fertility rites of the Egypt they had left behind. The sexuality of the bull not only has caused people to associate it with the fructifying powers of the earth, but with the dark animal passions in man. Gods and heroes in several ancient legends kill monstrous or supernatural bulls, which has led to the opinion that slaying the bull represents not just man's wish to overcome nature but to subdue the beast that hides in his own breast. Perhaps this is why the bullfight has survived long after other spectacles of mortal combat between man and beast have vanished.

The Latin bullfight of today evolved from fights to the death between high-born warriors and bulls that were staged in the Middle Ages. When not fighting each other, Christian and Moorish nobles of Spain armed themselves with lances, mounted their war horses, and challenged the bulls to combat. Charles V of Spain killed a bull in the ring to honor the birth of his son in 1527.

The combats were not confined to the Iberian peninsula. Knights of the Roman aristocracy staged a grand battle against bulls in 1332. Afoot and armed with spears, they took on the bulls in the crumbling ruins of the Colosseum, while the great families of Rome watched. Apparently, however, the bulls won the day, for eleven of them survived while eighteen spearmen were killed and nine wounded.

DEALERS OF DEATH

As time went on, bullfighting lost its appeal for aristocrats, and by 200 years ago it was a job for professionals, men from the lower classes who saw the bullring as a means to rise in economic and even social status.

The first of the great Spanish matadors was Francisco Romero, a carpenter's helper who lived in the early eighteenth century. He is credited with originating the form of the bullfight as we know it today. According to the story, Romero was watching a combat between a mounted noble and a bull when the rider was unhorsed. Romero leaped into the ring and by waving his broad-brimmed peasant's hat drew the attention of the bull from the fallen aristocrat. Thus he became the first matador.

The word "matador" means "dealer of death." Its origins are interesting, in the light of the significance of the bull to the ancients, for it stems from the Latin word "mactare" meaning to sacrifice. Mactare, in turn, evolved from "mactus," meaning sacred. In truth, much about the bullfight and the ceremonies that distinguish it has the aspect of a holy sacrificial ritual.

The Spanish fighting bull is an agile, light-bodied but powerful creature, believed to retain many of the characteristics of the extinct aurochs, the large wild ox that was the ancestor of most domestic cattle. For most of their lives, the fighting bulls live on vast ranches, roaming freely like wild cattle. When of an age and size for the ring, the bulls are tested for bravery and if their courage merits, they are chosen to meet the matadors.

In the ring both the bull and the matador are bound by ritual to behave in precise ways. The rules followed by the matador are dictated by custom and culture. If he broke them he would be shamed, but the choice remains his; he can do as he wishes. The bull, on the other hand, has no choice; its behavior in the ring is ritualized in a biological sense. Subject to the conditions of the bull ring all bulls can behave in only one way. They respond to the matador's challenge in the same way as to a rival bull in mating season.

To clarify this point I will refer to observations of animal behaviorist Fritz Walther. The horns of such animals as cattle and antelope are only secondarily used for defense against enemies, but mainly serve the males in battles for sexual dominance. There is a definite pattern to these battles, which can be ended at any time if the weaker male assumes a "submissive posture." It amounts to a subservient crouch, similar to that of a sexually receptive female.

In the light of these facts, says Walther, the bravado of the matador in kneeling down before the bull is sheer sham. Why? Because, Walther asserts, the kneeling position mimics that of the submissive male when it signals the end to a fight. The instinct of the bull forces it to call a truce, which is not binding on the matador. The bull is at a complete disadvantage, for nothing in its behaviorial patterns prepares it for the continued onslaught of the matador. This is but one instance, according to Walther, of how the ritualized behavior of the bull works against it.

Nevertheless, bullfighting is a perilous way to earn a living. Death waits for the matador in every contest, and while usually it is the bull which loses, many bullfighters also lose their lives in the ring. Among the matadors who have been killed by bulls are two of the greatest of all time, José Gomez Ortega (Joselito) and Manuel Rodriguez (Manolete).

Most, if not all, matadors bear the scars of the horns from any number of serious injuries. In 1975, during the most prestigious bullfights of the year in Madrid, three matadors were gored in one day.

The contest in the bullring has been denounced as cruel, barbarous and inhumane on one hand, and as a celebration of manhood and bravery on the other. Hemingway, in particular, dwelt on the latter theme. This book makes no judgments about the morality of the bullfight, except that the drama in the bullring stands as one of the best examples of how, like his prehistoric ancestors, modern man still must prove his dominance by combat with the beast.

BLOODY COMBATS IN THE ARENA

Like it or not, the bullfight is surrounded by an aura of romance and adventure. This cannot be said of another well-known example of staged combat between men and beasts, the bloody games of the Roman arena. From what we know about them, the combats between men and animals performed for the Roman mob were little more that mass slaughter.

The shows in the Roman arena were of mammoth proportions. Almost every species of large wild animal known at the time was goaded into combat with men, and also with other animals. Lions, tigers, bears, dogs, elephants, bulls, and a host of other creatures provided an endless variety of killers and of victims.

Often the beasts were matched against prisoners, sometimes sent into the arena unarmed, sometimes with the weapons of their country. The Roman general Pompey (106–48 B.C.) once staged a show in which captured barbarian warriors from central Europe, bearing the arms they had used in war, were forced to fight against twenty elephants. When the Roman legions razed Jerusalem in 70 A.D., many of the captured Zealot warriors were thrown to the beasts. So, of course, were unarmed Christians, who were slaughtered by starving lions and tigers.

We usually think of the Roman arena in terms of the human life lost there, which was considerable. Forgotten, however, is the fact that the

Today, as in the past, men still meet the bull in the arena. Many cultures have staged bullfights in the past. Today, the bullfight is a mark of Spanish influence and tradition.

number of animal victims was colossal. During the festivities that marked the opening of the Roman Colosseum in the first century, 5,000 animals were slaughtered in a single day. The Emperor Augustus once sponsored a series of twenty-six spectacles in 3,500 African animals died.

The animals in such spectacles were killed by men known as *bestiarii,* who were specially trained for the task.

THE BEAST KILLERS

With bow and arrow, spear, and sword, the bestiarii were matched alone and in groups against the beasts. Sometimes one man would distract an animal, in the manner of a rodeo clown, while another attacked it. Other men fought while strapped to a giant wheel which carried them in and out of the animal's reach. Many works of art from Roman times portray the bestiarii and their adversaries. A mosaic from the fourth century shows an animal fighter, lacking armor or other body protection, spearing a charging leopard. One of the most haunting depictions of the *bestiarii* at work was found deep within the maze of chambers that lie under the stands of the Colosseum. There, on a slab of masonry, someone scratched a scene of spearmen opposing six snarling bears. Who was this man of centuries ago who left the drawing as testimony of his passing? Was he a prisoner awaiting his fate? Was he a professional *bestiarii* whiling away time before his turn came to take on the beasts?

The most avid supporter of the animal games was the crazed emperor Commodus, who ruled from 180 to 192 A.D. Commodus himself participated in the slaughter, sometimes dressed as the hero Hercules. Once from a platform he shot arrows into 100 bears, an elephant, a hippo and a tiger.

To find animals for the arena, Roman beast catchers combed the known world, organizing vast collecting expeditions to bring back big cats, ostriches, elephants, bison, and possibly even gorillas. A mosaic found in North Africa shows one of the expeditions in the field. Beaters afoot and hunters mounted on horses drive oryx, lions, leopards, and ostriches into a hidden pen. The hunt is successful, but while it is under way, a man is lost as a leopard leaps on him and savages him.

The demand of the Roman mobs for more and newer animals to die in the arena sent the collectors farther and farther afield, throughout the Empire and probably beyond as well. The arena consumed so many creatures that entire wildlife populations were decimated. By the time the wild beast combats ended in the sixth century, elephants had vanished from North Africa, the hippo was exterminated in Nubia, and the lions of Mesopotamia, once the royal game of fierce Assyrian kings, were only a memory.

CONFRONTATION IN THE CAGE

Today in the United States men still brave the claws and fangs of lions, tigers, leopards and bears for the entertainment of audiences. These modern *bestiarii* are the circus animal tamers, who risk death by demonstrating their mastery over wild beasts.

The life of the trainer depends not on his ability to kill animals but to impose his will over them. His stock in trade is to do so in a manner that leaves the audience in doubt as to whether he can, to bring his watchers to the edge of their seats in tense anticipation of a disaster before their eyes.

Every moment he is in the cage, the trainer is forcing conflict with the animals, simply because he and they are confined together at such close quarters. It is a situation that can explode at any moment. So dangerous is the job of the wild animal trainer that Clyde Beatty, famed trainer for the Ringling Bros. and Barnum & Bailey Circus, several decades ago was the only performer in the show unable to obtain life insurance. Beatty appeared with a mixed group of animals, including lions, leopards, and bears, and had several close calls.

While he was still a novice, Beatty turned his back for a moment on a male lion, which jumped him and mangled his shoulder. Beatty's instructor drove off the cat. Several years later, Beatty had another encounter with a lion which was much more serious. While he was putting a group of lions and tigers through their paces, Nero, a big male lion, suddenly pounced on him, knocked him to the ground, and bit his leg to the bone. In the midst of the attack, however, the lion let go, and cozied up to a lioness, leaving Beatty alone. Beatty, who almost lost the leg, afterwards claimed that the reason for the attack was that the male lion viewed him as a rival for the favors of the lioness.

One of the best known of big-cat trainers today is Charly Baumann, also of the Ringling Bros. and Barnum & Bailey Circus. Twice daily when the circus is touring, Baumann strides into a steel cage with a dozen huge tigers to make them jump from pedestal to pedestal, roll in unison on the floor, and leap through fiery hoops in an act calculated to leave his audience breathless.

Baumann distains the familiar chair and pistol loaded with blanks and instead relies on his own brand of firm patience coupled with his understanding of how to get the most from his animals without pushing them too far. When teaching his tigers their routines, Baumann says, he takes into account not only the behavior of the species but the quirks of individual animals, which he learns by careful observation.

Baumann spends considerable time studying a new tiger until he has a good idea of its likes and dislikes. He says he will not try to force an animal to perform an act that it abhors, but rather tries to reinforce the natural behavior of his cats.

Tigers naturally roll on the ground when in high spirits, Baumann explains, and cubs often sit up to box with one another. Building on these behaviors, Baumann gets his animals to roll over on the floor of the cage and to sit up on their pedestals.

When Baumann is training his tigers he rewards them for completing a trick by feeding them pieces of stew beef at the end of a broomstick. This type of conditioning takes longer than the usual way of forcing a cat into a routine, which is accomplished by menacing the animal with the legs of a chair and tugging it about with a rope around its neck. However, reward training makes the cats much more stable.

As Baumann trains his animals, he also lets them bite on a stick, which they view as an extension of his body. Soon, he says, they learn that their bites do not hurt him.

Even so, Baumann must remain constantly alerted to the possibility of attack. The life of an animal trainer can hinge on how quickly he recognizes the danger signals which a big cat gives off when it is preparing to launch an assault. A tiger ready to spring will fix its eyes unswervingly on the object of its attention. If a tiger in Baumann's group looks at him in this way, the trainer distracts its attention by loudly calling its name.

Despite his watchfulness, Baumann has been attacked several times. The worst was a mauling by a tiger in 1961 that sent him to the hospital for two months. "I expect it will happen again," he says.

THAT'S SHOW BUSINESS

Performers who work with wild animals must accept the risk of injury—and, in some cases, death—as an inescapable hazard of their particular branch of show business. It is the price that has to be paid for using animals in this way. Very often the damage is not done by creatures that are particularly large or menacing. In dealing with these animals, it is natural to be on guard. It is easy to relax, however, with animals that are small and cuddly, or apparently friendly, and more often than not these are the ones that nail you. I have handled all sorts of creatures in front of television cameras and live audiences, but have been bitten during performances only by the coatimundi mentioned earlier, and by a gerbil.

Even an animal that is accustomed to working with performers can suddenly become a danger. Recently at a nightclub in Miami Beach, a python used by an entertainer in a sketch about Adam and Eve unexpectedly looped itself around him and started to squeeze. Gripped in the tightening coils of the serpent, which was sixteen feet long, the man fell to the floor unconscious. Stagehands saved him by wrestling with the snake and unwrapping it from around its body. The python had been used in the sketch for some time, and its sudden change in behavior could not be explained. Its owner, when he recovered his senses, said he planned to keep the snake in the act.

Often all it takes to make a performing wild animal strike out is a sudden noise or change in its routine. One of the three men killed by the elephant Mandarin, described in the preceding chapter, was a substitute trainer, strange to the elephant. The act called for the trainer to place his head under the upraised foot of the elephant. Mandarin, who performed the trick perfectly with his regular trainer, stepped on the head of the substitute.

An outstanding example of how a strange noise can set off a rampage by circus animals occurred in 1888 on the streets of Munich. The

Bloody man-animal battles were staged for the benefit of the Roman mobs. Animals were brought to the area from all over the known world.

sudden blast of a steam engine frightened four elephants in a circus parade into stampeding. Before the elephants were rounded up and calmed, they trampled several bystanders and triggered hysteria in which scores of people were pushed, shoved and knocked to the ground by the frantic crowd.

THE ELECTRONIC ANIMALS

Today animals provide diversion for more people than ever before in history. Never has man lived so far removed from nature, and yet never before has he had access to the innermost secrets of the animal world. Virtually any day in the week Americans can sit back and watch as animals of every size, shape and description go about the business of living in places as familiar as a city park or as remote as the polar ice. It is all possible, as they used to say, through the magic of television.

Television programs about wild animals have become a staple of mass entertainment in recent years. They appear in the television listings almost as frequently as game shows, whose sponsors sometimes may wish they had placed their money on the birds and the beasts instead of freezers and new cars. By programs about animals, it should be added, I do not mean shows about fictitious animal characters, which have been on the air for years; but documentaries which present, or purport to show, wild creatures as they really live in nature.

The immense audience such shows attract has created great faith among marketing people. During the 1973–74 season, for example, the flagship station of the American Broadcasting Company network devoted almost half its most marketable air time to nature programs.

The ideas millions of people have about wild animals and their relation to humanity has been shaped by nature as seen through the television. The only exposure many people have to wild animals in any variety, in fact, is electronic. What these people see on the television screen has a powerful effect on their thinking. A pet dealer quoted in *The Record,* a New Jersey newspaper, put it aptly when he explained the influence television has on his business: "People are always looking for unusual pets, and I think the television shows are mainly responsible. People want or think they want whatever they see on TV. I once had a request for 1,000 grasshoppers because of a TV show."

The formats of the programs differ. Some are life studies of particular species, or focus on the activities of naturalists and wildlife biologists. Others follow the alleged adventures of a specific animal. The latter, such as the story of Castor the beaver, described in Chapter 1, tend to humanize their animal characters in the worst way.

The widely seen series "Animal World" has done this on occasion, in addition to its respectable studies of animals in the wild. One such program describes the adventures of a raccoon named Zorro and the "beguiling" female coon he meets in the dog pound. The kindly dog warden releases the raccoons in the forest where they "lived happily ever after." The program never mentions the one big problem that captive raccoons released in the wild almost always encounter—the bloody and almost unceasing battle they must wage to carve out a territory from those claimed by raccoons already living there. Mentioning that fact would have been a great service to the countless pet raccoons dumped in the woods by owners who tire of them and think that releasing the animals is a good deed.

Other programs go to the opposite extreme and show true, unvar-

One of the world's most famous trainers, Charly Baumann, puts his tigers through their paces at the Ringling Bros. and Barnum & Bailey Circus.

nished nature in the raw, with no holds barred. One of a series of specials starring behaviorist Jane Goodall, for example, showed in gory detail a pack of African hunting dogs making their kill. It may not have been pretty, but it was a true depiction of nature.

To me it is especially significant that the most popular television nature program—indeed one of the most successful television series in history—regularly shows not only combats between animals but also the naturalists who are its protagonists grappling with assorted wild creatures. The program is "Mutual of Omaha's Wild Kingdom," which went on the air in 1963 and is still running strong. Not only is the program one of the most long-lived on the air, but it has gathered a trunkful of Emmy awards.

Seen on more than 200 stations fifty-two weeks a year, "Wild Kingdom" stars zoologist Marlin Perkins, who usually is shown accompanied by one or two brawny and handsome young assistants. A recurring theme in the program, along with the motif that wildlife should be conserved, is that the beasts encountered by the human stars are likely to be dangerous. Words like "feared" and "killer" crop up often in the script. Perkins frequently tosses off lines such as, "Those powerful jaws can splinter a two-by-four or break your arm." The ability of animals to do harm is stressed. While watching gorgeous scenes of mountain goats on the peaks of the Canadian Rockies, for instance, viewers are told that the goats "can slash an attacker to pieces with those sharp horns."

Most episodes of "Wild Kingdom" have featured Perkins and his aides in the field. Usually they accompany other zoologists, game wardens, or similar people as they capture animals for zoos, tag them with markers for research purposes, or relocate them in sanctuaries.

It is always in a good cause, but sooner or later Perkins and his friends are likely to rope, wrestle or run down some creature or other, which may be then trussed up, or shoved into a bag, and hauled about the landscape.

The roughhouse on "Wild Kingdom" is bloodless, no one really gets hurt, and it is all supposed to be for the benefit of the animals, even though they don't know it. At the same time, the program gives people plenty of what they seem to want—the sight of men engaged in physical struggle with animals. Certainly there is nothing unhealthy about enjoying this sort of thing, or even the more violent but fictitious exploits of Tarzan. Deep down, however, our fascination with such things stems from the same urges that, at their cruelest, drew throngs to the Roman arena.

8. MAN AND THE
ALIENS

THUS FAR THIS book has focused on how our attitudes and actions towards animals not only drastically affect their existence but also generate a powerful feedback on our own lives as well. Until now, however, no mention has been made of one of the most profound changes that this interplay has wrought—the redistribution of animal life on the face of the earth.

Man, often to his own ruin or that of the environment, has rearranged the geographical distribution of the world's wildlife by carrying all manner of creatures from their native haunts to places where they are ecologically alien. Muskrats from North America infest European rivers, providing a source of furs for trappers but also digging away at riverbanks and chewing up vegetation. The American gray squirrel was released in Great Britain and now threatens to displace the smaller red squirrel that is native there. Asian porcupines which have escaped from captivity in England are chewing away at forests. The mongoose was introduced from the Old World on numerous tropical islands in the Western Hemisphere, supposedly to control venomous snakes. Instead it has slaughtered native birds. European red deer loosed by British settlers in New Zealand multiplied out of control in the absence of predators and so overgrazed the landscape, that serious erosion of the soil has occurred. South American fire ants which have been introduced in the southeastern United States have caused incalcuable damage to crops. In the past decade at least two people have died after they were swarmed upon by the biting, stinging insects.

Sometimes man has deliberately put animals where they do not belong; other times it has been purely by accident. Often, though not always, the introduction of alien species has resulted from some kind of exploitation of animals by people. The trade in exotic pets, for example, has been responsible for the introduction into the United States of several alien animals, some of which menace the livelihood and even the lives of Americans, to say nothing of the well-being of our native animals. The pet trade also has spread animals from one part of the country to the other. The garter snake, described in Chapter 2, which bit the youngster in California in November 1975 is believed to have been a pet that was released or escaped, for it was a variety not native to that area.

More often than not, if an introduced animal becomes established in a new environment, calamity follows in its footsteps. The nature and extent of the disaster can range from something as localized as the upsetting of the natural checks and balances in a small stream or a single spring to the unleashing of a disease that decimates the human population of a continent. The plague which ravaged medieval Europe was carried by the black rat *(Rattus rattus)*, which was introduced there from Asia in the thirteenth century as a stowaway on the ships and in the caravans of returning Crusaders.

ANIMAL INVADERS

When an animal is introduced into a new environment the chances are that it will perish, or at the most survive only in a small, isolated colony. Sometimes, however, a species is so adaptable, or else conditions in its new home so amenable to it, that it establishes a firm foothold. If this occurs, the odds are excellent that the creature will flourish, increase its range and dominate native animals, all at the expense of the balance of nature, and often to the detriment of human welfare.

One of the things that can give introduced species an edge is that it has left its natural enemies and competitors far behind in its homeland,

and the animals living in its new environment probably have not evolved a means of coping with the invader.

Some of the most familiar wild animals in the United States today are alien species which have become established here. They include the pigeons, starlings, and English sparrows that abound in our cities and suburbs; the black rat and its cousin, the brown rat; as well as the house mouse and even the ringneck pheasant.

The pheasant *(Phasianus colchicus)*, an Asian species introduced all across North America as a game bird, has been a welcome addition to native wildlife. It does not offer serious competition for any native birds, and moreover gives pleasure to both bird watchers and hunters. We have not been so lucky, however, with other birds introduced from abroad. Most of them have upset natural balances, and some are at least potential threats to health and agriculture.

Both starlings *(Sturnus vulgaris)* and English sparrows *(Passer domesticus)* have contributed to the decline of some native birds by taking their food and nesting places. The bluebird, which nests in cavities in trees, has been virtually eliminated in some areas because the foreign birds have appropriated their nest sites.

The introduction of starlings and English sparrows from Europe was accomplished during the last century on the Atlantic seaboard. In both cases it was deliberate. The starling was imported and set free by people who thought the speckled, intelligent bird would brighten up America's avian scene. English, or house, sparrows were released in Philadelphia, New Haven and other eastern cities to control caterpillars, and also because people thought that these birds, which get along well in the presence of man, would bring a touch of nature into despoiled urban areas.

Both species now live in vast numbers from coast to coast, particularly in towns and cities, where they have few enemies other than housecats and an abundance of places to live. The high adaptability of starlings and house sparrows is reflected by their unusually flexible living requirements. They can use any of a wide variety of sites to roost or nest, and buildings provide them plenty of places to do both. Because the birds are so favored, their concentrations have become unnaturally large in many communities, where the droppings of the birds have become an eyesore and a threat to health.

BIRDS AND DISEASE

Bird droppings sometimes promote the growth of fungi which can infect people and in some cases even kill them. Fortunately, these fungus diseases are rather rare, but the danger that people will catch them increases considerably in places where bird droppings accumulate in large amounts. Significant amounts of the infectious fungus *Histoplasma capsulatum,* for example, have been discovered around very large roosts of starlings and native blackbirds that have plagued some communities in Kentucky and Tennessee. One of the largest roosts, at Fort Campbell, Kentucky, contains 10 million birds. The disease which the fungus causes, called histoplasmosis, has two forms: one which creates no serious symptoms and seldom is detected in people who have it, and the other, exceedingly rare, which results in ulcers, anemia, and a host of other disagreeable symptoms. Sometimes it can be severe enough to kill.

The pigeons which flock in our cities also carry this disease, as well as one that is potentially more serious. Pigeons are the domesticated form of the Eurasian rock dove *(Columba livia)* which has become feral in cities all over the world. They prosper virtually unmolested by predators in urban areas, where lofts, window ledges, rooftops and air conditioners that protrude from windows mimic the rock ledges and caves in which their wild relatives nest.

Where pigeons congregate and their droppings pile up, the infectious fungus *Cryptococcus* grows profusely. Millions of the fungi can grow in a single dropping. The fungi are airborne, and people who pass by inhale them, but the natural resistance of the human body usually is sufficient to ward off infection.

A very few people, however, do not have natural immunity to *Cryptococcus,* and for such persons exposure to the fungi can cause a form of meningitis, which is usually fatal. Physicians do not know what the bodies of such people lack in the way of natural defense against the fungi, only that something is missing. Fortunately, the disease is rare.

POLLY IS A PEST

During the past few years, a brand new avian invader has begun to establish itself throughout the country. This one has caused something of a sensation because it is a large green and gray parakeet. The introduction of this bird, the monk parakeet *(Myiopsitta monachus)* is due solely to the pet trade, which brought thousands of the parakeets into the United States from their native Argentina.

Some of the birds have escaped while in shipment or from their owners. Other parakeets probably have been set free by people who purchased the birds then found out that they are extremely noisy. In one instance, monk parakeets were freed by a zoo.

Monk parakeets, which get their name from the gray plumage of their hood, are prospering in places as diverse as California, Michigan, Virginia, Florida, New England, New Jersey, and New York. At least two dozen states have reported the presence of these birds in large numbers. They are especially numerous and are breeding rapidly around New York City, where in 1969 a dozen birds may have escaped from a shipment at Kennedy International Airport.

The huge stick nests built by these birds—they are the only parrots or parakeets to make a nest of sticks—have turned up atop utility poles, on window ledges on church steeples, and even at the Cleopatra's Needle obelisk in Manhattan's Central Park.

On the other side of the country, in California, fifteen parakeets were released by the San Diego Zoo in November 1971 with the idea that the birds would liven up the city's Balboa Park. They did, so much so that people living nearby complained about the raucous cries emitted by the parakeets. The zoo responded by recapturing all of the birds—so its officials claim—but the California State Department of Agriculture says there was a discrepancy between the number released and that recaptured.

Agricultural and environmental agencies in several states are exceedingly distrubed about the introduction of the parakeet because in its native Argentina it is a major farm pest. Flocks of parakeets descend upon fruit orchards and fields of corn, millet, and sunflowers, and devour these crops. Argentina has waged war against the birds, and in one province alone more than 400,000 parakeets were destroyed in just two years. Even so, the bird continued to prosper.

The New York State Department of Environmental Conservation already has started to eradicate the parakeets, and the United States Fish and Wildlife Service has begun to examine the implications of the introduction on a nationwide basis. The climate of the southern half of the

nation is just right for the parakeet, but it also has displayed a strong tolerance for northern winters. In the northern states, however, the parakeet may need the help of man to survive the cold weather. It appears that in winter the bird is dependent to a large degree on sunflower seeds and other food available at bird feeders. Parakeets frequently show up at bird feeders in the north, and in some cases have driven off native birds. One parakeet was seen killing a bluejay near a feeder in New Jersey.

THE MOST DESTRUCTIVE WILD VERTEBRATES

While the consumption of crops, competition with native wildlife, and even the infrequent threat of disease are unpleasant enough, none of the examples cited so far provides a truly adequate view of just how much havoc an introduced animal can create. The extent of the harm introduced species can cause comes into much sharper focus when one considers the ruin brought about by the rats which man has spread throughout the world.

Of all wild vertebrates, none has profited more from the expansion of the human species that rats. From their original homes in Asia, the black rat and the larger brown rat *(R. norvegicus)* have been carried by man all over the populated world. The two rats are commensal to man, that is they adapt so well to man-made changes in the environment that they benefit from them. Rats do not flourish nearly as well on their own as they do in the world of man, where they find all the shelter and food they need. So superbly are rats suited to living with man that they even can develop resistance to poisons used against them and pass it on to their offspring.

The arrangement between rats and man is all one-sided, however, because rats are man's worst enemies among the higher animals. Diseases spread by rats have killed more people than all the wars ever

The monk parakeet has been introduced into the United States and is viewed by many people as an agricultural pest. The bird, from South America, has been free-ranging in this country since the 1960s.

fought, and in a time when millions of people are starving, rats render a fifth of the world's food supply unfit for human consumption. Annually, rats consume 48 million tons of rice alone. That is enough to feed 1,000 million people for a quarter of a year.

Originally, rats were creatures of the wild. Black rats ranged from Asia Minor to the Orient, which also is believed to have been the original home of the brown rat. Black rats in the wild readily climb trees, while brown rats are burrowers, often living along stream banks. When rats live in association with man, each species follows its natural proclivities. The black rat nests aloft in roofs and attics while the brown makes its home in basements.

It has been thousands of years, however, since rats were purely creatures of the wild. Probably rats moved in alongside man when people developed agriculture, creating a ready source of food for the rodents. Rats have been residents of Asian cities since time immemorial, but not until the Middle Ages did they arrive in any numbers in Europe. The first to come was the black rat, which was brought home by the Crusaders. As soon as the first Europeans reached the Americas, so did the black rats. Brown rats scurried into European ports from the holds of ships from Asia in the middle of the sixteenth century. They quickly spread throughout the continent and by the time of the American Revolution had crossed the Atlantic. Today there are as many rats in this country as people.

Although the two rats do not compete for living quarters they do for food. The confrontation always is won by the brown rat, which is therefore the species that most commonly infests our cities. The black rat lives mainly in rural areas, although it also inhabits some seacoast towns as well.

The brown rat has adapted so well to living with man that it cannot survive in substantial numbers without the presence of large human populations. In fact, even a dump may be less desirable than human habitations as a home for the brown rat. A study of rats in a Hartford, Connecticut, ghetto in 1975 showed that more of the rodents lived in a housing project where garbage was not properly stored and collected than in the city dump.

When conditions suit them, rats multiply very rapidly. Up to seven litters a year, with as many as a dozen young in each, can be produced by either species. Extremely wary, rats have excellent senses of hearing and smell, although they see poorly. They are capable of astonishing physical feats. A rat a foot long can squeeze through an opening slightly larger than a half-inch square. Rats can climb wires and pipes, both horizontally and vertically, jump vertically about three times their length from a flat surface, and withstand a drop of fifty feet without injury. Excellent swimmers, rats can make a half mile in open water. Cinderblock, lead and aluminum sheeting, and adobe brick all can be penetrated by the rat's chisellike teeth, and a rat can burrow straight down into the earth to a depth of four feet.

Rats eat just about everything people do, and more. Garbage or food left exposed quickly attracts the rodents. Even keeping pets to discourage rats can have the opposite result, for rats swarm to food left out for dogs and cats. Rats have been known to live under a doghouse and emerge at night to feed on the dog's rations as it slept.

Not only are rats voracious eaters—one of them can consume up to forty pounds of food a year—but they also foul vast amounts of food with their droppings. All told, rats render between $500,000,000 and $1,000,000,000 worth of food unusable each year in the United States alone!

Although rats do not wander far from home in search of food and water they are always frantic when away from the nest. The slightest threat to them at such a time prompts them to respond with hysterical fury. A cornered rat will attack cats, dogs, and people with equal savagery. A person who tries to poke the rat with a broom handle or stick may find that the animal has run up the stick and bitten his hand. For one reason or another, at least 10,000 Americans a year are bitten by rats.

Often people become victims because they have attempted to catch or kill a rat or have accidentally shoved a hand into a cupboard where a rat is feeding. But there is another far more horrifying side to the story, for rats also sometimes bite people with the express aim of feeding on human flesh. The rat is one of the predators of man.

MAN IS THE PREY

The danger of rat bite is something that people who live in urban slums must contend with as part of everyday living. Not only must they watch out for accidental encounters with rats, but they also must protect themselves from rats which view them as prey. The inclination of some rats to consider humans as food is not generally realized, but it has been known to public health authorities for many years.

In 1945 Dr. Curt P. Richter of the Johns Hopkins Hospital in Baltimore published the results of a four-year study which demonstrated with frightening clarity that rats do try to eat people. The predation of the rat on humans, Richter explained, arises from the unique relationship between rat and man:

> "Wild rats, even more than domesticated animals, enjoy very intimate living arrangements with man. They live in the same house, share the same beds, eat the same foods, carry the same internal and external parasites, and suffer from the same diseases and plagues." Noting that man has tried to discourage such intimacy, Richter added: "Rats, on the other hand, are less discriminating, even seeking contact with man and treating him much as they do the dying and dead members of their own species—running over him, licking him, biting him, and finally trying to eat him."

Richter based his conclusions on analysis of rat-bite cases treated at the John Hopkins Hospital, which is located near a black ghetto. Although the victims ranged in age from two months to sixty-five years, most were infants less than a year old. In most cases, the rats attacked while the victims slept, biting the hands or face.

A person who is sleeping, Richter suggested, provokes the same reaction in a rat as a dead member of its own species. The scientist explained that "wild rats eat dead and dying rats with great relish. They start at the head and work down and often devour the entire body. . . . They often prefer dead rats to other foods."

For some reason, rats have the same appetite for the flesh of sleeping humans, which in the rat's eyes become a source of food. Moreover, Richter asserted rats develop a "real craving for fresh human blood."

Driven by this hunger a rat may return again and again to the same victim. One child whose case was examined by Richter was bitten on eleven different nights!

Usually, of course, the bite awakens the victim, and either the victim or the family usually can chase the rodent away. But a monstrous potential for tragedy hangs over families who must live in the slums. It is the danger that a sleeping baby, left alone even for a short time, will draw rats greedy for human flesh and blood, and that no one will hear the infant's cries as it feels the slash of rodent teeth.

THE BLACK DEATH

The threat that the rat poses to man as a competitor and predator pales besides the misery and destruction that rats have caused as carriers of several dread disease germs and the fleas that transmit them to humans. The most serious of the illnesses carried by rats are a form of typhus fever and the plague, the "Black Death" of the Middle Ages.

Much of the terror once associated with both diseases has been dispelled by the development of antibiotics, which are very effective in curing these sicknesses. In past centuries, however, epidemics of typhus and plague spread by rats killed countless millions of people. Plague, especially, has been the ravager of entire continents.

Plague, which so terrified the people of medieval times they believed it a sign of divine wrath, results from infection of a germ known to science as *Pasteurella pestis,* which infects several species of wild rodents. Of these animals, only rats readily live close to humans, so because of adaptability of rats to the world of man they are mankillers without parallel among the higher animals.

The usual route for transmission of plague from rats to humans is through fleas, which live on the rodents. The plague germs enter the fleas when they bite the rats. Anybody who happens to be bitten next by such fleas will be infected by the germs. A person does not even have to be in contact with rats to be infested by the fleas, however, for pets can serve as intermediaries. The fleas find dogs and cats as much to their liking as rats. One of the eight people stricken by plague in the United States during 1974 was a twenty-two-year-old student who came down with the disease after sleeping with his cat, which probably picked up the fleas from a rat or other rodent. He survived, as did all the other victims in that year, the last for which statistics were available.

All of the plague cases in the United States during 1974 occurred in the southwest, where some wild rodents are known to carry the disease. During June 1974 plague germs were discovered in ground squirrels and chipmunks which scavenged refuse at a campground in the Rocky

Mountain National Park of Colorado. The camp was closed until the rodents were exterminated. The only other reservoir of plague germs known to exist in the nation is in rats living near Tacoma, Washington.

The year 1974 was typical as far as plague cases in the United States are concerned, for few people in this country ever contract the disease, and appropriate medical treatment almost always ensures survival of those who do.

Plague is a serious problem in some other parts of the world, notably northern India, parts of Indochina, and central Asia. Cases occur regularly in these regions and from time to time, vast epidemics erupt. One of the world's last major outbreaks of plague swept from southern China to India shortly before the end of the last century. Millions of people perished.

The epidemic most notorious in the western world was the Black Death, which arrived in Italy from Asia Minor about the middle of the fourteenth century and in a few years spread through central and northern Europe to England and Scandanavia. The catastrophe was a direct result of the introduction of the black rat. Millions perished as the disease wasted Europe, much of which already was in ruins from the Hundred Years' War. All told, Europe lost a third of its population. In some places such as the thickly populated cities of Italy, more than half the people died. Spain is said to have lost 80 percent of its population. Rural regions fared somewhat better than the jam-packed cities, which were less than healthy in the best of times.

Where the ravages of the plague were worst, people lost all hope, and ran wild, giving themselves over to rapine, corruption, murder and witchcraft. Many people blamed the disaster on Jews, who were unmercifully slaughtered in some localities. Within less than a decade, the epidemic expired. Periodically, over the next three centuries, local outbreaks occurred, but never again on the scale of the Black Death.

In the wake of the Black Death, Europe was a land of deserted cities, empty monasteries, and untilled fields. The society that emerged from the maelstrom was considerably different than the one that preceded it. This is not the place to describe in detail how the plague influenced the development of modern Europe, but in general the Black Death left the old social order in such a shambles that it could never be reconstructed. While not the only factor, the epidemic which the black rat brought to

Europe in the fourteenth century was a major force in ending the medieval way of life.

SNAILS SPREAD DISEASE

The Black Death is an extreme case of what can happen when introduced animals spread disease. However, a disaster of that magnitude still can happen at any time as a result of the introduction of exotic creatures. Today, in fact, because of the introduction of a species of tropical snail in Florida, the possibility exists that one of the most serious of all major tropical illnesses could break out for the first time in the United States. The disease is schistosomiasis, second only to malaria among tropical diseases in the number of people it afflicts. From Puerto Rico to the Far East, schistosomiasis infects at least 200,000,000 people.

To understand the role of the snail in spreading schistosomiasis, the nature of the disease should be understood. First of all, it is parasitic, caused by flatworms called schistosomes. At one point in their life cycle the flatworms use certain species of aquatic snails as hosts. Like other parasitic diseases, schistosomiasis is perpetuated by an endless round of infection and reinfection. Humans contract the disease when they enter water inhabited at the flatworm larvae, called "cercariae." On contact with human skin, the cercariae burrow through it into the bloodstream. It takes as little as a half second for the minuscule young worms to penetrate the body, so even a short exposure to infected waters can mean trouble.

In the bloodstream the worms mature, mate and produce huge volumes of eggs, usually in the blood vessels, bladder or intestines. The blood carries the eggs to most other organs, even the brain, where the eggs cluster in vast numbers. The lungs of one victim contained 100,000 schistosome eggs. The worms, moreover, are long-lived and may go on producing eggs for twenty years. Although not always fatal, the disease so impairs the organs that in its later stages it can render a person helpless. Treatment does not always work, and besides, it requires administration of drugs that can have highly toxic side effects.

The eggs leave the human body in urine and feces, and if the feces happen to enter freshwater, the eggs hatch into the first of the flatworm's two larval stages. These primary larvae enter the body of aquatic snails, and in them reproduce asexually into thousands of cercariae. Eventually the cercariae kill the snail, enter the water, and attack a human host, thus completing the cycle.

Aside from good sanitation, the best way to control schistosomiasis is to drain or poison the waters where the snails live. Obviously this approach is not always desirable from an ecological or economic point of view. In some parts of the world, moreover, new habitat for the snails is being created, rather than destroyed, in the form of irrigation projects. It is feared, for example, that the Aswan Dam project in Egypt will spread the snails and thus increase the number of Egyptians infected with schistosomiasis.

The presence of the snails alone is not enough to start an outbreak of schistosomiasis. Either the snails must already carry the larval flatworms, or else urine or feces from someone infected with the disease must contaminate water where the snails live. Literally all it takes, however, is one snail and one infected person in the same place.

One of the snails that can play host to schistosomes has been introduced into Florida's fresh waters. The snail, known by the scientific name *Tropicorbis obstructus,* probably arrived via the tropical fish trade. Snails from abroad often arrive in shipments of tropical fish and aquarium plants. After the fish and plants are removed from the vessels that carry them, the water containing the snails is sometimes dumped into streams and ponds.

So far as is known, the snails introduced in Florida have not been infested with schistosomes and thus pose no threat at this time. However, thousands of people living in the United States carry the eggs of schistosomes in their bodies, and thus potentially could transmit the disease to the snails. Public health authorities estimate that 10 percent of the Puerto Ricans who have come to the United States from the island are infected. So, undoubtedly, are many people who come here from other tropical lands where schistosomiasis is prevalent. If even a single carrier of the disease were to urinate or defecate in one of the waterways in Florida that harbor the snails, schistosomiasis could break out in the United States.

THE LAND OF EXOTICS

Florida has become the adopted home of more than eighty-five different kinds of exotic animals and has the worst problem with introduced species of any place in North America. The state, to the sorrow of many of its residents, provides a natural laboratory in which the effects of widescale introduction of alien species can be observed.

There are several reasons for the success of so many introduced species in Florida. One reason, obviously, is the mild climate, particularly in the south, which approximates that of the tropical and subtropical lands from which many of the animal invaders have come. Moreover, aquatic animals that find themselves in Florida's waterways quickly spread over the countryside through the network of drainage and irrigation canals that crisscross much of the state. This network connects almost all stream systems in the state, so that a species introduced in one stream can quickly turn up in another.

Another reason for the problem in Florida is the proximity of the state to the islands of the West Indies. Frogs, lizards, and other small creatures have migrated from the West Indies to Florida aboard boats and ships, often as stowaways in cargo. The prime source of exotic animals in Florida, however, has been the pet trade. Many animal importers and dealers make Florida their base. All sorts of creatures have escaped from dealers, and some animals even have been set free when they have proven unmarketable. Pet owners have released many more.

Among the most unusual beasts from elsewhere which now make Florida their home are the following.

—Squirrel monkeys *(Saimiri sciureus)* from tropical America, believed to be released pets and their offspring, inhabit several areas around Miami.

—Rhesus monkeys *(Macaca mulatta),* large, aggressive macaques from southern Asia, live along the Silver River in central Florida. The monkeys descend from animals that escaped during the filming of early Tarzan movies in the area.

—Ocelots, most likely escaped pets, have been seen in several parts of the state.

—Jaguarundis *(Felis eyra),* wild cats which like the ocelot naturally range from the extreme southwestern United States to South America, also have escaped from pet owners in Florida. About twenty pounds, the jagaurundi is not viewed as any sort of a threat to man or the environment, and may in fact help right the natural imbalances which have resulted from the decline of native predators such as the cougar and bobcat *(Felis rufa).*

—Rose-breasted cockatoos *(Kakatoe roseicapilla),* a species that feeds on fruit and grain crops in its native Australia, are often seen in the southern part of the state.

—Spectacled caimans—South American relatives of the native American alligator, have been sighted in several parts of the state. The introduction of these bellicose reptiles probably was accomplished by people who released pet caimans because the animals either grew too large or as is the nature of the beast, became too feisty.

—South American piranhas, the small flesh-eating fish which are the subject of so many horror stories, also have been dumped into Florida waterways. The culprits, according to state game and fish officials, are home aquarists and tropical fish importers. Several species of piranhas have been found in the state, including some which belong to a group, scientifically known as *Serrasalmus,* which in their native waters have bitten many people. Despite the tales of piranhas converging in vast schools on swimmers and eating them, there is no well-documented case of a human being killed by these fish. Even so, few people would relish the thought of entering the water with them, for they do sometimes kill animals as large as man.

—Giant marine toads *(Bufo marinus),* which have a native range from the Rio Grande Valley to South America, were released in Dade County to eat insect pests in sugar-cane fields. The toads, now firmly established in southern Florida, eat not only insects, but also the young of the endangered Florida burrowing owl, which nests in holes in the ground. Marine toads have skin glands which secrete a poison powerful enough to sicken any dog which happens to mouth them, and to irritate human skin.

—The notorious walking catfish *(Clarias batrachus),* an air-breathing creature from southeast Asia, is a permanent resident of canals, streams and ponds in the southern part of the state. The catfishes, which arise from specimens that escaped from a tropical fish farm near Fort Lauderdale, have decimated populations of native fish, which the invaders either kill or crowd out of feeding areas.

It is difficult to predict just what kind of odd or unpleasant creatures one is likely to meet on a stroll about the Florida countryside. A jaguar was shot near Vero Beach in the early 1960s. The big cat apparently had been roaming free for some time. In October 1975 two men driving along a road near Orlando discovered an eight-foot boa constrictor stretched out on the pavement. The snake, which was turned over to a local zoo, apparently had been living in the wild for some time, probably existing on a diet of rabbits and rodents. A few weeks after that, an eleven-foot Indian python *(Python molurus)* kept as a pet by a Kissimmee man slithered out of its cage to freedom, creating a case of jitters in the neighborhood.

Rumors of exotic snakes roaming the countryside of Florida have been rife for years. Anacondas have been reported for years around Lake Okeechobee, a 700-square-mile body of water in the south-central part of the state. A reticulated python was reported seen recently near Tampa and, worst of all, cobras may be living in the area south of Okeechobee.

Such stories may seem farfetched, but not so remote that biologists do not pay heed to them. The cobra story is a case in point. Several biologists of unquestionable veracity say that it may be true, and one of them has seen a specimen of the snake, whose species has not been identified. One scientist says he believes specimens are in the hands of agents of the State Fresh Water Fish and Game Commission, but the director of the commission denies any knowledge of it.

Biologists who have studied the problem of introduced species in Florida have feared for a long time that exotic venomous serpents such as cobras will be transplanted to the state. Florida has an abundance of reptile dealers and a reputation for having more than its share of snake freaks, including some people of rather dubious mental stability who even might go as far as releasing a cobra or a mamba. Considering how foolish it is to keep venomous snakes as pets at all, the possibility of a deliberate release is not improbable. The release or escape of one or even a few venomous serpents might not create a breeding population in Florida, but then again, it very well might.

It is not so much that exotic serpents are more venomous than those already native to Florida. As noted previously, the eastern diamondback rattlesnake, which ranks among the most deadly living snakes, is common in the state. The rattlesnake, however, fits into the natural scheme of things in its native environment and more importantly is a known quantity. Antivenin is readily available and physicians know how to treat rattler bites. An introduced cobra would be something else again.

It is impossible to predict how an exotic animal will behave in its new home. Often, in fact, introduced species act quite differently in new environments than they do in their places of origin.

For example, a serpent that in its native land hunts prey in the bush far from human habitation could be transplanted to a place where suitable prey is abundant only in suburban backyards. The snake would begin to prowl around homes, and thus begin to encounter large numbers of people. The new pressures such contact would entail could make the serpent extremely nervous, and perhaps aggressive—traits it might never exhibit in its native bush country. Forced to live side by side with people in its new home, the snake could become a major mankiller.

The case just described is hypothetical, of course, but the point it makes central to understanding how man can make a menace out of an animal which normally threatens him very little, or even not at all. Man does it by changing the conditions under which the animal evolved, and to which it is adapted. This disturbs the animal's relationship with its world and compels it to act unnaturally in an attempt to survive.

Man's manipulation of the animal kingdom is not always deliberate. Just by being in the animal's world, people can alter it. Ever since man was half-beast himself, he has made his presence felt upon animals, but never so pervasively and indomitably as today. All over the globe human encroachment upon the animal kingdom has inspired increasing conflict between man and beast, and while the latter always loses in the long run, the clash also bodes ill for man.

9. SIDE BY SIDE

SCIENTISTS DIGGING FOR fossils in the Swartkrans Cave of South Africa in 1949 unearthed part of the skull of a juvenile apeman whose kind had inhabited the region more than a million years ago. While by no means unimportant, the skull fragment in itself is not especially remarkable, for the cave has yielded the remains of more than seventy prehistoric subhumans, members of a breed known as australopithecines. What is intriguing about the ancient piece of bone, however, is a pair of small holes punched in it. Judging from the flaked condition of the bone around the holes, they were made when it was still fresh—perhaps only moments after the apeman died.

Some anthropologists believe the holes were from the fangs of a leopard, which killed the young apeman and then dragged off the carcass to feast. Leopards characteristically seize the head of their prey in their jaws when they carry it away to feed.

It is highly probable that leopards and other large flesh eaters regularly preyed on some of the apelike ancestors of man, just as they do baboons and monkeys. The predators even may have helped shape the course of human evolution by eliminating the lines of apemen who were

The leopard prowls Africa today just as it did in prehistoric times. Leopards seem better able to adapt to man than the other big cats.

259

the least able to take care of themselves, leaving the field open for others, including the strain that evolved into the first true men.

According to this theory, the line leading to modern man was intelligent enough and probably combative enough to fend off the big flesh-eaters, at least much of the time. The sort of competition that existed between our prehistoric predecessors and the creatures which preyed on them was conflict between man and beast at its most basic level —a fang-and-claw struggle for survival in the wilderness. Leopards exploited primal man as a source of food, hyenas may have fought with him over carrion, but when man managed to kill his enemies, most assuredly he ate them as well.

Man as a species is no longer a creature of the wilderness. Today, except in a few remote places, people do not have to struggle against wild animals for basic survival. This does not mean, however, that man has nothing to fear from the beasts of the wild. People still are killed and maimed in forest and field by wild beasts, but often for vastly different reasons than our ancestors were. No longer is it only a matter of a leopard seeking human prey to fill an empty belly, or an elephant trampling its hunters. Such things sometimes still occur, of course, but when a person is attacked by a wild animal today, more often than not it is because ruthless exploitation of the wilderness has compounded the conditions that inspire such violence.

THE SHRINKING WILDERNESS

Man has all but destroyed the wilderness and the isolation it provides for wild animals. Most of the animals—especially those whose interests run directly counter to man's—have vanished with the wild country. The beasts which survive must confine themselves to the bits and pieces of wilderness which remain, mostly in parks and preserves, or try to live alongside man.

For many creatures, neither alternative is happy. Both situations can breed conflict between man and beast, because under such conditions the two are forced into unnatural contact, as if caged together. Thus, even though there are fewer wild animals than ever, in both cases the chances of disagreeable meetings between animals and people have increased.

The problems arising from large or predatory wild animals living in the midst of human society are obvious; those which plague the survival of such creatures in sanctuaries are less so. But although there may be fewer animals, many of those which are left are packed into parks and other havens; crowded into them in numbers that are much too large for the amount of land that is available. This puts a strain not only upon the land, but means that if people wish to savor these fragments of wilderness, they will be surrounded by dense concentrations of wild animals, many of which can be dangerous.

An example can be drawn from the lamentable state of the grizzly bears which survive in a few national parks in the western part of the United States. The grizzly would rather stay away from man, but if the two meet, the bear is more often than not disposed to attack, with devastating results. It stands to reason if there is plenty of wilderness available, meetings between people and grizzlies will be few. About the only type of country in which grizzlies can live south of Canada, however, is in a handful of national parks and forests heavily utilized by people. Thus, although fewer grizzlies exist than ever before, the chances that they will kill someone are increasing. It is not because of anything the bears have done, however, but because of people.

Both people and bears are suffering. Grizzlies have killed or injured several park visitors. And, although the United States Department of the Interior has the responsibility for preserving the grizzly from extinction, that same arm of government also is destroying bears which menace people.

Such a state of affairs is just another reflection of the paradoxical nature of the relationship between man and beast. It bodes ill for both because not only does it mean that people are being killed and hurt unnecessarily, but it also contributes to the further decline of wildlife. Man does not tolerate animals which threaten his welfare.

In this chapter we will examine how the shrinking wilderness sets the stage for strife between man and some of the animals which have the capability to threaten people or their livelihood. Whether or not these animals are dangerous to meet in the wild, and if so, why, will be discussed as will the outlook for such creatures in a world changed by man.

Consider the grizzly, modern relative of the cave bear of prehistoric times, but even more savage than its predecessor.

NIGHT OF THE GRIZZLIES

One summer night in 1967 grizzly bears emerged from the dark forests of Glacier National Park and killed two young women who were camping there. The killings, by different bears, took place about twenty miles apart in the space of just a few hours.

It was about midnight when the first grizzly struck. A group of young people camping in a part of Glacier known as Granite Park awakened to the screams of one of their number, Julie Helgerson, a nineteen-year-old who was sleeping a little way from the main body of her companions. For a moment it looked as if the girl would escape, as the bear turned from her to savage a young man, sinking its yellow fangs into his legs and back. But then the bear resumed his attack on the young woman, seizing her in its jaws and dragging her away. After traveling several hundred feet the beast dropped the girl, barely alive. She died shortly after park rangers arrived, but the boy who was bitten recovered after hospitalization.

Four hours later, at the second campsite, another group of young people awoke to find a grizzly looming over them. Screaming and yelling, the campers emptied out of their sleeping bags and frantically scrambled into the trees. But Michele Koons, a nineteen-year-old from San Diego, never made it. The zipper on her bag stuck and she was caught by the rampaging bear. Her companions listened horrified as her cries ripped through the night.

"He's tearing my arm off! Oh my God, I'm dead!" the tormented girl screamed as the bear killed her, carried her body a short distance, and then dropped her before vanishing into the darkness.

The killings horrified the nation and prompted demands for vengeance against the bears. Park rangers shot and killed the two beasts responsible, which were found to have human blood clotted on their muzzles and claws. The rangers also killed two more grizzlies for good measure, but it was not enough for some Montanans. A Butte newspaper called for extermination of all grizzlies in the park on the grounds the attacks would discourage tourists from visiting the area.

The excitement over the deaths in Glacier Park quickly merged with a larger controversy over grizzly bears that has been going on for years. Stockmen operating within the great bear's range have long declared that the grizzly must go because now and then it preys on sheep and cattle. Scientists, conservationists, and government bureaucrats have been wrangling for years on the best way to manage and preserve the grizzly bear, especially south of the Canadian border where only several hundred of the animals survive.

CREATURE OF THE WILDERNESS

The grizzly is a creature of awesome power and savagery which, if encountered in the wilderness, can be the most dangerous of big land animals in North America. Few creatures on this continent adapt so poorly to human presence as the grizzly, for it is much more likely than other bears to attack when it encounters someone, especially unexpectedly. People who surprise a grizzly in the field should prepare for a charge by an enraged brute weighing up to 1,000 pounds, with huge yellow fangs and the power to mash a man with one blow of its great paws. The chances of emerging from such an encounter with a whole skin are slim, but the grizzly often will not stay around to finish the job after it has mauled someone. This tendency saved a father and his two children who surprised a grizzly on a trail in Glacier Park in August 1975. The bear attacked the trio, bit and clawed them, but then ran off.

A month later in the same park, two men walked into a backcountry berry patch and startled two or three grizzlies which were feeding there. The men were mauled on the head and body but not killed. Another attack occurred in Yellowstone about the same time. A grizzly bear suddenly charged out of the brush and chased a hiker up a tree. The man was unable to climb out of reach of the brute, however, and it bit his leg, dragged him down, and gripped him in a crushing hug. Remembering that grizzlies sometimes release victims who play dead, the man did, and the bear dropped him and ambled away. Its victim lay there for a while and then got up and walked seven miles to a park installation for help.

At least some of the attacks in 1975, according to the National Park Service, probably were by sow grizzlies with cubs. This is the last kind of grizzly that one wants to bump into on the trail, for the sow is ferociously protective of her offspring. In July 1974 a college professor who had hiked off the trail in Glacier Park had a close call when he arroused the maternal instincts of a sow. She charged, but then ran when he hit her with an ice axe.

The best way to avoid chance meetings with grizzlies in the wilderness other than keeping out of grizzly country, is to make plenty of noise. Even most grizzlies will move along if they know people are approaching. Once at close quarters, however, it often is too late to avoid a charge.

Obviously the grizzly bear needs enormous stretches of country to roam without coming across humans. Plenty of this kind of wild country exists in Canada and Alaska, where grizzlies still abound, but there is little of it left in the lower forty-eight states. The only places south of Canada where grizzlies live in any numbers are in the national parks and national forest areas of Wyoming, Idaho, and Montana.

Parks such as Glacier and Yellowstone and the wilderness areas around them support a total of several hundred grizzly bears—perhaps 1,000—although nobody knows for certain. Sufficient wilderness exists within these regions for the bears, but there is an important catch. The bears sometimes wander out of the wilderness and, increasingly, people seeking communion with nature, or just scenic grandeur, are pouring into it. Visitors to our national parks in 1974 totaled 218,000,000 and that figure was expected to increase by 9,000,000 for the year ending December 31, 1975. Moreover more people than ever before are hiking the back country, where the grizzlies live.

Some biologists believe that grizzlies in national parks and forests have encountered so many people that they have become frighteningly bold, like the smaller black bears in the same areas which beg for food from people in automobiles. If indeed this is true, then the grizzly could lose the only thing that tempers its savagery: the fear of man that, as a wild beast, it has almost as an instinct.

Certainly many grizzlies are bold enough to scavenge for food around garbage dumps and campsites in national parks, a practice which was once encouraged by the parks so people could see the bears, but which has become a nightmare. It is very likely that the bears who killed the two girls in Glacier National Park were looking for garbage of campers' rations.

THE GREAT GRIZZLY DILEMMA

The National Park Service, an Interior Department agency which has come under fire for its somewhat confused policies on grizzly bears, is trying to handle the problem with such measures as closing garbage dumps, and imposing strict regulations on trash disposal and on handling of food by campers. Signs posted in grizzly country warn people

The magnificent grizzly bear is one of the most dangerous of flesh eaters and adapts poorly to human presence.

to stay in their cars, and at times of year when the bears may be especially cantankerous, such as when they awake from winter dormancy, areas where the bears live are banned to the public.

Grizzlies that make a nuisance of themselves by repeated forays into areas where visitors congregate are not routinely shot as in the past but are drugged and removed to the back country. Habitual violators among the bear population, however, are killed. Sometimes the bears return to the same site again and again. Not long ago, for example, a female grizzly that persisted in prowling around the home of an employee who lived in one park, even once shoved its paw through a window. It was relocated, but continued to return, so it was killed. According to a publicist for the National Park Service a bear gets about three chances before it is eliminated.

Some of the pitfalls of trying to keep big, dangerous animals in national parks will be examined later in the chapter. It may, in fact, prove impossible to make parks for people as well as for some wild beasts. Despite the sincere efforts of the National Park Service, for example, grizzlies continue to attack people in parks. Three dozen people have been mauled in the last two decades, and in the summer of 1972, at Yellowstone, another camper was killed by a grizzly.

The victim was a young man from Alabama who was killed by a bear as he returned to his tent, which was pitched near Old Faithful in an area where camping was prohibited. According to the National Park Service, the bear was drawn by garbage left near the tent, but that did not stop a judge from ordering a substantial award for damages to the dead man's parents.

The attack happened a year after the National Park Service had closed all of the garbage dumps in Yellowstone, a move which some biologists said was too abrupt because the bears had come to depend on the trash heaps as an easy source of food. The critics said that the dumps should have been closed gradually, over many years, so the grizzlies could be weaned back to more natural feeding behavior. A sudden closing of the dumps, critics warned, could send grizzlies into camps in quest of scraps for dinner.

The National Park Service is not the only Interior Department agency which is embroiled in the grizzly problem. The United States Fish and Wildlife Service, which has authority over wildlife in danger of extinction, has classified the grizzly bears in the lower forty-eight states as a threatened species. This is an official designation with a very specific meaning. It indicates that the species is imperiled, but not so critically that it needs complete protection. As a threatened species, the grizzly still can be hunted in Alaska and in one part of Montana—the wilderness area which surrounds, but does not include, Glacier National Park. Only up to twenty-five bears a year may be killed by hunters in Montana, however. As a threatened species, moreover, the grizzly also can be killed in cases when they are proved to be killing livestock or, as noted, threatening human life.

Some conservationists question the wisdom of the Fish and Wildlife Service decision to classify the grizzly as threatened rather than as endangered, which would have guaranteed it absolute protection. However, few conservationists or biologists would argue that grizzly bears can be tolerated around heavily populated areas. The western states—including the ones which still have grizzlies—are experiencing a surge of population growth, so it may be that the numbers of grizzlies below the Canadian border will have to be reduced even further.

The outlook for the great bear seems to be this: A few grizzlies will remain in the western states, and perhaps some of the bears even may be reestablished in suitably isolated parts of their former range, but all of the grizzlies in the lower forty-eight states will have to be carefully managed and watched. The bulk of the grizzly population should be able to survive in Canada and Alaska, at least unless conditions there change radically, which always is possible.

MAN AND BEAST IN THE WILDERNESS

What to do with the grizzly bear is one of the most ticklish dilemmas facing conservationists today. It serves as a classic example of the difficulties that arise when large numbers of people encroach on the domain of animals that can kill them or interfere with their livelihood. People not only compete with the grizzlies for land to live on and grow food, but even for the right to walk in the forest, and the bears do not take to sharing.

If the problem presented by such animals was merely the old-fashioned question of survival, it would be settled in short order. The animals that challenged man would be eliminated. But it is not so simple, for although we are continuing to ravage the wilderness, at the same time we are trying in an unprecedented manner to save a fragment of the world's wildlife—even animals that can kill people.

Grizzlies, tigers, elephants, and most other large wild animals survive in the wild today only through human sufferance and often only because people have taken positive action to preserve them. The more people flood into the last wilderness refuges of such creatures, however, the more tolerance for them is eroded, for sooner or later the people and animals come into conflict. It matters not at all that the conflict usually is triggered by human actions; the animals are the ones that are held responsible.

Consider some of the other big animals of the wilderness, why they are dangerous—if indeed they are—and how the real or imagined threat they offer to man affects their future.

BEARS, LARGE AND SMALL

The grizzly bear belongs to a very widespread species, known collectively as the brown bears. They inhabit Europe and Asia as well as North America. None of the others is as savage as the grizzly, although the brown bears which inhabit the southern coast of Alaska can be murderous when provoked.

The Alaskan brown bears, though not as irascible as grizzlies, are even larger. The biggest of the Alaskan browns can exceed 1,600 pounds in weight, and are the largest living carnivores. Most of the time the Alaskan browns will flee from the approach of man, but if wounded or with cubs, they are likely to attack. For the most part, however, the brown bears of the Alaskan coast have enjoyed the isolation of the northern wilderness, and their contact with men other than hunters has been relatively rare.

All that may change, however, as Alaska is developed. In the mid-1960s, for example, more than a score of brown bears were killed by ranchers on Kodiak Island after bears killed some cattle. Unlike the grizzly, which ranges all of Alaska's vast interior, the brown bear is strictly a coastal species, inhabiting only a narrow strip of territory from the Alaskan Peninsula south along the Panhandle, and on islands close to shore. The country inhabited by the brown bear is some of the richest, most scenic, and from a standpoint of climate, optimum part of the state. What Alaska's current boom and the people it is bringing to the state will mean to the big brown bears remains to be seen, but it cannot be good for the big animals, and their range probably will shrink.

This is what has happened to the brown bear of Eurasia, which has vanished from most populated regions, although a few bears remain in two national parks in Italy. Substantial numbers of brown bears still live in the Soviet Union, however, and smaller populations inhabit some of the other eastern European countries.

Every so often brown bears from the east wander westward. Those from the Soviet Union sometimes stray into Poland, while bears from Yugoslavia occasionally roam into eastern Austria. The reception these wanderers get is usually hostile, as old prejudices and fears quickly take over. When four or five brown bears from Yugoslavia crossed the border into Austria a few years ago, newspapers demanded the animals be killed as a menace to schoolchildren.

Such reasoning was regrettable, for while wandering the eastern Alps the bears almost certainly would have kept away from people, that is, unless someone did something to attract them.

As the grizzlies of Yellowstone have proved, even the wildest of bears will venture amidst concentrations of people if they make food available. If bears have easy access to garbage, for instance, they will enter settlements located in the wilderness.

One such community is Churchill, Manitoba, which stands at the edge of the Canadian tundra on the rocky shores of Hudson Bay. Populated largely by Indians and Eskimos who hunt for white whales, or belugas, in the bay, the town is within the southern range of the polar bear *(Thalarctos maritimus)*. When I visited the town in 1967, on an expedition to bring back belugas for the New York Aquarium, residents told me that at times polar bears would wander into Churchill to raid garbage cans.

Almost as large as the Alaskan brown, the polar bear is a creature of the true Arctic, often wandering on pack ice hundreds of miles from land. The great white bears are said to stalk men as prey, but that is probably because to the bears men resemble the seals on which polar bears regularly feed. Normally, because of their isolation, the bears encounter few people, except for Eskimos and Indians who know enough about the big animals not to get in trouble.

Polar bears in the streets of a town, however, are something else again. People living in Churchill told me that, especially at night, they had to keep a sharp eye out for unexpected meetings with the bears, which might be tempted to turn from garbage to man—or in the bear's eyes, seal—for a meal. A few years after I visited Churchill, just such an episode occurred. A bear wandering through the town and a young man met, and the bear killed him. Because garbage was available in Churchill, a meeting between man and bear which might never take place in the wild occurred on the streets of town.

Considering the obvious hazards presented by bears which feed near people it is hard to believe that countless visitors to our national parks deliberately encourage bears to come near by offering them handouts. The bears in this case are not grizzlies—people at least seem to know better than that—but the smallest North American species, the black bear *(Euarctos americanus)*.

The black bear is small only in comparison to its big relatives, and often reaches a weight of at least 400 pounds. Like most other species, black bears have a varied diet, often feeding innocuously on berries, honey, and grubs, but essentially they are predators that can bring down animals as large as deer.

Rarely, moreover, black bears have tried to eat people. This seems to be the motivation behind a highly unusual series of attacks by black bears in Alaska during the summer of 1963. Blueberries—customary staple of the bears at that time of year—were short, and the bears apparently were driven by hunger to attack humans.

The first victim was a fisherman asleep in his sleeping bag whom a bear bit and tried to drag away. The man was saved by a companion who killed the bear with a rifle.

A few days later a bear stormed a tent in which four hunters were sleeping and chased one of the men until it was able to pounce on him and knock him down. As the bear stood over him, tearing at his chest and neck, the man shoved his arm into the animal's mouth, keeping it away from his throat until one of the other hunters shot the beast twice, killing it. The bites were serious, but the victim survived.

About the same time an employee of the Fish and Wildlife Service who was canoeing down a river noticed a bear following him from the shore. When the canoeist was forced to leave his boat because of a log jam, the bear charged him and chased him up a tree. As the bear snarled just below him, the man dropped a sack of provisions to the ground, distracting the animal so he could get to a larger tree. After devouring the food, however, the bear went after him again, and climbed high enough up the tree trunk to bite him on the leg. By that time, however, another Fish and Wildlife agent arrived, and the bear fled. The worst incident in the series was the death of a fifty-one-year-old miner from Anchorage, whose ripped body was found lying near his mine, with a bear standing over it.

Because of its smaller size, the black bear is not as powerful as the brown bears but even so it can hit like a piledriver. An example of how strong the creature is can be found in the writings of the famed naturalist Ernest Thompson Seton, who described how a black bear charged three Canadian loggers, caught one and broke his neck with a single swipe.

Although the grizzly is by far more ill-tempered and formidable, the black bear has mangled and killed many more people than its larger relative. Except for freak rampages such as the one in Alaska during 1963, the main reason for the bad record compiled by the black bear is people's lack of respect for it as a wild animal.

No other reason can explain why thousands of visitors to national parks persist in feeding the black bears, which have become so bold that they beg handouts from the occupants of vehicles. Why do people ignore the real nature of the black bear? Perhaps because the like of Smokey, Yogi, and the other bears of the media have convinced them that bears which stand up, beg, and act like people in furry suits really are just like us.

A QUESTION OF FEEDING

In years past, park officials encouraged feeding of bears on the grounds that it was fun, and also because it brought more people to

Park officials at Yellowstone National Park immobilize a black bear for removal to the back country.

national parks. If there is a surplus of anything in the national parks today, it is people and, moreover, the dangers involved in feeding bears have become tragically clear. Now visitors are bombarded with warnings to leave the bears alone. Judging from the 100 people hurt by bears annually in national parks, the campaign is falling upon deaf ears. The same inability to comprehend warning signs and the desire to touch wild animals that seems to grip many visitors to drive-through zoos also takes hold of people in national parks. In 1971 a man visiting Yellowstone walked right up to a huge bison bull and stood next to it so his wife could take a photograph. While other visitors looked on, the bull gored and killed him. In the same park a woman tried to pet an elk calf in front of its mother which kicked her so hard she suffered several broken bones.

Only a few years ago, the Park Service took photographs like this one at Yellowstone to make feeding bears look like fun. Today the Service discourages the practice.

Of all park animals, however, black bears seem the most attractive to people.

Lines of cars stack up along the park roadways where bears have learned to wait for handouts. Forgetting that the bears, despite their comical behavior, are wild animals, people place themselves perilously near the beasts and shove a variety of tidbits at them. I have heard and read of some incredibly stupid acts by people with bears in the national parks. A husband supposedly tried to shove a bear into the front seat of his car to take a picture of it next to his wife. The parents of one child allegedly coated his face with candy so they could photograph the animal licking the youngster.

Such tales may be apocryphal, but they are not as preposterous as they may sound, for people take similar risks with park bears all the time. Hands, arms, legs, and faces all are offered to the bears along with food, and it is surprising that the beasts do not sample more of them.

Black bears are intelligent creatures. Once they learn to associate people with food, they naturally go where the people are. Bears can be very persistent. In September 1975 a Glacier Park bear followed six hikers all the way to their canoe, then jumped into the craft, tore open their packs, and devoured their rations while the hikers scattered and watched helplessly from shore.

The bears also invade campgrounds in search of easy meals. National park authorities have tried to make it more difficult for the bears by insisting that wilderness campers hoist their supplies high in trees when they settle down for the night. Although the black bear's intentions may not be aggressive when it enters a camp, any number of things can make the animal turn on people. Campers who spill bacon grease on their sleeping bags or fail to wash food off their hands after eating, are inviting the bears to visit them during the night. A sleeper who awakes to find a black bear sniffing him and screams or strikes out may be attacked. It is better to lie still and pray the bear will go away.

Once a black bear becomes a danger or a pest at campsites it is treated just like grizzly pests. The animal is relocated if possible or killed if deemed necessary. The bears that must be killed are either shot or given a fatal overdose of tranquilizer. In a park like Yosemite, about a dozen black bears may be destroyed in a single year.

The tragedy about it all is that if people only treated black bears like the wild beasts they really are, few people would be hurt and few bears would have to be killed. Unless encouraged by food, black bears are unlikely to approach dangerously close to people. Since the black bear does not need the vast wilderness required by grizzlies, the smaller bears could do very well on their own in national parks and could be enjoyed from a distance by people who bother to look for them.

If the black bears of our national parks and forests continue to feed off the handouts and leavings of man, however, the outlook for them is grim. More bears will be killed, while others will become slavish clients of man, fawning over people for food, and ill-practiced at getting it on their own. Robbed of their noble wildness, the bears will become shadows of their former selves, perhaps unable to survive alone in the wild.

THE LAST OF THE ASIATIC LIONS

Such is the fate that has befallen a magnificent race of lions, whose likeness was used to symbolize nobility by some of the world's greatest empires—Persian, Assyrian, and Babylonian among them. The cat is the Asiatic lion, which belongs to the same species *(Panthera leo)* as the lions of Africa, but a different geographical race. The most obvious difference in the Asiatic lion is that it has less of a mane. The Asiatic lion—the lion of biblical times—once ranged from Israel as far east as India, where it still graces the national crest, and where its last remnants survive.

About 200 Asiatic lions live in a sanctuary called the Gir Forest, which is located on the north-central coast of India. A few of the big cats have been transplanted to other preserves in India, although for the moment the Gir is the only place where the lions live in any numbers. (There is a chance that Asiatic lions have survived in remote parts of Iran, but no one is certain.)

The Gir Forest, which no longer is really a forest at all but a collection of second growth, scrub and accacia thorns, affords the lions only marginal protection. It is ringed by the herds of poverty-stricken tribesmen, whose domestic water buffalo and cattle have made repeated incursions into the forest and have all but eaten it away.

Most of the deer and other wild game that once furnished prey for the lions have left the stripped forest, and the big cats survive only by preying on the livestock, plus occasional handouts from the game wardens who constantly watch the lions. It is a way of life that is completely unnatural for the lions, and observers say they even are losing the ability to hunt wild game.

So docile have the lions become that they sit calmly while their wardens walk among them, a sight witnessed by millions of Americans when it was shown on a National Geographic television special a few years ago. Imprisoned in a wasteland, the lion that fought Samson and was hunted by the fierce Assyrian kings is now totally dependent on man.

An Asian lioness with its prey is shown in the Gir Forest of India, the last refuge of the breed.

THE SOUND OF THE PRIMEVAL

Even in Africa, which still has a couple of hundred thousand lions, the territory available to the tawny cats is shrinking, perhaps by half in the last twenty years, according to some experts. Nevertheless over an area of about 2,000,000 square miles south of the Sahara, the wild music of the lion still rumbles over the grasslands in the night.

The call of lions in the darkness is the sound of the primeval, guaranteed to raise the hackles and send chills over the spine. The sound is not really a roar, but a series of coughing grunts which begin in staccato fashion, but mounting in intensity, gradually merge into a thunderous wave that rolls over the darkened landscape, permeating the night and even, I suspect, one's soul. It is a sound that can make a modern man feel as naked and exposed as our half-human ancestors must have felt when they heard it huddled together on that same African savannah millions of years ago.

Lazing in the grass by day, the lion is not as imposing as the mental image conjured up by its thunder at night. When stalking game, however, the lion leaves little doubt it is the mightiest predator of its grasslands home. Lions have been described as the most social of all cats and they hunt as they live, in groups. Usually the lionesses do most of the stalking, often accompanied by several cubs of varying ages.

The tawny coat of the lion blends so well with the brown savannah grass and scrub that lions can be close by and yet undetectable. I have been just a few yards from lions sitting in the shade of scrub and not seen them until they were pointed out by a knowledgeable friend.

Taking advantage of cover, hunting lions creep to within a hundred yards of so or their intended prey, and then burst from cover in a blood-chilling charge. Tail extended stiffly, head lowered, the cat aims for its victim's neck with its huge fangs.

Once its teeth have sheared into its victim's flesh the lion uses its weight—up to 500 pounds—to wrestle its prey to earth, or else snaps the neck of the victim with a blow of its forepaw. Sometimes the cat also breaks the neck of prey by twisting it.

Zebras, wildebeest, and even animals as large as buffalo make up much of the lion's diet, but it also feeds on small animals as well. Every so often, in addition, a lion will stop killing animals and will begin to kill and eat men.

MANEATERS, PAST AND PRESENT

No one knows what makes lions or other big cats turn maneater, but there are many theories. Some lions which have grown old and weak may find men the easiest prey to obtain, or else a lion may kill a man by accident, and acquire a liking for human flesh purely through chance. Perhaps changes in the ecology of the lion's surroundings, or even in the biochemistry of its body are causes, but no one really knows.

The fact remains that without warning, lions may begin to attack people. This occurs even today. While visiting Africa in 1974 I was told by a well-known professional hunter that a colleague of his had just been attacked and killed by a lion as he slept outside his tent in Zambia. Between 1955 and 1964, the deaths of seventeen people killed by lions were reported in Uganda.

Of all killer lions, the most notorious were two which harried workers building a railroad to the sea in the Tsavo River region of southeastern Kenya shortly before the turn of the century. The ill-famed Tsavo maneaters, two maneless males, appeared like phantoms one day in 1898. No one ever had seen them before in the region, and their origin remains a mystery today.

Night after night the lions entered the camps of railroad workers, mostly coolies from India, seized men, and bounded off into the night with them, often while their victims still screamed in terror and agony. Sometimes the killer beasts would crunch the bones of their victims within earshot of the camps, where the workers huddled in fear. Sometimes the morning would reveal pieces of flesh, limbs, or the head of victims where the lions had eaten.

So terrorized were the laborers that they stopped work on the railroad. The cessation of the project was noted far away in the British Parliament, where the Marquis of Salisbury explained that the lions had "conceived a most unfortunate taste for our workmen."

Preying on poor coolies might be tolerated, but not halting the progress of the railway. The destruction of the lions was ordered by British authorities. The man picked to eliminate the lions was Colonel J.H. Patterson, who also had a prime interest in getting work on the railroad started again, since he was the engineer assigned to bridge the Tsavo River.

Patterson persistently hunted the mankillers until he managed to ambush one from atop a platform he had ordered erected, and the other while perched in a tree. The two beasts were mounted and exhibited in the Field Museum, Chicago.

Not all would-be killers of maneaters were as proficient as Patterson. Some years after the Tsavo incident, another lion began to harry an East African railroad. After the animal killed several people near a station, the district superintendent of the line set out in his private railway car to kill the lion. The car was stopped on a siding near where the lion had been seen, while the superintendent sat by a window with his rifle to wait for the beast.

After a while, the superintendent dozed off, then fell into a deep sleep. While he snored the lion arrived, pushed open the door of the car, padded up to the sleeping man, and killed him. Then the beast carried off its victim and ate him.

LIONS, PARKS AND PEOPLE

Maneaters tend to return to the same places for victims again and again, so eventually the killer cats can be ambushed. Once the lions responsible are killed, maneating in a district ceases, for it is not likely other cats will take up the habit. Only rare, abnormal lions yearn for human flesh; most take only four-legged prey.

If the four-legged victims are cattle, as is increasingly so in Africa today, control of the problem is far more difficult than stopping maneating. Any lion that gets the chance will kill a cow, so either the cows or the lions must go. Seldom do stockmen choose the lion.

The opportunity to feed on beef is being presented to lions throughout Africa as cattle ranching spreads across the grasslands that are the hunting grounds of the big cats. In most areas outside of parks and preserves, the endless herds of game are gone. Here and there gazelles, giraffe, or zebras may be seen on the landscape, but the predominate animals in many places are herds of cattle. And while they continue to kill what is left of the game as well, the lions are taking advantage of the new food supply.

Like stockmen everywhere, African ranchers react violently to predators which kill their animals. For most cattlemen, the only solution is to kill lions, as many as possible. The Masai herders may do it with their spears, but in Africa today most cattlemen use much more devestating weapons—such as poison and rifles. And the lion is declining.

Perhaps 200,000 lions remain in Africa. That may sound like a lot of animals, but not considering the vastness of the lion's range—all of the continent below the Sahara except for jungles and extreme desert. Furthermore, a few decades ago there probably were twice as many lions living in the African wilds.

Naturalist Norman Meyers, who conducted a study of the African lion for the International Union for the Conservation of Nature and Natural Resources, says that by the end of the century only a few thousand lions may remain, and only in national parks and similar preserves.

The efforts of African ranchers to eliminate lions reveals a curious facet of human nature. Animals are persecuted more severely for threatening people's wildlife than their lives. Conserving wildlife has become largely a matter of making wild animals economically acceptable. As long as lions remain an economic liability they are in peril but if they can become an asset, people will keep them around.

Wildlife conservationists are trying to persuade the governments of the new African nations of this, and some, especially in East Africa, have responded. Lions, buffalo and other animals have become a means of attracting dollars from abroad through the tourist industry. For the time being, wild beasts can be very profitable. The largest source of foreign trade in Kenya, for example, is tourism, and it is the animals in national parks that visitors come to see. The national parks and preserves of Kenya are among the best in Africa, equaled only by those of South Africa.

National parks in Africa exist primarily as places to see wild animals, and are not operated to serve a wide variety of recreational needs like the parks in the United States. Visitors to most Kenyan parks, for instance, do not go hiking about the landscape on their own, but are carefully supervised and not allowed outside of their vehicles in places where dangerous animals are to be found.

The possibility of hair-raising episodes in the national parks of Africa cannot be entirely discounted, and there is plenty of wild country in some of the parks where travel remains an adventure. Earlier in this decade a lion—or, more likely, a lioness—killed and ate a young woman walking within a quarter-mile of a lodge in the Amboseli Reserve of Kenya. The fact remains, however, that you can watch wild beasts with a cocktail in hand from the safety of a game lodge patio, or from the security of a mini-bus packed with senior citizens from the United States.

Outside of the parks, people still can rough it on their own among wild animals, but they are not nearly as concentrated as in the sanctuaries, so the chances of unfortunate encounters are rather low. And the wilds are dwindling.

The function of the African parks as animal preserves rather than multipurpose recreational areas dictates that the lions in these sanctuaries will not be caught in the same squeeze that has trapped the grizzly bear in Glacier and Yellowstone. Moreover except for rare maneaters, lions abide much better than grizzlies when living side by side with large human populations—cattle killing aside, of course. A score of lions lives in the national park on the borders of Nairobi, Kenya, a city of the same population as Denver, Colorado. It is impossible to conceive of a few dozen grizzlies roaming the outskirts of Denver, or any city, for that matter.

In addition, lions are ideal among the big cats as a tourist item, for unlike the others they live in groups, spend most of the day in one place, and in the open to boot. No other large flesh eater, for that matter, is so visible.

As a last-ditch alternative, a few thousand lions in parks would be better than no lions at all, but it also might mean that the African lion would be a different beast than in the past. Already lions in national parks spend much of their time surrounded by vehicles full of tourists. Game guides who escort visitors around parks no longer look for lion signs, but for clusters of vehicles in the savannah grass. Almost invariably, within the cluster are one or more lions, playing, sleeping or perhaps feeding. The halted vehicles draw almost all others within sight and they careen over the landscape towards the cluster like bees heading to the hive.

The lions put up with all the commotion, and seem unconcerned about it, but the presence of an endless stream of tourists must place untold new stress upon the animals. Just by being there, the people in their vehicles change the surroundings in which the cats exist; what change it will have upon the behavior of succeeding generations of lions is unknown, but naturalist Meyers, writing in *International Wildlife* magazine, described how a lion actually used his Land Rover for cover while stalking zebra.

Ideally, therefore, wildlife conservationists would like to see lions surviving both in parks and on suitable land outside of them. The prob-

While still numerous, the African lion is losing ground as its habitat is converted to ranches.

lem is to find some way to make the lions economically valuable, even beyond mere compensation for the cattle they kill. After completing his study of the lion, Norman Meyers suggested that the lions on some lands outside parks could be the basis of a profitable trophy hunting industry. As long as the lion populations are carefully managed, Meyers said, hunting them might be the best way to keep them from the brink of extinction.

When its natural prey, like this African impalla, vanishes, the lion may turn to killing stock. In turn the lion is killed by stockmen.

What supreme irony it would be, if man's desire to overcome fierce wild beasts becomes the only reason why they are permitted to exist. This turn of events, of course, is by no means certain; but the way things now stand, it is entirely possible.

STRIPED CAT OF ASIA

The options that exist for preserving the lion as a wild animal have all but disappeared in the case of the tiger *(P. tigris),* which is very close to becoming extinct in the wild. In all of Asia, from the Siberian snows to the steaming forests of Java, only a few thousand tigers survive. Only 2,000 tigers still live on the Indian subcontinent, which had 40,000 of the striped cats only fifty years ago. Perhaps that many also live in Indochina and Burma. In Java, where tigers still were common a century ago, only a dozen tigers cling to existence. Sumatra has 800 of the animals, small but unknown numbers survive in Iran and Afghanistan, and a few hundred tigers still live in the Asian heartland, scattered in remote pockets from Korea to Siberia.

People often think of the tiger strictly as a tropical beast but the species probably originated in the north of Asia, and today the biggest of all tigers—indeed, of all cats—live in Siberia. The Siberian tiger, as it is called, can reach a length of thirteen feet, including its tail, and weigh 600 pounds; more than a lion and as much as a small grizzly bear.

Unlike the lion, the tiger is a solitary animal of wooded country rather than grassland. It stalks large prey like deer slowly and silently until it is very close, then pounces, seizes its victim in its forepaws, and tries to fasten its jaws in the victim's neck. Deer, antelope, water buffalo, and boar all fall to the tiger, but the big cat also eats fish, ground birds, and even frogs. The record shows, too, that man is the prey of the tiger much more often than of the lion, a fact which makes it more difficult to avert the extinction of the striped hunter.

THE DOWNFALL OF THE TIGER

The decline of the tiger stems from multiple causes, as usually is so when an animal has become endangered. Thousands of tigers were killed in hunts organized by Indian maharajahs and British government officials during the last century of colonial rule in India. One hunter in the mid-1800s shot 400 tigers in twenty-five years and then continued to kill them until he lost count. The Maharajah of Gwalior shot 800 of the cats.

While visiting India, King George V of Britain killed 39 tigers in the course of just one hunt.

The lion never has had to face such organized slaughter in the name of sport hunting, nor have lions ever been so ruthlessly hunted for their skins as has the tiger. The striped coat that enables the tiger to blend so well with the light and shadow of the forest has served the animal poorly in man's world, for tiger skins have been among the most valuable commodities in the fur trade. Until recently, hunting and trapping of tigers for the fur trade was rampant in India and Southeast Asia, but although stores in Hong Kong and Singapore still display tiger skins, the market has diminished because of public pressure and protective laws. Some illegal hunting and commerce still goes on, and although it is minor compared to what went before, the tiger's predicament is so critical that the loss of even a few of the animals can be perilous.

Most of all, however, the tiger has suffered because much of the vast region it inhabits, except for the northern fringe of its range, is also the part of the earth where man is most abundant. There is very little territory left with sufficient cover, game and isolation for the tiger to survive. Even where there is enough forest and prey, people are pressing in from all sides; the closer people get to the last tigers, the more they threaten human life and property, and the less chance the tiger has of surviving.

With the moral and financial support of the World Wildlife Fund, the governments of India, Bangladesh, Nepal, and other states which have tigers within their boundaries have pledged to try and preserve the species. Under the auspices of the fund, "Project Tiger" was launched a few years ago in these countries. Thus far the most tangible results of the effort have been to focus attention on the plight of the tiger and to stimulate some badly needed research on how tigers can be permitted to exist in sanctuaries located among millions of human beings. India also has beefed up protection at preserves with tiger populations.

MANKILLERS AND MANEATERS

If the tiger survives in the wild at all, it probably will not be outside of carefully maintained sanctuaries, except in some extremely remote

The tiger is making its last stand. Only a few thousand tigers remain in the wild.

regions of northern Asia. There simply is not enough land left for any other way.

Even if there were additional land, conservationists who desperately want to save the tiger are bedeviled by the fact that tigers regularly kill humans—not great numbers, perhaps, but enough to keep alive people's deep fear of the striped cats. If the tiger is to be saved from extinction, not only must sanctuaries be provided, but people must be protected from the fangs and claws of tigers. So scientists are trying to learn what makes tigers attack people.

When considering why tigers kill people it is important to realize that not every mankiller is a maneater. Many deaths caused by tigers are strictly accidental, although that does not make being killed by one any less horrible. People luckless enough to stumble across a big cat at its kill or a tigress with cubs may provoke a terrifying response, but in such incidents the tiger's instincts are self-protective, not predatory.

Occasionally, however, the accidental killing of a human can trigger an episode of maneating by a tiger. It is believed, although unproven, that many maneaters first taste human flesh by chance, and then find they like it. A few years ago a tiger which had restricted itself to preying on cattle near one Indian village killed a man in a cane field. The cat then started to prey on the inhabitants of the village and killed eight people before it was shot.

Some maneaters also may get their start when they cannot catch their normal game, either because it is in short supply or they are incapacitated. Whatever makes a tiger relish human flesh, once it turns to maneating it becomes a striped nightmare, terrorizing entire districts, so fearless that it will burst into homes and carry off their inhabitants. In one incident not too many years ago, a tiger invaded the home of one Indian couple while they slept and snatched the young wife away from her husband's side.

American troops operating in the jungles of Indochina during the recent conflict there found that sometimes they had to contend with hungry tigers as well as human enemies. It is likely that over the years more than one G.I. was attacked by a tiger, but I know of one incident for certain, which was recounted for me by an officer in the U.S. Special Forces.

Deployed behind enemy lines, a contingent of American troops was camouflaged in the jungle, with Vietcong all around them. Suddenly a tiger rushed from the trees, picked up a soldier in its jaws, and started to carry him off. Shooting the tiger would have alerted the enemy so the other soldiers began to club if with the butts of their rifles, until the animal dropped their companion and ran away.

That particular tiger might have become accustomed to feeding on the bodies of people killed in the war, and could easily have mistaken a soldier lying motionless in the jungle for a corpse. Perhaps this is why the animal merely seized the man, rather than killing him outright as tigers usually do with live prey.

More recently, another tiger in Indochina attacked under equally unusual circumstances. The beast jumped from a tree into a boatload of people headed down a river to vote in Thailand's national 1975 election. After mauling one of the nine people aboard, the tiger leaped off the boat and vanished in the jungle.

KILLERS OF THE SUNDARBANS

The region of the world that is most notorious for its maneating tigers is the Sundarbans delta, a vast tangle of mangrove swamps and forest that fringes the Bay of Bengal where the Ganges and Brahmaputra rivers empty into it.

Mangrove swamps are weirdly beautiful places, halfway between land and sea, where tidal creeks snake among the gnarled, twisted roots of the mangrove trees in an endless maze of muddy channels. Sea snails patrol the roots of the trees, which can grow in saltwater, and monkeys chitter overhead. Wading birds such as egrets and herons roost in the branches. A swamp might seem like a strange place to find tigers, but they swim well and sometimes paddle for miles between the mangrove islands.

The tigers of the Sundarbans have inspired fear for centuries. As long ago as the mid-seventeenth century, a Frenchman who had traveled through the area wrote of them:

> Among these islands it is in many places dangerous to land, and great care must be had that the boat, which during the night is fastened to a tree, be kept at some distance from the shore, for it

constantly happens that some person or another falls prey to tigers. These ferocious creatures are quite apt, it is said, to come into the boat itself while the people are sleeping, and to carry off a victim, who if the boatmen are to be believed, generally happen to be the fattest members of the party.

Whether or not the tigers of the Sundarbans are quite so selective as alleged, their dread reputation is in good measure justified, even today. Between 1961 and 1971 the tigers killed 275 people and mauled many more. During the month of April 1973, when a thousand people fanned out to gather honey in the forested parts of the region, the tigers claimed the lives of five people.

SAVING TIGERS AND PEOPLE

Much of the Sundarbans region has been operated as a forest reserve where a limited amount of lumbering, honey gathering, hunting and fishing is allowed. Wild enough to support game and tigers, the area also must be shared by a moderate number of people. If the interests of both animals and people can be resolved, the Sundarbans could prove to be a secure haven for the tiger. Obviously, however, it is difficult to convince people who stand a chance of being eaten by tigers to preserve them.

Hoping to find a way out of the impasse the World Wildlife Fund has sponsored a study by a German scientist, Dr. Hubert Hendrichs, who has examined maneating in the Sundarbans as a preliminary step towards a means of preserving both man and the tiger there.

Hendrichs observed that the behavior of tigers towards people in the Sundarbans varied widely, and he grouped the cats accordingly:

A. Tigers that never seem to attack man even when startled, with cubs, or on a kill.

B. Tigers that generally do not attack man but may if they are provoked or surprised in difficult situations. The victim often is only mauled, and if by chance killed is not carried off and eaten.

C. Tigers which do not hunt human prey but if molested readily attack, kill, and sometimes begin to eat their victim. If driven off, they usually do not return to their kill. These tigers, responsible for a substantial number of deaths, sometimes grow increasingly aggressive towards man until they cross the line to become true maneaters.

D. Tigers that are really maneaters in the sense that they will deliberately hunt men, even to the point of ignoring other prey. They are responsible for more than half the deaths caused by tigers. Once they make a kill they return to the site and if the body has been removed may circle the areas for days. This habit is the Achilles heel of the maneater, for once it strikes, it can easily be ambushed when it comes back to the scene of the attack. Hendrichs proposed that if this procedure would be followed in the Sundarbans, the casualties from maneaters could be sharply reduced.

The more a maneater kills, Hendrichs discovered, the greater its appetite for human flesh. At first the maneater begins by killing about one man a month, while the rest of the time it continues to eat animal food. Sometimes at this stage the tiger may stop maneating entirely. If the animal persists, it ends up by stalking only men, and can kill as many as fourteen people a month. Preying on men is not very productive, however, for tigers often make several trips back to a kill before they finish it. Because the bodies of most human victims are recovered before the tiger fully consumes them, the beast can be cheated out of so many meals its condition deteoriates until it cannot hunt at all. Then it may starve or fall to disease.

Maneaters, Hendrichs also observed, account for only 3 percent of the cats living in the Sundarbans. Tigers in the "C" category, however, are more numerous, but more than 66 percent of all the tigers in the region followed the more normal pattern of not attacking man except under unusual circumstances.

Hendrichs has proposed that confirmed maneaters could be eliminated and that certain areas where "C" tigers seem to concentrate could be designated as sanctuaries. Such a move would mean that forest industries no longer could be conducted in these places, but Hendrichs pointed out that "the alternative is not tiger or men but tiger or revenue. If one is sacrificed, the other is safe."

The scientist did not conclude what makes some of the Sundarbans tigers more dangerous than others, but he did perceive that attacks on people seem to increase when the level and salinity of water in the swamp is high, in other words, during periods of unusually high tides. Moreover, he noted that the attacks decrease when the variety of plants and animals is greatest.

The correlation could result from the fact that when the region is flooded by the sea, many types of land plants, which cannot grow in saltwater, perish. The animals that feed on them also may decline, contributing to a decrease in the variety of species living in the region, and therefore in the types of prey available to tigers. Man may become a substitute.

Other authorities have uncovered additional clues about the pattern of tiger attacks in the Sundarbans. Forest industries are at their height during the big cats' mating season when the tigers are considerably more touchy about being disturbed. Some tigers also have learned to raid the nets strung across small tidal creeks by fishermen, who may stumble across the tigers on the way to gather the catch. One Indian forestry official has proposed that not all the deaths attributed to the tigers of the Sundarbans really are their work. Some of the bodies found in the swamps, he says, may be murder victims killed not by beasts but by their fellowmen.

It must be admitted, however, that if tigers are preserved among the teaming human populations of southern Asia, mankilling will never entirely cease. Despite all precautions, tigers and man still will meet in the forest, sometimes with fatal results. But does this mean we cannot afford to keep tigers? A compelling answer to this question has been provided by Professor Paul Leyhausen, chairman of the I.U.C.N. committee specializing in saving the world's wild cats. He said:

> Certainly the tiger is a potential maneater, in the sense that every car driver is a potential mankiller, i.e. if he wants to or is irresponsible he may kill a human being by driving a car. If a tiger wants to, he may kill and even eat a human being. However the fact is that tigers very rarely do so. Normally it is quite possible to walk through tiger-inhabited country with no fear of being attacked. Furthermore, in the majority of cases, even when a tiger becomes a maneater, this is mainly only because human carelessness gives him an opportunity; just as there are numerous people who will cross a busy road without first looking right and left, there are people living all the time in the neighborhood of tigers who become rather too careless when there has not been an accident for years and years. For obvious reasons we do not abolish cars, and . . . we must not abolish tigers.

The tiger can be saved but it will be enormously difficult and expensive. Governments whose people are starving will have to justify some stock killing and not turning vast acreages of forest into farmland. Each tiger needs ten square miles of territory and to prevent harmful inter-breeding a healthy population of tigers must number at least 300 animals. The ideal tiger sanctuary, therefore, should cover 3,000 square miles, about the size of Puerto Rico or three times the size of Rhode Island. No such place exists where the bulk of the world's tigers survive.

The solitary, secretive life-style of the tiger in its native forest make it far less attractive for the tourist trade than the lion. Seeing a tiger in the wild is a thrill, but it is very difficult.

It is marvelously convenient for tourists who can afford it to see lions in places like Kenya without sacrificing any comfort. A view of lions is practically guaranteed even on the most cursory motorized tours of wildlife parks in East Africa. But seeing tigers never will be that easy, and it will be very expensive, all because the country tigers inhabit is not as accessible as that in which tourists can find lions, although I saw a tiger in Khao Yai National Park, less than 150 kilometers from the city of Bangkok. Nor will the tiger ever be the basis of a sport-hunting industry, no matter how well managed. There are not enough tigers, not enough land on which to hunt them, and there never again will be. If the tiger is to be preserved in the wild, it will have to be for the sake of the animal and for people who take pleasure in knowing that somewhere out there tigers roam free.

SPOTTED SURVIVAL EXPERT

Of all the big cats, the one most likely to survive in the world of man is the beast which preyed on the apemen of Swartkrans. The leopard *(P. pardus)* will make it not so much because people are trying to preserve it, but on its own. The key to the leopard's survival is the remarkable ability of the creature to adapt to an amazing spectrum of living conditions, from suburban backyards to deserts and mountains too barren to support lions or tigers.

Just like other large animals, of course, leopards have lost ground, for once leopards ranged over more of Eurasia than lions and tigers combined. Even today, however, the leopard still lives throughout most of Africa and Asia, from Morocco to South Africa and from the Cacausus to Korea south to Java. Africa alone is the home of 100,000 leopards, and no one knows how many live throughout the rest of the vast expanse claimed by this cunning and adaptable cat.

At home on the ground and in the trees, the leopard is not very large —males average about 150 pounds—but pound for pound it is the most powerful of all big cats. The prey of the leopard is extremely diverse, ranging from antelope to tortoises, but leopards especially like to eat monkeys. Sometimes leopards develop a taste for other primates as well and once in a great while the list includes man. It does not happen often, but when it does the loss of life can be severe. Leopards have been implicated in some of the worst outbreaks of maneating ever recorded. Newspaper reports from one district in India during the late 1950s and early 1960s claimed that leopards had killed more than 300 people there. During the British rule of India, the notorious maneating leopard of Rudaprayag slaughtered more than 100 people before it was tracked and killed by the famed author and hunter of maneaters, Jim Corbett.

Most leopards, however, leave people alone and are so unobtrusive they can live even on the fringes of large metropolitan areas. Leopards can frequently be seen in the suburbs of Nairobi, for example, but they seldom cause more of a stir beyond occasionally carrying off someone's dog. In one particularly posh neighborhood a few minutes drive from downtown Nairobi, a leopard regularly appeared at night to sit atop the roof of a house, just as leopards from time immemorial have perched on rock outcroppings to survey the African savannah. The presence of leopards in settled areas shows how little threat they are, for if they were dangerous, they would be quickly driven away or killed.

The remarkable ability of the leopard to survive even amidst a modern industrial society was demonstrated quite dramatically by the recent return from seeming extinction of leopards in Israel. The so-called Sinai leopard was believed to have become extinct several years ago, but in the early 1970s a few paw prints were seen in the Judean desert. In 1974 zoologists working for Israel's Nature Reserves Authority discovered the remains of an ibex which apparently had been killed by leopards in the desert. The scientists maintained a watch over the kill and in short order two leopards emerged out of the darkness and began to feed on the goat.

In the months that followed, other leopards were sighted, and it was established that at least eight of them had survived in the Judean wilderness.

The recovery of the Sinai leopard was hailed by conservationists around the world, but there was more to come. In the autumn of 1975 I visited the head of the Israeli Nature Reserves Authority, General Avraham Jaffe, and found him elated over the discovery of a second population of leopards, more than 100 miles away from the first group.

The new sightings were in the Jordan Valley—only twenty-five miles from the city of Jerusalem. Israeli soldiers reported seeing some large cats in the area, so wardens from the Nature Reserves Authority set out to take a look. They saw three leopards, which because of the distance from the sightings in the Judean Desert, undoubtedly represent a brand new population. The survival of the Sinai leopard in two different parts of Israel including one area near a major city, has raised hopes that the animals also has held on in a few other parts of the country as well.

The Sinai leopard probably has been able to persist not only because of its own tenacity but because of indirect help from Israeli conservationists, who have restored the population of the ibex, the leopard's chief prey, from 300 animals nine years ago to 4,000 today.

Because the leopard thrives alongside man as well as in the deserts, mountains and other places of marginal use to people, its chances for survival as a truly wild animal are higher than that of any other big cat.

CAT OF MANY NAMES

About the same time as Israeli zoologists were sighting the resurrected Sinai leopard their counterparts in the United States recognized the existence of an American big cat which, like the Sinai leopard, had been thought to be extinct. The cat was the eastern race of the cougar *(Felis concolor)*, which shares with the leopard an ability to cope with an astonishing variety of surroundings.

Several races of cougar, which equals the leopard in size, inhabit both North and South America, from coast to coast. Few animals have been given so many different names; in English alone the cougar also is known as the mountain lion, puma, painter, panther, screamer, and catamount. The cougar's choice of habitat is also quite diverse. From

British Columbia to Patagonia it can be found in forests, jungles, wetlands, deserts, mountains, and even, like the leopard, even in urban areas.

Cougars still can be found within the city limits of Los Angeles, and, as it has turned out, not very far from New York City. In 1973 the United States Department of the Interior officially recognized that cougars still roam from eastern Canada to the Carolinas, chiefly in the forests of the Appalachians. By doing so, the department gave credence to reports that had been circulating for years of cougars prowling about Connecticut, New Jersey, and New York, often less than 100 miles from the busy streets of Manhattan.

For many years zoologists believed that the eastern cougar had joined the ranks of vanished animals. Cougars have been persecuted ever since Europeans settled in North America, and the eastern race was the first subjected not only to deliberate campaigns of extermination but to the pressures of habitat destruction. A handful of eastern cougars apparently survived, however, in the last pockets of wilderness left in the Appalachians.

Over the years a few reports of tawny cats being seen in the mountains persisted, but more recently sightings began to increase until they numbered in the hundreds. Many of the people who saw the beasts, moreover, classified as expert witnesses, for they included scientists, woodsmen, park rangers, and game wardens. Eventually even the most conservative zoologists had to admit that the cougar was still around.

One reason for the increase in sightings may be that the eastern deer herds, a main source of prey, have been restored in the last fifty years. Another may be that some rural areas have lost human population as people have abandoned farms and headed for the cities and suburbs. In addition, many parts of the east that were cleared of forest are again wooded, thus affording cover to the cougars.

The eastern race of cougar, and the one that still exists in Florida, are protected by the Interior Department as endangered species, but both are so few that their future is in doubt. Elsewhere cougars are not considered endangered, although in the western states they have been relentlessly hunted and poisoned by stockmen because of their livestock depredations. The extent of the damage cougars do to livestock probably has been exaggerated but, especially when they cannot obtain game, cougars do prey on sheep and cattle.

Whether cougars also attack man has been hotly debated for years.

The answer seems to be that they do, but hardly ever. The number of known attacks by cougars on people does not surpass two dozen, and probably is less than that. Some of the attacks probably have been the work of animals that were sick or mistook man for another kind of prey. But a very few attacks seem to be true acts of predation. One of these occurred in 1924 when the body of a teen-aged Washington boy was found partly devoured by a cougar. The next year a female cougar was shot and killed in the same vicinity, and the contents of the cat's stomach were examined. It contained a mass of human hair and blue denim cloth similar to that worn by the dead youth.

Mishaps involving people and cougars are so rare, however, that by no means can the cat be considered more than remotely dangerous. The well-documented presence of cougars in the residential hills and canyons of Los Angeles shows that the creatures can get along close to people without bothering them. Nothing the cougar does to humans or livestock warrants its persecution. Where it is rare, it should be protected; where plentiful, it should be permitted to prosper under control.

Wholesale killing of cougars is not the only answer to protecting livestock from them. Another way, increasingly favored by the western states where cougars are abundant, is to raise the creature's status from a varmint, which can be shot on sight, to a game animal, subjected to regulated hunting as long as its population is healthy.

The adaptability the cougar shares with the leopard of the Old World means that the American cat also might persist not only in the wilderness but relatively near settled areas; that is if the war against it is ended once and for all.

GRAY SHADOW OF THE WILDERNESS

Of all the predatory animals which man views as his enemies none has been the target of such endless and far-flung persecution as wolves (Canis lupus), which oddly enough in some ways act very much like men.

Throughout its range, which spans both hemispheres, the wolf has been reviled and rooted out by man. Legend, error, and superstition have combined to make people who never have even seen a wolf hate the creature. Even the very name of the animal is used to signify unsavory behavior, the least harmful being ruthless sexual exploitation.

Actually the wolf has been the target of the worst smear campaign ever conducted against an animal. The male wolf is not a lustful beast but a faithful mate and father, which unlike most male mammals, helps rear the young. Wolves, in addition, get along well together and within a pack cooperate magnificently in such tasks as getting food for all.

The foul reputation of the wolf, more than its actual deeds, has led to its persecution, so conservationists are working feverishly to change its image. In 1973 an international group of wildlife experts met in Stockholm to develop plans for changing "the public image of the wolf from that of a bloodthirsty killer to that of a highly developed social animal which is no threat to man."

The idea that the supporters of the wolf are trying to get across is that the creature is not really an evil, slavering mankiller. In their zeal, however, the friends of the wolf sometimes go overboard. The unhappy consequences of making the wolf seem too loveable have been described in the chapter on exotic pets. Moreover, while the wolf is in no sense the devil incarnate neither is it a friendly wilderness version of Rin Tin Tin.

The wolf is a savage, highly intelligent flesh eater that is one of the most relentless of all predators. It is a deadly hunter, not cruel, but a wonderfully efficient killer. Fleet and powerful, wolves range in size from about 60 pounds to 175 pounds; the largest are the huge wolves of the Arctic. Wolves have very long, curved fangs and bite with much more power than dogs of comparable size. Pound for pound, in fact, wolves are far better fighters than domestic dogs, which is why the dogs developed to guard flocks against wolves or hunt them are huge breeds such as the Great Pyrenees and Irish wolfhound.

Scientists who have studied wolves in North America estimate that the average wolf pack numbers between one and two dozen animals. Working together, sometimes coursing over the landscape at speeds up to thirty miles an hour, the wolves operating as a pack can bring down game as large as moose. Often the animals killed by wolves are infirm for one reason or another, so in addition to keeping populations of game animals within bounds, wolves also keep them healthy.

The coordinated attack of the wolf pack has been described in detail by biologist L. David Mech in a book he wrote for the Department of the Interior.

Mech's description of one such hunt, witnessed on Isle Royale National Park in Lake Superior, follows:

> The sixteen wolves were traveling along the shore when suddenly they veered inland about 2:30 P.M. toward a lone cow [moose] standing on a ridge 200 yards upwind. The animal ran when the pack was 100 yards away, and the wolves charged up the ridge and continued on her trail. The cow ran slowly and stopped to look back at the approaching pack, which caught up within 100 yards. She stood next to a bushy spruce for protection, and as the wolves lunged, she charged and kicked at them with all four feet. Although she seemed to connect with her hind feet, apparently no animals were injured.
>
> Meanwhile, the whole pack caught up. The moose defended herself for about 3 minutes while backed against the spruce, but suddenly she bolted and fled toward the end of the ridge. The wolves attacked her rump and flanks but released their hold as she brushed through some thick spruces. They pursued the animal for 25 yards to the end of the ridge, where all plunged down the steep slope.
>
> When the moose landed at the base of the ridge, the wolves were attached to her back and flanks, and one held her by the nose. The downed animal attempted to rise, but the sheer weight of the wolves seemed to anchor her. The wolf grasping her nose held on firmly while she violently shook her head. Most of the animals continued working on her rump and flanks, while two tore at her shoulders.
>
> The moose struggled for more than 5 minutes while the wolves, packed solidly around her, tugged away. Two individuals had to wait at one side, for there was no room around the moose. The "nose wolf" continued its hold for at least 10 minutes, while the others pulled from all sides. After about 10 minutes, the moose appeared dead.

Isle Royale, where Mech conducted his studies, and the adjacent mainland of northern Minnesota constitute the last real stronghold of the wolf in North America below the Canadian border. A handful of wolves lives in Yellowstone, and a few inhabit the mountains of northern Mexico, but only in Minnesota do the gray hunters persist in any numbers —perhaps 1,000 animals.

Even those last remnants are too many for some Minnesota farmers and deer hunters, who have pressured the Interior Department to lift its protection of the wolf below the border. Farmers who lose a few animals may have some reason to complain, but the argument of the hunters— that the wolves compete with them for deer—has no merit. The presence of wolves may mean fewer deer, but it also keeps the herds healthy and in accordance with the rules of nature. And if wolves have sufficient natural prey, they are likely to avoid livestock.

Even people who should know better sometimes are blind to the role of the wolf in maintaining the balance of nature. The Alaskan Fish and Game Department has blamed wolves for a decline in the numbers of moose under its jurisdiction and views the situation as justification for a wolf-killing campaign.

For the time being, however, wolves remain abundant in Alaska and in Canada. Elsewhere they are holding out in the Soviet Union, Turkey and parts of the Balkans and Central Asia. Wolves have disappeared, however, from all of western Europe except for a few mountain hinterlands such as the Apennines and the Pyrenees. In all of Scandinavia, only a few dozen wolves remain; the rest have been exterminated, largely in the past several years.

Although the wolves of Eurasia and North America belong to the same species, their behavior towards man has differed in that Old World wolves have been considerably more aggressive. A few people may have been attacked by wolves in North America during pioneer days, but not one case has been documented in recent times. Not long ago a wolf which had been slightly injured by a car on a highway in Ontario even allowed a dog catcher to muzzle and chain it. The dog catcher, a woman who was newly appointed to the post, was summoned by police who reported an injured animal on the road. Thinking it was a dog, she approached it, but the wolf ran off, the woman in pursuit. When she finally cornered it, the animal growled and snapped, but did not bite. Only after it was chained did the woman realize what it was.

The wolves of the Old World, however, have a more sinister reputation, one which goes back to ancient times. It is not entirely undeserved. The slaughter of twenty-two children in Finland by a single wolf between 1880 and 1881 has been documented to the satisfaction of scientists. So have a number of other attacks in Europe, but these were single episodes probably triggered by rabies. However, a few years ago, news reports from Turkey told of huge wolf packs, apparently starving, attacking snowbound villages in a remote mountainous region.

A year after the Stockholm conference had urged tolerance for wolves, they attacked three children in northwestern Spain in the province of Orense. Two of the youngsters died, and the other was badly hurt. The people of the region were enraged and in response to public pressure, the local government set out poison baits, which killed not only several wolves, but also feral dogs.

Defenders of the wolf blamed the dogs for the attack upon the children, and the feral animals are highly suspect, although there is no proof. It is important to note, however, that every year thousands of young campers visit Canada's Algonquin Park, which is in the heart of wolf country, but an attack by wolves never has occurred there.

The disparity in behavior between Old World and New World wolves is as confounding as the reasons why some big cats become maneaters. The fear of firearms sometimes is said to underlie the reluctance of American wolves to attack man, but the wolves of the Old World also have been exposed to guns, and for a longer time.

The difference could be nothing more than a matter of where the

Highly social, elephants will come to the defense of embattled herd mates.

wolves live. Wolves have never had to live among heavy concentrations of people in North America. The animals were eliminated from settled areas with shocking suddenness; the wolves that were left reteated into the wilderness before the advance of civilization, and none stayed behind. In the Old World, however, there are farms, villages and towns even in many of the remote places where wolves have endured. Wolves there have been trapped in small islands of wilderness surrounded by mankind, while in North American they have fled beyond the first wave of civilization. Even in Minnesota, wolves live much farther removed from heavy concentrations of human populations than they do in the Apennines.

Crowded together, it is natural that wolf and man will continually trespass on each other's territory. Of the two, man reacts to the invasion more viciously, but as incidents in zoos show, when the wolf has nowhere to go it greets trespassers with bared fangs. The alleged agressiveness of the Old World wolf may only reflect the fact that since the Middle Ages, it has lived hemmed in by man.

Even in Europe, however, wolf attacks are so rare that they happen only once in a great while. Nowhere in the world is the risk to man from wolves so great that it should be an excuse for exterminating the animal. If the number of people bitten and killed is to be the sole reason for waging war upon an animal, we must exterminate the dog before we go after its wild cousin.

It is not the menace to man but to his livestock that prevents the wolf from persevering among people. But in the wilderness, with a reasonable amount of country to roam and game to eat, the wolf offers no threat to people or their interests. Unlike the grizzly bear, the wolf will not dispute the right to walk in the woods; there is no reason why people cannot use wolf country for outdoor recreation—they do it now in Algonquin Park. As for the risk involved, there is immeasurably more danger entailed in strolling down the street when the neighborhood dogs are loose.

THE ROOTS OF THE CONFLICT

If the wilderness continues to vanish, however, the wolf and most of the other animals mentioned in this chapter will exist only as zoo animals and, perhaps, like the lions of the Gir Forest, in artifically maintained preserves.

National parks and game preserves may seem to be an obvious solution, and they will help, but they are not the only answer. What is happening to the lion in Africa and grizzly bear in America raises serious questions about the role of parks in preserving large and dangerous beasts.

It can be argued that the grizzly, the tiger and the lion are extreme cases, because these animals, after all, are predators that are natural foes of man. But the destruction of the wilderness has had the same impact upon big plant-eating animals such as elephants, which even in parks, face an uphill struggle for survival.

TROUBLE FOR THE ELEPHANT

Largest of living land creatures, the elephants of Asia and Africa are the mightiest animals of their respective wilderness realms. The African species reaches a height of thirteen feet and can weigh almost seven tons, while the Asiatic elephant is somewhat smaller but still big enough to derail a train. This is precisely what happened in 1906 when a Siamese elephant met a locomotive head-on, spilling it and several freight cars from the tracks. The impact killed two members of the train crew—and the elephant.

The colossal size of either species makes an adult elephant too formidable for even a lion or tiger to kill, and generally elephants are challenged by no other wild animals. The bulk that gives the elephant the advantage in the wild, however, is a liability in a world where wilderness no longer exists in unbroken expanses, but in isolated fragments which are being eroded by a tide of humanity. There simply does not seem to be enough room left for the elephants—particularly the African species—and it seems as if even large game parks may not be able to contain the huge beasts. The next few years, it appears, will tell whether the elephant's size has made it incompatible with man.

Just by virtue of size, of course, elephants can be dangerous but unless frightened they usually are peaceable. There are exceptions, however, such as the so-called "rogues," bulls which have been driven from the herd by a stronger male, and which stalk the countryside looking for trouble. Such a beast may charge people it meets on sight.

Bulls of the Asiatic species also can be extremely dangerous when they are seized by a peculiar condition called *"musth,"* which occurs about once a year and lasts for several days. Musth produces bouts of bad temper that make even tame bulls unmanageable. The condition is accompanied by the swelling of the temporal glands which are located in the elephant's temples and produce an oily black fluid. The reasons for *musth* are obscure, but it may somehow be connected with the breeding cycle.

Musth probably is responsible for unexpected rampages by Asiatic elephants such as one which occurred in Bangladesh late in 1975. Nine people were trampled to death and ten hurt when an elephant suddenly ran amok through two villages.

Normally, however, the Asiatic elephant is a placid animal, as demonstrated by the fact that it has been domesticated in southern Asia for at least 5,000 years. The elephant has been utilized in warfare, but it also has been a beast of burden and ceremonial animal, and is valued —even beloved—by people in the lands where it lives.

Working elephants usually are not bred in captivity, but are captured from wild herds which have dwindled but still roam preserves and in what open country remains. In some regions, domestic elephants range freely over the countryside, behaving much as they do in the wild. The line between such animals and wild elephants, in fact, is very thin.

Because the Asiatic elephant has been exploited by man for thousands of years, it has become a familiar beast in its part of the world, a part of the lives and culture of the people. It is taken for granted that elephants, wild or tame, are supposed to be there. Meanwhile, during its long association with man, the Asiatic elephant has adapted very well to living with man; except for a few ill-tempered bulls the elephant gets along quite well with humans. Therefore, even amidst multitudes of people, and despite the destruction of the wilderness, the Asiatic elephant seems to be able to survive.

The outlook for the African elephant is much more grim, for several reasons. To begin with, African elephants are not as docile or tolerant of man as the Asiatic species. Even in places such as game parks, where African elephants have become used to people, they can react in devastating fashion when threatened. This is why great care must be taken when approaching elephants in the bush, even when riding in a truck or automobile.

Although some animals such as lions do not associate people with vehicles and perceive no threat from them, elephants may take offense if a motor vehicle approaches too closely. Ears fan out, trunks begin testing the air, the cows gather their calves in a knot, and the young bulls feeding at the edge of the herd turn questioningly towards the source of alarm. It is the time to think about departing; the elephants may be bluffing—they often do—but they also may be in earnest, and even *one* of them can smash a vehicle to scrap metal.

An African game guide in Kenya told me of how he was trapped in a car for more than six hours while forty elephants milled ominiously around as if trying to decide whether to flatten the vehicle. The guide had been escorting an American couple and their driver through the Masai-Mara game preserve in southwestern Kenya when he sighted the elephants browsing on acacia trees.

He told the driver to stop and they watched the elephants for a while as the big creatures moved through the bush, tearing off entire branches and stripping them. When the elephants began to feed in the direction of the car, the guide told the driver to leave. He tried the ignition but the engine would not start.

Meanwhile the elephants were slowly moving towards the automobile, and although the driver frantically worked the key, the ignition would not turn over. Like a slow but relentless tide, the elephants came closer, unconcerned about the car at this point and intent only on their feeding. Soon they were tearing down branches all around the car, while its occupants sat frozen, fearing that a single move would arouse the huge beasts.

For about forty minutes the elephants fed in the bush surrounding the car, and then they moved on. The driver switched on the ignition again, and this time the engine started. The sound of the engine coughing to life aroused the elephants, however, and they turned from their feeding and headed back to the car.

This time they were curious about the vehicle and circled about it cautiously, sniffing at it, and eyeing it intently, much to the fear of the people within. For six hours the animals remained there, sometimes stopping to feed, but much of the time milling about the vehicle. The people who sat inside the auto knew at any moment they and the car might be smashed. As the afternoon waned, however, the elephants seemed to lose interest, and eventually they trooped away, this time for good.

When confined within the artificial boundaries of national parks, elephants eat themselves out of habitat.

Fortunately for the guide and his party, the elephants of the region were not especially bad-tempered towards man, as are elephants in some other neighborhoods. One such place is the lower slopes of the Aberdare Mountains, a range in Kenya which rises 13,000 feet above sea level to chill, fog-shrouded moorlands. The lower slopes, however, are heavily forested, with lush glades opening up here and there among the trees.

Here and there, too, one can see large potholes, partly overgrown with vegetation, their sides crumbling, and bottoms slick with mud that provides fine wallowing for wart hogs. While traveling through the region with a well-known professional hunter who has lived in Kenya for decades, I asked him what had caused the potholes. The holes, he said, were craters blasted in the red earth by the British during the Mau Mau uprising of the 1950s, which led to Kenyan independence.

The Mau Mau insurgents had used the forest as a haven. The bombing failed to accomplish its goal, but according to my hunter friend, had another effect. It was the cause, he said, of the testiness of the elephants of the region.

If I doubted the bad reputation of the elephants, the caution exercised by the hunter, who for political reasons cannot be identified, changed my mind. As we traveled over a dirt track through the forest, he asked me to stand in the rear of our Toyota Land Cruiser and keep watch for elephants through the photo hatch in the roof.

We had been traveling for a half hour through thick forest which walled both sides of the road, and had seen buffalo and wart hogs aplenty, but no elephants. But then a gray trunk snaked out of the roadside tangle about a hundred yards ahead. I ducked into the hatch and whispered, "Elephants," then rose again to watch one of the creatures cross the road and silently merge with the forest on the other side.

Meanwhile, my friend eased the gear shift into reverse and slowly backed the vehicle a hundred yards or so down the road. Up ahead, another elephant had crossed. We waited for several minutes and when no more elephants appeared, we started forward again. As we did, a third elephant materialized out of the trees, heading after the others. But this one sensed us, stopped, and turned in our direction. Ears spread, it slowly weaved its trunk in the air, seeming for a moment to move in our direction, but then stopping. It stood in the middle of the road for about five minutes, considering what to do, while we waited, knowing that the roadbed was too narrow in that place for the vehicle to turn around. Then the elephant turned abruptly and strode into the forest on the other side of the road.

The Aberdare region is a national park, or else we probably would not have seen elephants, for the beasts have vanished from most areas outside of parks. The need for farmland to feed the burgeoning populations of emerging African nations has meant that elephants have had to forfeit their traditional feeding grounds. In addition, parks are the only place elephants have any sort of protection—even if marginal—from the ceaseless slaughter by ivory poachers, who threaten to make the African species extinct if they are not curbed.

Much to its misfortune, the African elephant has tusks that are considerably longer than those of the Asiatic, and thus is more prized for ivory. The largest tusks carried by African elephants can surpass ten feet in length, and both sexes carry them, whereas only the bull of the Asiatic species is tusked.

Killing the African elephant for ivory, or for its hide and meat, has been the only way man has found to exploit it, until recently when it has become a tourist attraction. Although the African elephant can be tamed, rarely has it been domesticated; even the elephants that the Carthaginian general Hannibal brought with him to Italy from North Africa may have been Asiatic. Part of the reason there is no tradition of domesticating elephants in Africa is that below the Sahara it has not had the long history of civilization that southern Asia has. Five thousand years ago, for instance, India had sophisticated city-states which had not only the ability to train elephants, but uses for them.

For many years elephants were trained and used for work at a station in the Belgian Congo, but the project never approached a commercial success. Even so, some conservationists believe that if a major effort were begun today to domesticate the African elephant, it could become a valuable asset, and thus have a better chance of survival in the future.

Right now it seems as if the only chance the African elephant has is in national parks, but even there the fate of the species is uncertain. Imprisoned in the artificial boundaries of the parks, surrounded by humanity, the elephants are literally eating themselves out of a home.

A single elephant needs up to 600 pounds of leaves, grass, and other fodder a day. No wonder that a herd can strip a forest in an entire night —not just strip it, moreover, but demolish it, for in their desire to feed elephants uproot whole trees to get at all the twigs and leaves.

Only a few decades ago there was enough open country left in Africa so elephants could move on, again and again, after consuming all the food in an area. Meanwhile, in the absence of the elephants, the food supply would be renewed.

Today elephants no longer have limitless foraging grounds. In many places farmers have planted crops to within a few feet of national park boundaries. If the elephants try to move out of the parks to new feeding grounds, they are greeted with great hostility, and no wonder for they can wipe out a farmers crops in just a few hours.

Confined in the parks, the elephants return again and again to the same feeding sites, not allowing nearly enough time for the vegetation to regrow. As a result, not only are they in danger of starving, but they are destroying the very habitat in which they and other animals live. During the early 1960s, in the Tsavo National Park of Kenya, for instance, elephants stripped the landscape of so much vegetation, that many black rhinoceroses, which also foraged there, died of starvation.

Like the grizzly bear, the elephant is proving to be an animal that is simply not suited for life in national parks, the way such preserves are established and managed today. There seem to be only two alternatives to the elephant question: either the parks must be extended—it can be done if conservationists are willing to pay the price—or elephants must be culled—the number of elephants must be kept in check by killing surplus animals. Carried on to any great degree, the latter option is a bitter one, with elephants becoming so rare.

Seeking more alternatives, such scientists as Iain Douglas-Hamilton are studying the behavior and life cycle of African elephants in relation to their surroundings. It seems to be, however, that the only alternative to culling elephants, as it is to killing off grizzlies, and allowing wolves to vanish, is somehow ensuring that the animals have more wilderness to roam. The price may be too high to pay, especially for emerging African nations faced with a choice of preserving elephants and other wild animals and feeding ever-expanding numbers of citizens.

This is the decision that early in 1975 confronted the government of Rwanda, a central African nation of 10,000 square miles and 4,000,000 inhabitants. Most of the traditional foraging grounds of the nation's 140 surviving elephants had been converted to farmland. The elephants had been pushed into a few small areas of wilderness that had not been cultivated, but they continued to emerge from these havens, to feed where their ancestors had—but now it was not natural forage, but crops that were disappearing down the gullets of the animals.

A white rhino is readied for removal from a preserve in South Africa. So many of these creatures have been bred in preserves that the species is no longer endangered in that part of the continent.

At the order of the country's president, riflemen were dispatched to end the problem. By June they had killed more than 100 elephants and were searching for the rest. All but 26 of the animals were slated for death; those left alive were drugged, transported to the nation's only national park, a 970-mile tract that hopefully can support a small herd of elephants, unless it multiplies too quickly.

The operation in Rwanda showed how totally man dominates even the largest animals to walk the land. It took only a few weeks for the riflemen to decimate the herd. The animals that were saved were taken to the park unconscious, in trucks and in slings suspended from helicopters. Without really too much effort, man had rearranged and redistributed the elephant population of an entire nation.

Ironically, this vivid demonstration of mankind's dominance over animals was accompanied by a tragic reminder of how vulnerable individual humans still are when matched against the awesome natural prowess of wild beasts. Lee Lyon, a twenty-nine-year-old California woman, was knocked down and trampled to death by one of the elephants which had been saved from the slaughter. Her mission there was one peculiar to our times; she was a wildlife photographer filming the relocation of the beasts.

Miss Lyon's death was not only shocking to people who had worked with her in Africa but it was also somewhat puzzling. She was an old hand at her job, and she had photographed elephants before under extremely risky circumstances. This time, however, she was filming a well-organized project. She was within the fences of a corral when she was trampled by the elephant, which had just been released after its relocation. It should not have been a dangerous assignment, and yet she was killed.

A QUESTION OF RISK

No matter how dominant man has become, as long as animals like elephants, lions, tigers, and grizzly bears continue to exist somewhere on earth, so will the risk that they will harm somebody. It is only natural to wonder about how much risk is involved and whether it is worth taking; particularly when many of the animals capable of doing the damage need the help of man to survive.

Before the continued existence of many of the wild animals described in this book is assured, we will have to access the risk they pose, and see how much of it we have brought upon ourselves. We need to seek ways of reducing it, as well as to put it into perspective. After all, if you think about it, grizzly bears are much less of a menace than the dogs in our streets.

What we need most of all is to clarify exactly why animals which threaten us or compete with us should be kept around, and to define exactly the problems they create.

I would be immensely saddened at the loss of the last tiger, but I would not want to be eaten by one. Nor would I know what to tell a hungry African peasant who needed elephant feeding grounds to grow crops to feed his own family.

Ecological justification often is offered in behalf of preserving wildlife. The argument is familiar: all living things have a role in maintaining the balance of nature. If we permit an animal to vanish, there is no way of telling how it will throw the system out of order. The results may be ruinous even to man.

There is considerable meat in that argument, but it is not as persuasive as conservationists would like to believe, because not all creatures have equal impact upon natural checks and balances. The loss of the few thousand tigers or handful of lions that remain in Asia would hardly upset nature's applecart. And if ecological considerations were all that mattered, we could do more easily without the grizzly bear than the diamondback rattlesnake. Both eat rodents, but the rattler kills so many that its loss would be measured in rodent hordes. Besides, the grizzly is either so rare or so remote from most of us that we would hardly notice its passing.

Even animals that become economic assets have little hope over the long run if our reasons for saving them are totally materialistic; eventually the scarcity of land will dictate more profitable ways of using it than as game parks or hunting preserves. Mankind will have to search its collective soul to find out why the beasts of the wilderness should be permitted to survive.

What would the world be like without a single tiger in the wild? How would it be to know that nowhere in any forest on earth does a beast roam which is both magnificent and savage, unchanged from the days when we had barely emerged from the beast ourselves? Would the forest then be just a patch of standing timber, its mystery and magic vanished with the great striped cat?

Perhaps a little risk is good for us; we never really have been afraid of it, and it has spurred on the evolution of our species. And it could be that the distance we have put between us and the beasts which were our ancestors can be measured by whether or not we can live side by side with animals, even if they serve us in no material way.

PHOTO CREDITS

INDEX